Postsecular Catholicism

Postsecular Catholicism
Relevance and Renewal

MICHELE DILLON

OXFORD
UNIVERSITY PRESS

OXFORD
UNIVERSITY PRESS

Oxford University Press is a department of the University of Oxford. It furthers
the University's objective of excellence in research, scholarship, and education
by publishing worldwide. Oxford is a registered trade mark of Oxford University
Press in the UK and certain other countries.

Published in the United States of America by Oxford University Press
198 Madison Avenue, New York, NY 10016, United States of America.

© Oxford University Press 2018

CIP data is on file at the Library of Congress
ISBN 978-0-19-069300-8

1 3 5 7 9 8 6 4 2

Printed by Sheridan Books, Inc., United States of America

Contents

Acknowledgments

A SABBATICAL IN the fall of 2015 after six years of being department chair recharged my intellectual energy. Paul Wink, my husband, was also on sabbatical and experiencing the new reality of an empty nest we were privileged to spend several weeks in Rome and Verona, an exciting time coinciding with the Synod on the Family. I am grateful to the University of New Hampshire for its support, and also to the Provost and the Senior Vice Provost for Research for research grants that were helpful in the formation and analysis phases of the book. I have benefited from colleagues' comments and questions on portions of the book's findings presented to symposia at the University of Leuven, Saint Anselm's College, the University of Connecticut, and at the American Sociological Association meetings. Conversations about all things Catholic with family, friends, colleagues, and many others over the years who have formally and informally talked with me about their understanding of Catholicism have greatly deepened my understanding; and for this I am grateful. I also appreciate the insightful comments and helpful suggestions of Gene Burns and anonymous reviewers, and Theo Calderara, Lincy Priya, and Oxford University Press's staff for shepherding this book through the editorial and production process. And with great pleasure I acknowledge Paul, and our now-grown sons, Michael and Andrew, for enriching the joy of love.

I

Contrite Modernity, Contrite Catholicism

ON FEBRUARY 11, 2013, Pope Benedict stunned the world by announcing his resignation. Within days, as speculation about his successor mounted, news stories emphasized a divide among American Catholics. Half of those surveyed said the next pope should "maintain traditional positions." The other half said he should "move in new directions."[1]

But, contrary to the pollsters' framing, the two options are not mutually exclusive. Catholicism is a living tradition, one in which faith and reason interact, helping the Church stay relevant in an increasingly secularized society. Yesterday's new directions are today's traditional positions. For example, the separation of church and state and the view that civil laws do not have to accord with Catholic doctrine are institutionalized Church teachings. But as recently as the 1950s, the Church actively rejected such views.[2] By the same token, what are regarded as traditional positions are often nourished by the incorporation of new directions. Generations of Catholics internalized the deeply felt obligation to attend Mass every Sunday. But the 1983 revised Code of Canon Law allowed attendance at Saturday evening Mass to fulfill the Sunday obligation.[3] Thus, moving in a new direction reinforced a traditional position. This is how any living tradition maintains vitality, and it is especially true of Catholicism—it is committed to tradition but open to change.

The purpose of this book is to explore how Catholicism negotiates the tension between the forces of tradition and those of change. Catholicism is a global faith, and therefore it operates in an array of historical, political, social, and cultural contexts. Although the Church is universal, the everyday realities in any particular location give rise to a great deal of pluralism in how the faith is practiced and understood. Each particular societal setting presents its own nuances, complexities, and challenges. Therefore, I anchor my inquiry in the context of American Catholicism, though some of the tensions I write about are also present in Western Europe, Australia, and Latin America.[4] Amid the crosscutting tensions and ties between America's religious and secular currents, how does Catholicism maintain public relevance? And what are the expectations of the Church hierarchy's engagement with Catholics and non-Catholics alike? In a time when pressing economic, social, and political problems call for urgent attention, can the Church give new voice to its strongly embedded commitment to the common good? And can it forge new directions in language, doctrinal thinking, and institutional practices that find greater resonance with the lived experiences of increasingly secularized Catholics and other citizens? This book addresses these questions from the standpoint of contemporary American Catholicism.

Contrite Modernity

The age-old questions "What shall we do?" and "How shall we live?" have renewed pertinence in light of the ills currently confronting the United States and Western Europe.[5] These problems include the exacerbation of economic inequality, the marginalization of certain social groups (e.g., the poor, immigrants, refugees), climate change, declining confidence in democratic political institutions, and new strands of alienation reflected in the feeling of being "a stranger in one's own land."[6]

Modernity, as ushered in by Enlightenment thinking and the democratic political revolutions of the eighteenth century, promised a new future. It gave rise to an unprecedented epoch of human progress, scientific achievement, and political equality. Yet, despite great progress, we can see from the problems I've mentioned that modernity has not completely fulfilled its promises. Scientific reasoning was not expected to answer, and indeed cannot answer, questions about how we should arrange our lives. It was assumed, however, that trust in the scientific method would provide the objective knowledge that could be used to achieve progress and remedy problems. With data in hand, issues would be resolved by democratic debate. Yet today, not only is democratic deliberation failing to solve problems but also public trust in science itself cannot be taken for granted.[7]

These various problems—failures of modernity—do not mean that modernity has failed. Instead, as the German theorist Jurgen Habermas argues, the problems of modernity require contemporary society to own up to them and to commit to a new way forward. He thus suggests that we think in terms of a "contrite modernity."[8] A contrite modernity, just as a contrite heart, does not give in to despair over past failings. Rather, it has the values and cultural resources to amend its shortcomings, and to steer society back on track so that it can better realize its potential. A contrite modernity thus has confidence in its overarching commitments (e.g., to reason, human equality, democracy, science) and in its ability to turn things around. To do so, however, it needs to put its resources to use.

Reassessing the Legacy of Modernity

The current moment is not the first time that the legacy of modernity has been called into question. Over the course of the twentieth century, there were times when the consequences of rationality and human achievement prompted a second look at what modernity had wrought. In particular, the quick succession of World Wars I and II prompted agonizing questions over how Enlightenment values and scientific and technological progress could produce such systematic human destruction. Scholars and religious leaders alike drew attention to the tragic inhumanity of modernity. Pope John XXIII denounced the darkness and "spiritual ruin" ushered in by an ethos of scientific conquest. He pointed to the gap between human capacity and human values, and pushed modernity to recognize its limitations and to reassess its goals. He elaborated:

> Scientific progress itself, which gave man the possibility of creating catastrophic instruments for his destruction, has raised questions. It has obliged human beings to become thoughtful, more conscious of their own limitations, desirous of peace, and attentive to the importance of spiritual values.[9]

But he was no pessimist. Rather than being negative about the course of history, he looked to it for lessons on how to improve upon the problems of modernity. In this spirit, he explicitly disagreed with:

> those prophets of gloom, who are always forecasting disaster, as though the end of the world were at hand . . . [and the] voices of persons who . . . in these modern times . . . see nothing but prevarication and ruin. They say that our era, in comparison with past eras, is getting worse, and they behave as though they had learned nothing from history, which is, none the less, the teacher of life.[10]

John was confident that the Church—and society—can "look to the future without fear."[11] And this is the aspiration of a contrite modernity today. As with the lessons of history, the resources of modernity can be drawn upon to shape a better future.

John surprised the world with his view that the Church required a new openness to modernity and with his confidence in its ability to renew itself in ways that would ensure its public relevance in the modern world. This marked a major turn from the Church's earlier stance, which took a dim view of modernity. Vatican II—the Second Vatican Council—was a meeting of almost 2,000 Catholic bishops between 1962 and 1965. It accomplished a lot of important things and reworked a lot of assumptions that Catholics had long taken for granted.[12] Many of Vatican II's developments were intended to ensure the Church's public relevance, a commitment underlined by the fact that for the first time in history, the Church addressed itself to "the whole human family."[13] This has been highly consequential both for the Church's role in society and for how Catholics construe Catholicism and interact with the Church; such consequences underpin much of this book's analysis.

Religion and Contrite Modernity

Public religions like Catholicism have a role to play in a contrite modernity. Their long-preserved values and moral and ethical principles are useful, Habermas argues, in helping to remediate contemporary ills and thus to rescue modernity and steer it out of its dead-end. Religion can also motivate the moral solidarity and political action necessary to overcome social and economic injustices.[14] Members of a religious tradition share moral vocabularies (e.g., "Love your neighbor") and narratives (e.g., parables) that inject meaning into concern for the vulnerable. By contrast, a purely secular discourse of individual rights that is unmoored from religion provides a weaker basis for collective action. It conveys a more abstract image of the individual, and is relatively silent on the individual's social relationships and the obligations they impose.[15] As such, an appeal to individual rights may fall short of the moral and emotional charge needed to mobilize individuals on behalf of others.

The Catholic Church is very much a public religion.[16] This is an identity consonant with its institutional self-definition as catholic (lowercase), universal, and committed to the public common good, its on-the-ground presence in diverse activities (e.g., religious worship, health, education, social services, public policy), and its amplification through media. Catholic social justice teaching is particularly pertinent to the problems of a contrite modernity. Similarly, Catholic doctrine on sex and gender extends beyond private morality and the Church's internal institutional practices (e.g., women's ordination) to variously impact individuals' and groups' public identities, and personal and social relationships.

Secularism

The forces of change unleashed by modernity were supposed to bring about the public retreat, if not the disappearance, of religion. Modernity's emphasis on reason opened the door to scientific thinking, which was expected to displace religious beliefs and deference to religious authority. It followed that if all individuals are created equal and endowed with reason, they should be able to reason about all things, including religion, and should be free to govern themselves in all things. This idea is the bedrock of democracy. And it conferred a new mindset that was—and is—not only critical to the democratization of political, economic, and social life but also to how people understand religion.[17] As such, democratic revolutions are secular revolutions. They transform how individuals and collectivities think of themselves, and they unhook the motivations of individuals, families, institutions, and whole societies from the hold of religious beliefs, interests, and authority. Modernity therefore pushes secularization. How and when it occurs in different societal domains (e.g., education) and who and what are its main drivers vary, however, across specific sociohistorical contexts.[18]

The reality today is that America and the Western world is secular. Secular principles and norms undergird our legal, economic, political, and social institutions, as well as the conduct of everyday life. Thus, for example, the secularization of economic activity is such that the motivation to accumulate wealth is not for the purpose of glorifying God, as it once was for the early Calvinists, but to enjoy an affluent lifestyle and secure the well-being of one's family.[19] Yet, religion has not disappeared. In the United States especially, it is a salient force. Notwithstanding the (secular) legal-constitutional separation of church and state, religious ideas, influences, and interests continue to be relevant in politics and law, in various other institutional fields (e.g., education, health care, social services, media), and in public culture. They are also relevant in individual lives. Three in four Americans self-identify with a religious tradition, and churches and religious institutions are highly visible in everyday life.[20] Therefore, while secularization is the settled reality, it is uneven in its reach and in its consequences.

The Secularization of Religious Authority

Secularization is sufficiently consequential that it penetrates religion itself. Thus, amid the (uneven) persistence of religious affiliation and church attendance, there has been a decline in the scope of religious authority.[21] The secularization of religious authority is evidenced by the limited influence of religious actors, ideas, and teachings. Religion's authority is constricted not just in the public sphere where, in accord with secular principles of church-state differentiation, one would expect the Church to have limited authority. Also, the secularization of religious authority is such that religious believers largely rely on their own individual authority rather than on Church officials in determining the terms of their religious engagement.

The secularization of religious authority has long been a feature of Protestantism. Its theological development emphasized the role of the individual in their own salvation. And this ethos of individualism was subsequently reinforced, especially in the United States, by the incorporation of everyday democracy into Protestantism. Democratization emphasized that it was a person's choice whether or not, and how, to be religious; and given the broad range of Protestant denominations, one was free to move from one to another.[22]

In Catholicism, the secularization, or individualization, of religious authority is a more recent development. But it has become a central part of being Catholic. Interpretive autonomy—the individual's freedom to disagree with official Church teaching—is critical to Catholics' understanding of their faith.[23] Vatican II affirmed several values (e.g., personal conscience, freedom of inquiry, honest dialogue) that give Catholics the authority to actively inquire into and evaluate the doctrinal import of Church teachings and practices. And successive cohorts of American Catholics have translated this into a practical interpretation whereby one can disagree with the Church hierarchy and simultaneously maintain loyalty to Catholicism. Interpretive autonomy (as I will discuss in chapter 2) is especially evident in the domain of sexual morality, but it extends far beyond that. This autonomy points to how secular expectations, such as the authority of the individual and of everyday practical reason, get institutionalized by the Church itself (e.g., at Vatican II) and routinized into Catholics' interactions with the Church.

Postsecular Society

In the context of Western society, the (uneven) persistence of religion in the face of secularism could be considered a partial failure of modernity, in that it defies the Enlightenment expectation of religion's demise. Yet, ironically, its persistence makes it newly relevant to the task of rescuing modernity from its economic, social, and existential failures. As previously noted, Catholicism's long-preserved ethics, its communal bases, and its public openness position it as an important resource for a contrite modernity. Thus, Habermas argues, the realities of Western modernity require a change in public consciousness and an appreciation of religion, what he calls a postsecular consciousness. A postsecular consciousness recognizes that while secularization is the settled reality, religion has public relevance and culturally useful resources for addressing contemporary societal ills.[24] Thus, postsecularity does not mean that we have moved beyond secularism or that secularization has not occurred. And nor does it denote the return of religion, as religion never, in fact, disappeared from Western society. Rather, postsecularity requires appreciation of the mutual relevance and intertwined pull of the religious and the secular.

This postsecular mutuality, Habermas argues, requires ongoing dialogue, tolerance, and active engagement between religious and secular actors. They are required to speak *with* and not merely *about* one another. In this normative view, each is a cultural resource for the self-understanding of the other.[25] In other words, religious and secular actors should each be open to the perspective of the other. And they should be open to reconsidering their own assumptions and convictions in light of those with whom they differ. This dialogue is not intended to persuade the other of the rightness of one's own convictions, or to ignore or to paper over differences. The goal, rather, is to forge new understandings and to integrate differences, however partially, in ways that can help society move forward in addressing its challenges.

The normative expectations for the conduct of religious–secular dialogue are relatively straightforward. Religious actors are entitled not only to participate in the public sphere but also to be given due respect for their contributions to public debate. "Secular citizens in civil society," Habermas argues "must be able to meet their fellow religious citizens as equals." Thus, secular citizens and institutions (e.g., government, mass media, the courts, universities, etc.) cannot treat "religious expressions as simply irrational." To the contrary, they have to sincerely recognize and respect the fact that religious-based arguments "can make a meaningful contribution to clarifying controversial questions of principle."[26]

Secular Translation

Religious arguments, however, Habermas emphasizes, require translation into an accessible secular vocabulary. Because secularization is the settled reality, and because secular principles underpin the everyday conduct of individual and societal affairs, secular expectations also apply to religion's engagement in public debate. This means that religious arguments have to be conveyed in an everyday secular language that has resonance with a broad range of individuals regardless of religious background.[27] Such secular reasoning includes acceptance of democratic principles (e.g., equality, civil law) and acceptance of the validity of scientific findings in informing public debate. Indeed, in everyday settings, so-called religious language tends to be broad-based. This is evidenced, for example, in the culturally resonant arguments used by the U.S. Catholic bishops in the abortion debate.[28] Further, as Robert Wuthnow notes, individuals, including those who are religious, participate in several diverse speech communities (associated with work, leisure, and other activities). All language, therefore, including religious language, is shaped by this diversity.[29] In any case, postsecularity requires the active translation of faith beliefs into a meaningful secular vocabulary. For example, religious participants could translate the Christian belief that Jesus died and was resurrected for the salvation of all people into the secular argument that all people have equal dignity.[30] Building on this, the argument could be developed that all people deserve a standard of living allowing them to live in dignity, and accordingly society must resolve the problems of poverty, homelessness, hunger, and the like.

Communicative Openness

The postsecular expectation of reciprocal dialogue between religious and secular actors also requires recognition that they may not agree. Neither religious nor secular actors have a monopoly on correct interpretation. Rather, the interpretations posited are open to mutual contestation and reciprocal counterargument. In the public sphere, Church officials (and Catholics in general) must not rely on the primacy of magisterial or papal authority.[31] When they engage in public debate, they are expected to rely on secular reasoning, and not on Church-based, hierarchical authority.

Within a contrite modernity, therefore, the questions of what to do and how to live may find fruitful answers if society draws on the mutual relevance and resources of the religious and the secular. Postsecular society thus rejects a defeatism that sees the problems of modernity as being beyond reason, beyond fixing. It similarly rejects remedies that—while relying on technical, scientific solutions—pay little attention to ethics and values.[32] I am drawn to postsecularity because empirically it captures the fact that religion still matters and that public religions such as Catholicism have something meaningful to say in contemporary society. Additionally, its expectations of religious–secular dialogue make good sense. Religion's relevance is bounded by secular realities. The expectation that religious arguments should be couched in accessible secular language and authority, and in conversation with secular lived realities, is thus highly pragmatic.

Contrite Catholicism

I interpret the postsecular turn as extending an invitation to Catholicism to embrace reciprocal dialogue between the religious and the secular. I am not suggesting that the Church should develop a postsecular mentality. Nor am I suggesting that the public relevance of Catholicism is contingent on its embrace of postsecular expectations. What I am arguing, however, is that the postsecular recognition of the mutual relevance of the religious and the secular opens up new lines of dialogue, and thus of action, both within the Church and for its role in secular society. Analytically, the postsecular frame can be used to illuminate the priorities of the Church's diverse actors—laity, priests, bishops, and the pope—and to understand the interpretive claims and strategies deployed in intra-Catholic and in Church–society engagement.

The postsecular turn may provide the Church with a way forward from the defeatism that has creeped into the Catholic narrative.[33] Such defeatism is driven by a number of factors. Foremost is the Church's sex-abuse scandal and the moral and financial costs it has exacted in the United States and elsewhere.[34] Also of concern is the ever-widening gap between lay Catholics and the Church hierarchy, especially over issues of sex, gender, and family (a phenomenon not confined to the U.S., but evident also among self-identified Catholics in Europe and Latin America).[35] Related to these forces, but with its own cultural dynamic, is the exponential growth in religiously unaffiliated Americans. Just within the past twenty-five years, the proportion of the unaffiliated has tripled so that they now account for a fourth of all Americans.[36] More generally, more than one in ten Americans are former Catholics.[37] Apart from this drift from the Church, the high proportion of young adults who have no religious affiliation or who have weak ties to the Church further sharpens the challenge posed to the Church's future relevance.[38] Thus, amid talk of crisis, fractiousness, and irrelevance, I want to probe whether the emancipatory potential of a postsecular consciousness may be beneficial not only to a contrite modernity but also to what might be called a contrite Catholicism.

The postsecular assessment of Catholicism befits the current moment in the Church. Pope Benedict's formal public apology in 2010 for the Church's sex-abuse scandals might well be viewed as the annunciation of a contrite Church. He sincerely apologized for the grievous suffering caused to victims and their families. And of particular significance, he owned up to the Church's own failings in leadership. He admitted "serious mistakes . . . grave errors of judgment . . . [and] failures of leadership" on the part of bishops.[39] Failures in leadership had previously been conceded by bishops in the United States and some other countries, and as fallout from the sex-abuse crisis continues still today, additional bishops are admitting their failures, too.[40] Benedict's apology was not without controversy, however. In it, he pointed to increased secularization as a contributing cause of the problem. Nonetheless, the apology—coming from the pope himself, the embodiment of magisterial authority—marked a significant symbolic moment of contrition for the Church after many years of institutional evasion. It gave voice, too, to Benedict's recognition that the Church needs to engage in reflexive self-critique—"honest self-examination"—in an effort toward its renewal.[41]

Benedict has long been a critic of modernity's one-sidedness. Prior to becoming pope, as Cardinal Ratzinger he was head of the Vatican's Congregation for the Doctrine of the Faith for twenty-five years. In that role, he frequently denounced modernity's materialist view of progress, its secularism, its moral relativism, and the drive toward human self-destruction.[42] Less frequently noted, however, is Benedict's acknowledgment of the relevance of a reflexive critique of Christianity. He made this acknowledgment, as Cardinal Ratzinger, in a public conversation with Habermas in 2004—a striking dialogue between a noted Vatican official and a famous secular intellectual.[43] Though they came from different intellectual perspectives, the two men acknowledged the mutual relevance of faith and reason and the necessity of critiquing them. Their conversation conveyed the need to be conscious not only of modernity's failings but of the Church's failings, too. As Benedict subsequently elaborated:

> A self-critique of modernity is needed in dialogue with Christianity and its concept of hope. In this dialogue Christians too, in the context of their knowledge and experience, must learn anew in what their hope

truly consists, what they have to offer to the world and what they cannot offer. Flowing into this self-critique of the modern age there also has to be a self-critique of modern Christianity, which must constantly renew its self-understanding setting out from its roots.[44]

The postsecular expectation of mutual self-critique of the religious and the secular thus finds particular resonance in a contrite Catholicism. And, in the wake of Benedict's resignation, Pope Francis is significantly amplifying the Church's commitment to renewal and relevance. He displays, as I will show in subsequent chapters, a remarkable postsecular sensibility, whether intended as such or not.

Catholic Interpretive Diversity

Can Catholicism fulfill postsecular expectations? This straightforward question belies the complexity of who and what speaks for Catholicism. Vivid photographs a few years ago showed Tucson Bishop Gerald Kicanas and a handful of other Catholic bishops distributing Holy Communion to outstretched hands through the narrow openings between the high steel bars of the U.S.–Mexican border fence.[45] Symbolically, this is highly significant. Communion is the bread consecrated during Mass, and it is core to the Catholic sacramental, theological, and communal tradition.[46] Bishop Kicanas's actions demonstrate a Church that is capable of prodding the nation's secular conscience. They show a Church that rejects exclusion and believes instead not only in the sacrament of communion but also in the building of an inclusive society. This image of inclusivity is complicated, however, by some other bishops who, for example, maintain that Catholic politicians who support abortion or same-sex marriage should be denied communion or other forms of public recognition by Catholic institutions.[47]

These contrasting faces of the Church reflect the fact that there are multiple doctrinal strands within the Catholic tradition. They also reflect the tension in Catholicism—and in postsecular expectations—between openness to secular realities and the simultaneous obligation to preserve certain ethical values. Of further postsecular relevance, they point to the interpretive diversity within Catholicism. The intertwining of religious and secular currents is encapsulated in the Church's structure itself. It is a hierarchical institution with a great deal of interpretive and legal authority vested in the Church hierarchy. The hierarchy, embodied by the pope and the bishops, is the Church's religiously grounded "teaching authority." At the same time, the Church is a community of discourse in which individual reason and lived experience hold sway. Catholicism is thus an interpretive community with multiple and diverse voices in ongoing conversation over doctrinal and other matters that have an imposing relevance in the everyday lives of Catholics. This is a model of the Church that was itself confirmed by the bishops themselves at Vatican II.[48]

The interpretive diversity within Catholicism means that no single voice speaks for, or on behalf of, Catholicism. This is so notwithstanding the significance of the pope and the bishops. Moreover, as has been illuminated here, individual bishops themselves vary in their doctrinal priorities. Further, both as individuals and in their collective assembly, such as the U.S. bishops' conference (USCCB), they enjoy relative autonomy from Rome—a point increasingly evident in the public tensions between some bishops and Francis. Interpretive diversity is further deepened by the interpretive autonomy of lay Catholics. As I noted earlier, the secularization—or individualization—of religious authority is strikingly evident among American Catholics. They bring secular expectations to their participation in the Church and to their reflexive engagement with various elements of Catholicism. This allows them to claim, and to act on, an interpretive freedom that underscores the limited influence of the Church hierarchy in their everyday lives. Yet, importantly, their interpretations of Catholicism, as well as the interpretive diversity within the hierarchy, are all variously legitimated within Catholicism.

Catholic interpretive diversity means that the invitation extended by postsecularity is applicable to the pope, to the bishops, and to the laity. They are all active co-creators in the maintenance of Catholicism.[49] All are participants in conversation with one another, with the larger Catholic tradition, and simultaneously in and with secular society. The intermeshing of the religious and the secular within the Church and within society presents the hierarchy and lay Catholics with different pragmatic challenges. It is the same Church, however, the same Catholic tradition whose resources are engaged in encountering and negotiating these crosscutting, intra-Church and Church–society pressures.

For Catholics, the religious and secular elements of their identity intersect. Lay Catholics should thus be thought of as Catholics who are secular-religious citizens, and not as Catholics who compartmentalize their secular roles and experiences from their participation in the Church. (My point here contrasts with Habermas who, as noted earlier, makes a theoretical distinction between "religious citizens" and "secular citizens.") By the same token, the intertwining of religious and secular citizenship means that the Church hierarchy is a religious–secular actor who interacts with Catholic and secular audiences alike. When the hierarchy engages with secular audiences, it is simultaneously engaging Catholics. And when it specifically addresses Catholics, it cannot simply silence the embedded expectations of a secular society that simultaneously inform their Catholicism. In my view, therefore, a postsecular Catholicism recognizes that, in practice, one cannot separate within-Church processes, including issues of language and authority, from Catholic Church–secular society processes. I thus maintain that the postsecular expectations Habermas outlines for religious–secular engagement are the same expectations required of Catholicism as it negotiates both its public role in a contrite modernity and the array of doctrinal issues of particular relevance to Catholics. I turn in the next chapter to American Catholics and to how they embody the postsecular mutuality of the religious and the secular in their understanding of Catholicism and in their engagement with the Church.

2

Postsecular American Catholics

AUTONOMY, IRONY, AND FRACTURED SOLIDARITY

AMID DRIFT FROM the church, many Catholics stay Catholic. They are able to do so largely because they bring their secular expectations and experiences to their understanding of Catholicism and their interactions with the Church. Yet Catholics' interpretive autonomy vis-à-vis the hierarchy and various Church teachings is not wholly secularized. It highlights, rather, the continuity between Catholics' religious and secular expectations and the ironies entailed. This chapter illuminates those ironies. These include the fact that interpretive autonomy is partially legitimated in Church teaching, that it contributes to preserving attachment to the Church, and that it is simultaneously used to seek the imprimatur of the Church for behavior that contravenes its teachings.

Being Catholic Amid Societal Change

Catholics have long maintained a one-fifth share of the U.S. population. This remarkable stability underscores the continuing relevance of religious attachment despite wide-ranging societal change. It also highlights the resilience of the Church despite the negative impact of the sex-abuse crisis on its finances and the credibility of many bishops. Today, 21 percent of Americans are Catholic—slightly less than a decade ago (23 percent) but relatively similar to the 1950s. This stability, however, masks significant demographic changes in American Catholicism—specifically, a growing Hispanic population. And of central importance to this book, it also masks the fact that attachment to the Church is largely preserved by Catholics' exercise of their own authority in interpreting its obligations and doctrines.

The strong trend toward religious disaffiliation in the United States—from less than 10 percent in the mid-1990s to 25 percent today—includes large numbers of Catholics. Highlighting the relative ease with which an inherited religious identity can be discarded, 13 percent of Americans who were raised Catholic have left the Church.[1] Amid this exodus, the stability in Catholics' share of the U.S. population is largely due to Hispanic immigrants and to Hispanics' comparatively high fertility rates. Hispanics account for a majority of the current growth in the American population, and over half are Catholic (58 percent).[2] Immigration is a major social force; it has long impacted Catholicism, and religion and society more generally, in America and elsewhere. Hence we shouldn't be surprised that it is a salient factor in the current religious landscape.

What is interesting today is that Hispanics are slowing down Catholicism's numerical decline, and thus dampening secularization. At the same time, their approach to what it means to be Catholic reflects and reinforces a secular sensibility. They show, more or less, the same individualization of authority characteristic of white Catholics. Their socioeconomic circumstances are highly disadvantaged compared to whites—the implications of which I discuss later in this chapter—and they are somewhat more devout in their attachment to specific faith beliefs (such as the Resurrection of Jesus). Nevertheless, their attitudes on sexual morality and other issues show that they too variously disagree with official Church teachings.[3] Thus despite the current demographic transformation, the relatively settled character of American Catholicism remains intact. This is a moderate Catholicism. As will become evident here, it entails the prioritization of certain aspects of faith and doctrine over others, and the balancing of attachment to Catholicism with a strikingly autonomous—highly secular—view of hierarchical authority and Church teachings. In a variety of ways, American Catholics show both the draw and the limited relevance of religion, and they embody the ironies maintaining this tension.

Interpretive Autonomy

It is impossible to talk about Catholics, especially American Catholics, without confronting the issue of authority. They have long taken an autonomous interpretive stance vis-à-vis Church authority, whether on religious or on secular matters. For Catholics, the continuity between their Catholicism and their everyday secular roles makes sense: being Catholic is not an overarching identity that eclipses all other aspects of the individual's life. Rather, in most of the everyday contexts in which Catholics move, including church-related activities, their secular roles (as parents, workers, volunteers, citizens) take precedence. And, importantly, their secular experiences shape the expectations they bring to religious matters. Thus, the secular is interwoven into their Catholic identity.

The Persistence and Unevenness of Faith

Historically, the Church has differentiated between its binding authority on matters of faith and morals and its lesser authority on social and political questions.[4] However, the secularization of faith is such that even core tenets of faith are not fully accepted among Catholics. One in three, for example, say that a person can be a good Catholic and not believe in the Resurrection of Jesus (34 percent), and over a third do not believe that in the Eucharist, the consecrated bread and wine are the real presence of Jesus (37 percent). Many also say that the Church's teaching that the Blessed Virgin Mary is the mother of God is not important to them personally (36 percent).[5]

For large numbers of self-identified Catholics, however, these beliefs are important. They are central to the constellation of beliefs and practices that demonstrate the persistence of faith despite secularization. The many Catholics who look to the sacraments as a significant source of personal meaning is one of the most compelling manifestations of the persistence of faith. In Catholicism, the Mass is the core liturgical and communal celebration at which the Eucharist (Communion) is sacramentally consecrated. Very large majorities of Catholics say that the Mass (84 percent)—and the sacraments in general (80 percent)—are personally very meaningful and very important to them, and are essential to their relationship with God (75 percent).

Yet—again reflecting the unevenness of faith's persistence—the valuing of the sacraments does not translate into rigorous practice. Over three-fourths of Catholics (78 percent) say that, despite its obligation in Church teaching, one can be a good Catholic without going to weekly Mass. And consistent with this view, only around a third (32 percent) report weekly Mass attendance. But, over half altogether go at least once a month (55 percent), thus integrating church community and some routine reminder of spiritual transcendence into their life. Private daily prayer is also salient (52 percent), and many too report going to confession at least once a year (43 percent). Moreover, a large majority of those who attend Mass say they do so *not* because it is required by the Church but because they feel the need to receive Communion (81 percent), and they enjoy participating in the liturgy (85 percent). For many, the sacraments have additional relevance as markers of the rites of passage. The sense of social belonging and comfort they provide is underscored by the fact that many Catholics who are infrequent churchgoers, nonetheless, turn to the Church at significant points in the life course—weddings, baptisms, and funerals.[6]

The mix of findings presented here shows that faith today clearly matters, *and* its hold is uneven and inconsistent. This is not necessarily a new phenomenon. Nevertheless, the postsecular recognition of the mutual draw of religious and secular influences captures the dynamic tension in the pull toward faith and its simultaneous counterbalancing by individual autonomy in what is believed and practiced. It helps illuminate that while being religious is largely determined by the self and not Church authority, it is simultaneously in ongoing conversation with the Church and gives selective deference to certain faith and other elements of Catholicism.

Irony #1: Interpretive autonomy is legitimated in Catholic teaching

One of the ironies of contemporary Catholicism is that interpretive autonomy finds legitimacy in Catholic teaching. It is not simply imported into Catholicism as a consequence of lay Catholics' secular roles and expectations, though it is bolstered by these. A consequence of the search for relevance in the modern world is that once you let modernity into religion, you cannot then forestall its implications. With Vatican II (1962–1965), Catholicism intentionally opened itself to modernity and engagement with the "signs of the times."[7] Such openness, however, cannot be selectively applied in one domain of thinking or being and silenced in another. Individuals' religious and secular roles comingle and intersect, and secular expectations and attitudes inevitably cut across religious activity.

The Church itself has contributed in no small way to this understanding of both individual and institutional Catholicism as an interwoven religious and secular entity. In 1891, Pope Leo XIII issued the papal encyclical *Rerum Novarum* (Of New Things), which focused on the mutual rights and duties of employers and workers amid the expansion of industrialization. Stating that "the condition of the working classes is the pressing question of the hour," its publication marked a significant turn in the Church's acknowledgment of the new realities of modern society. The encyclical was also an institutional claim by the Church that modernity required its public, ethical commentary on its changing character. It further communicated the Church's assumption that Catholic individuals and organizations had an obligation to work toward the common good and the improvement of economic and social conditions.

In doing so, it conveyed that Catholics' religious and secular roles were of a piece, a view reinforced by numerous subsequent encyclicals discussing social change.[8]

The Rebalancing of Interpretive Authority

Lest a view persist that Catholics were expected to "act Catholic" only on Sundays or in the highly controlled arena of sexual behavior, Vatican II offered clarification. It explicitly collapsed the boundary between religious and secular roles, and advised that Catholics should not compartmentalize their religious beliefs from their secular activities. John XXIII convened Vatican II partly to ensure that the Church would not be a "lifeless spectator in the face of [societal] events." And he conveyed that Catholic individuals and organizations should not be lifeless spectators, either.[9] Vatican II emphasized the proactive engagement of lay Catholics in Church and societal issues alike. It outlined an agential view of the crafting of human society, stating that "Men and women are the conscious artisans and authors of the culture of their community." Individuals, therefore, are responsible for the progress of culture that, it was argued, should be guided by the extent to which it enables the development of "the whole human person harmoniously." Vatican II thus called for a "vital synthesis" that would integrate individuals' religious identity with their various everyday family, work, social, and civic activities. It declared:

> Let there be no false opposition between professional and social activities on the one part, and religious life on the other. . . . In the exercise of all their earthly activities [the laity] can thereby gather their humane, domestic, professional, social, and technical enterprises into one vital synthesis with religious values, under whose supreme direction all things are harmonized unto God's glory.[10]

Conscious of the various problems in society, Vatican II acknowledged that responsibility for human society may lead individuals to look "anxiously upon many contradictions which [they] will have to resolve."[11] It insisted, nonetheless, that there was a collective obligation to remedy such contradictions:

> Let the laity . . . by their combined efforts remedy any institutions and conditions of the world which are customarily an inducement to sin, so that all such things may be conformed to the norms of justice.[12]

Such remedialization, it affirmed, would be accomplished by the Church operating as a collaborative, interpretive community. This would require the active engagement of an informed and competent laity in tackling the issues and problems that arise in modern society. Thus, while Vatican II reaffirmed the hierarchical structure of the Church and the teaching authority of the bishops, it also emphasized that the Church as an interpretive community requires a rather different understanding of authority. This new understanding emphasized the importance of lay–clerical dialogue and honest discussion:

> Let the layman not imagine that his pastors are always such experts, that to every problem which arises, however complex, they can readily give him a concrete solution, or even that such is their mission. . . . Often enough, the Christian view of things will itself suggest some specific solution in certain circumstances. Yet, it happens rather frequently, and legitimately so, that with equal sincerity some of the faithful will disagree with others on a given matter. Even against the intentions of their proponents, however, solutions proposed on one side or another may be easily confused by many people with the gospel message. Hence it is necessary for people to remember that no one is allowed in the aforementioned situations to appropriate the Church's authority for his opinion. They should always try to enlighten one another through honest discussion, preserving mutual charity and caring above all for the common good. . . . [L]et it be recognized that all the faithful, clerical and lay, possess a lawful freedom of inquiry and of thought, and the freedom to express their minds humbly and courageously about those matters in which they enjoy competence.[13]

Vatican II's rejection of a false opposition between religious and social activities, and its explicit affirmation of human agency, lay competence, and honest discussion in discerning the issues of modernity marked a highly significant turn. It put forward for Catholics a new understanding of religious and secular citizenship. This new framing sought the integration of the two and their exercise through informed, deliberative dialogue. The significance of this development in a Church in which the overarching, unilateral authority of the hierarchy was the unquestioned view, cannot be overstated.[14] It should further be noted that this rebalancing of interpretive authority is—as Pope Benedict recently argued—in continuity, not discontinuity, with the Catholic tradition.[15]

Vatican II's acknowledgment that the hierarchy's expertise and competence were not all-encompassing, and that its authority should not be
assumed by default, pushed open a crack in the singular privileging of hierarchical authority (whether so intended or not). Now, Vatican II insisted,
people must "be free to search for the truth, voice [their] mind, and publi-
cize it."[16] The acknowledgment of such freedom was critical to Vatican II's
new affirmation of religious pluralism and the separation of church and state.
Importantly, too, it also gave Catholics themselves a certain freedom in their
understanding and practice of the faith.[17] Clear evidence of this is seen in the
unevenness in Catholics' faith beliefs (discussed earlier), and as I discuss next,
in their understanding of sexual morality and what it means to be "a good
Catholic."

Irony #2: Interpretive autonomy preserves attachment to Catholicism

The interpretive freedom unleashed by Vatican II decreases—or secularizes—
the authority of the Church hierarchy in Catholic life. Yet, ironically, it
simultaneously contributes to preserving Catholics' attachment to and participation in Catholicism. The modern self is not obliged to identify as religious. Neither is it obliged to adhere to teachings with which it may disagree;
an individual can simply walk away from religion, as indeed many do. Most
people who leave gradually drift away, and do so because of practical changes
in their life circumstances.[18] Many Catholics, however, tend to point to their
disagreement with Church teachings on sexual morality as the reason for
leaving.[19] This decision makes sense: it allows individuals to avoid dissonance
between their personal views and behavior and an objective Catholic identity
that prohibits such behavior.

Dissent and Loyalty

However, most Catholics who stay Catholic also disagree with the Church's
sexual teachings. This fact thus introduces the question of what motivates
them to stay. And what allows them to stay? I probed these questions in a
previous study of Catholics who advocate for change on LGBT rights and
women's equality. What I found was a strong sensibility that being Catholic
conferred the freedom to disagree with aspects of Church teaching and still be
loyal to Catholicism.[20] Testing this assumption among American Catholics in
general confirms this as a widely shared view: Almost nine in ten say that, for
them personally, a meaningful element of Catholicism is that one can disagree
with aspects of Church teaching and still remain loyal to the Church.[21] This

is the reality of contemporary Catholicism. And, importantly, it is not subjectively experienced as dissonance, precisely because interpretive freedom is pervasive among Catholics and, moreover, institutionalized in Church teaching (as discussed earlier).

Vatican II's rebalancing of interpretive authority included the affirmation of individual conscience as a person's "most secret core and sanctuary." Articulating the "rights of man," it emphasized "conscience and its freedom of choice," and stated that individuals should not be coerced into any religious behavior contrary to what they, in conscience, freely believe to be true.[22] Conscience, however, though private, is formed in a socio-communal context and is informed by thoughtful consideration of both Church teachings and lived experience. Post-Vatican II Catholics exhibit the realization that their lived experience confers competence and, combined with conscience, interpretive autonomy in the domain of personal and family morality. This view puts them at odds with the Church hierarchy's long-held insistence that it enjoys special authority on matters of faith *and* on matters of personal morality.

The breach between the laity and the hierarchy was spurred by Pope Paul VI's encyclical *Humanae Vitae*. Issued in 1968, it reiterated the Church's opposition to all forms of artificial contraception (as well as abortion), and reasserted the pope's "magisterial competence" to do so. Paul's decision was contrary to the recommendation of a papal commission evaluating the issue. It was largely driven by his concern that any such change would undermine the purported constancy and authority of the Church's moral tradition and the teaching of his immediate predecessors.[23] Prior to Vatican II, Catholics had ignored various aspects of Church teaching, including its ban on contraception, but they tended to keep their dissent private.[24] Using contraception is, after all, a private act. It does not infiltrate a person's public identity in the same way as being divorced, for example, or in a same-sex relationship. However, in the wake of Vatican II and the broader cultural ferment of the 1960s, *Humanae Vitae* violated the expectations of lay Catholics, priests, and theologians that the Vatican would moderate its opposition to contraception. Its failure to do so was highly consequential, and it ushered in a new way of thinking that redefined Catholics' understanding of Church authority and its limits.[25]

In the immediate aftermath of *Humanae Vitae*, many American Catholics stopped attending Sunday Mass; there was a drop from 70 percent to 64 percent. They believed that they could not in good conscience use contraception and participate in Mass and communion. Mass attendance stabilized in the late 1970s until the early 1980s at around 52 percent, and it has steadily declined since then to its current level of about a third of Catholic weekly attenders.[26] This is clear evidence of secularization. What is more interesting, however, and illustrative of the dual pull of the religious and the secular, is that the Catholics who continued to go to church did so with a new mindset. This is one that affirms the moral authority to use contraception, to selectively disregard hierarchical authority, and to participate fully in Mass and communion. This new way of being Catholic—Catholic with a "liberated conscience"—was supported by many priests and theologians who, even prior to Vatican II, were accustomed to developing "pastoral adaptations" to Catholics' sexual circumstances.[27] In the wake of Vatican II, they began to do so more publicly. Thus today, Catholics' use of contraception is essentially a settled issue of personal morality; 78 percent say that one can be a good Catholic and use contraception.[28] And it is one on which Church officials tended to remain silent—notwithstanding its new salience in the U.S. bishops' religious freedom campaign (see chapter 5).

Successive cohorts of Catholics have been applying a similar interpretive autonomy to other sexual issues. This includes cohabitation, divorce and remarriage, and same-sex relationships. In all these domains, large majorities of Catholics express attitudes directly contravening Church teaching; for example, two-thirds (67 percent) of Catholics today favor gay marriage. And their views further convey their assumption that they have the legitimate authority to do so. Beyond attitudes, such autonomy is evident in Catholic behavior. A fourth of American Catholics are or have been divorced; one in ten is currently cohabiting, while four in ten report having lived with a romantic partner at some point in their lives. And 14 percent of American LGBT adults identify as Catholic.[29]

Interpretive Autonomy Is Independent of Papal Popularity

Catholics' exercise of interpretive freedom, moreover, is independent of their views of the pope. American Catholics express highly favorable opinions of Francis; they were similarly positive about John Paul, but less disposed toward Benedict. Many appreciate the symbolism of the papacy and are drawn in by the charisma of individual popes. The crowds of Americans who visit the Vatican and who seek papal audiences, the thousands of young Americans who travel overseas for World Catholic Youth Day activities graced by the pope (e.g., at Krakow or Rio de Janeiro), and the throngs who turned out to greet Francis, Benedict, and John Paul during papal visits to the United States underscore the symbolic significance and emotional draw of the papacy.

Nevertheless, irrespective of who's pope, American Catholics make up their own minds about what it means to be Catholic. Eight in ten (81 percent) have a favorable view of Francis and an equally high number (77 percent) say that the Church should allow birth control. Similarly, over two-thirds say that the Church should allow priests to get married (72 percent) and women to be priests (68 percent), and half say that it should recognize same-sex marriages (50 percent). Less than a third (29 percent) assign high importance to its teaching opposing the death penalty.[30] Now is a more secularized time than even twenty years ago. Yet in 1999, when 85 percent of American Catholics had a favorable view of John Paul, they were similarly likely to disagree with Church teachings. Then, two-thirds or more said that one can be a good Catholic without obeying Church teaching on contraception (71 percent), marriage (67 percent), and divorce and remarriage (64 percent). Only a fourth said that celibacy (27 percent), and even fewer that the ban on women priests (17 percent) and opposition to the death penalty (22 percent), was essential to Catholicism.[31] In short, a Catholic's positive view of the pope should not be conflated with deference to his decisions, pronouncements, or authority.

The typical self-identified Catholic, therefore, is one who disagrees with Church teaching on sexual and other issues and continues to stay Catholic. Such Catholics illuminate the postsecular reality: the (partial) failure of secularism (to displace faith), *and* the secularization of religion. The persistence of Catholicism as a meaningful religious tradition is largely because many Catholics are empowered to hold together faith and reason and lived experience, and thus to interpret and own Catholicism in ways at odds with official Church teaching. This dynamic is most apparent in the lived Catholicism of those whose public identities as LGBT or divorced and remarried Catholics are in contrast with official Church teaching. But a similar interpretive autonomy is evident among Catholics more generally, almost all of whom disregard at least one or more elements of Church teaching (e.g., contraception). Catholicism both embeds and fosters interpretive diversity; and as such, it cannot be reduced to a checklist of compliance with a particular, unilaterally imposed, orthodoxy.[32] Interpretive pluralism is found not only among Catholic laity but also in the deliberations of theologians, ethicists, and bishops, as well as in the multiple doctrinal strands in papal and other Church teachings. This is the same interpretive pluralism that enables Catholicism to maintain its relevance as a source of personal and collective identity amid secularism.

Irony #3: Catholic advocacy of inclusive participation in the sacraments
is driven by belief in their sanctity

While interpretive autonomy undergirds the contestation of Church authority, it simultaneously empowers the push for doctrinal change. Again pointing to the mutual pull of secular and religious currents, many Catholics advocate for changes that, ironically, seek the imprimatur of the Church on its secularized integration in their lives. Catholic activism for change is grounded in Catholics' everyday experiences of sexuality, relationships, marriage, and family life that give them a perspective and an understanding at odds with the ideals and obligations articulated in Church teachings.

Doctrinal activism is also motivated by Vatican II's charge that the laity should remedy the contradictions within the Church, as in society. Heeding its call that the laity should "zealously participate in the saving work of the Church," various groups and organizations began mobilizing for change from within the Church in the late 1960s.[33] Their advocacy continues today on such issues as divorce and remarriage, LGBT rights, women's ordination, celibacy, and lay decision making. Catholic activism for institutional change was further energized in the early 2000s as a result of the Church's sex-abuse scandals.[34] Reflecting the comingling of religious and secular expectations, the activism within the Church coincides both historically (e.g., the 1960s and '70s) and today with a broader societal push for civil rights and social equality. It also contributes to the politicization of moral issues both inside and outside the Church, and to the so-called culture wars that continue to impact intra-Catholic and public debates.[35]

Of particular postsecular relevance, religion is maintained, in part, because those who are moderately religious push for the sorts of institutional changes that would make the Church more palatable to a secular sensibility. This drive is bolstered by secular expectations, but it is also rooted in religion. Specifically in the case of Catholic activism, it is rooted in the Church's doctrinal resources and shared solidarity. Demonstrating the postsecular mutuality of religious and secular resources, Catholics' expressed desire for change reflects a commitment both to the secular values enshrined in political liberalism (e.g., equality, pluralism) and to the values and meanings associated with belonging to Catholicism. When Catholics argue for doctrinal pluralism and a more inclusive Church, it is not a secular appeal to individual rights that they use. Rather, they ground their claims in the religious-sacramental and communal life of Catholicism. Their socialization within Catholicism—its culture of personal, family, and community relationships—and the deep resonance of its rituals, language, and meanings are what spur their advocacy of a Church that is affirming of doctrinal, attitudinal, and lifestyle differences.[36]

Divorced and Remarried Catholics

I focus here on divorce and remarriage because this subject sharply illuminates the entwined pull of the religious and the secular. The prevalence of divorce in American society, and its incidence among American Catholics, though lower than for non-Catholics, accentuates its salience as a Catholic issue.[37] It is also a pressing issue for Catholics in several other countries.[38] The complexities that divorce and remarried Catholics present were on display at the recent Vatican Synod on the Family (see chapter 6). But their relevance to ordinary Catholics is of long duration. In keeping with their interpretive autonomy, over two-thirds of American Catholics say that one can be a good Catholic without adhering to the Church's teachings on marriage or divorce and remarriage.[39] And acting on this ethos, many Catholics who are in "irregular" situations—in non-Church approved marriages or cohabiting—partake of the Eucharist (Holy Communion).[40] This pattern is emblematic of the secularization of religious authority such that individuals themselves determine the appropriateness of both their sexual and their Church behavior.

This secular ethos, however, does not penetrate deeply enough into the Catholic mind to suppress desire for the sacraments. The simultaneous threading of the religious and the secular is exemplified by the many divorced and remarried (and other irregular) Catholics who are not, as a general rule, allowed to receive Communion but who *want* to. The Synod—as I elaborate in chapter 6—has refined the doctrinal understanding of admissibility to Communion, and this is highly consequential. At the same time, formal Church teaching on marriage remains in place, and this is what informs my discussion in this section. In Catholic teaching, marriage is a sacrament, and all sexual relationships are expected to occur within marriage. Therefore, Catholics who live together in a sexual relationship outside of marriage, or whose civil marriages are not approved by the Church, are—according to official Church teaching—living in an ongoing state of objective sin.

Divorced Catholics who remarry without having had their first marriage annulled may attend Mass, but they are prohibited from receiving Communion.[41] An annulment is given if a Church tribunal concludes that the couple's marriage was not in fact valid at the time it was contracted. The marriage can be declared invalid for various reasons. These include the emotional immaturity of one or both of the partners, or other conditions (e.g., pregnancy, parental coercion) that at the time of the marriage impeded either partner's full consent to the obligations the Church imposes on marriage. An annulment is permission to remarry because it is based on the fact that the first (invalid) marriage was not properly a sacrament. Remarried Catholics without an annulment are thus excluded from Communion because they are considered adulterers and thus living in a sinful situation. This can only be absolved by confession, and only if the person commits to terminate the sin by refraining from sexual activity (or by seeking and being granted an annulment). Many Catholics, nonetheless, find it hard to understand the sinful status of remarriage without an annulment. They have difficulty reconciling how a Church that forgives human sinfulness also singles out divorce and remarriage as the sin that excludes an individual from receiving Communion, the Church's core sacrament.

Relatively few divorced Catholics seek an annulment (15 percent) and approximately half of those who do are granted one.[42] Yet, more than a third of all Catholics who divorce subsequently remarry.[43] Hence, there are many divorced and remarried Catholics in various states of "irregularity" in their practice of Catholicism. Some attend Mass and partake of Communion; some, though they attend Mass, do not go to Communion and as such are spiritually separated from their fellow Mass-goers.[44] Others don't go to Mass in the first place because they feel that their divorce and (civil) remarriage excommunicates them (though it doesn't). Additionally, there are many divorced Catholics who, though they have not remarried, nonetheless think that being divorced excludes them from Communion. This is an erroneous assumption on their part because Church teaching, in fact, allows divorced Catholics to partake of Communion if they maintain a celibate lifestyle. There has long been confusion among the laity on these various points, and local priests and Church officials do little to clarify them.[45]

Resisting Annulment

Amid their embrace of the secularization of marriage (e.g., divorce, remarriage, nonchurch weddings), Catholics' valuing of the sacramental life of the Church is further encapsulated by their views on annulment. Many Catholics, liberals more so than conservatives, express a negative view of the annulment process.[46] They are especially critical of its material costs, both the time and money entailed. They also denounce what they describe as the inquisitorial, evidence-gathering methods used in determining whether, for example, the partners were emotionally mature in contracting the marriage. On balance, despite acknowledgment by a small number of Catholics of its positive, heal-ing aspects, the process tends to be seen as lacking credibility. The recent pro-cedural changes instituted by Pope Francis, with the intent of streamlining the annulment process at the diocesan level, may help alleviate some of these concerns.[47]

Procedural issues, however, are not the whole story. Catholic pushback against annulments is also driven by religious-sacramental considerations. Some Catholics specifically object to the Church's attempt to dissolve what they themselves consider to be a full and valid sacramental marriage. Save Our Sacrament (SOS), is a relatively loose-knit group of divorced Catholics whose ex-spouses have sought an annulment against their wishes.[48] SOS lobbies Church authorities against the granting of such annulments and against the evidence-gathering process they are subject to as unwilling Respondents in a given annulment case. Their concern encapsulates the postsecular entwin-ing of the religious and the secular. Some Catholics who avail of divorce—a highly secular phenomenon—want a Church annulment in order to be in good standing with the Church in the event of a new Church or civil mar-riage. And others want to preserve the sacramental status of their marriage even though it may have ended in divorce and annulment. In either case, the sacrament is cherished despite the breakdown (and possible nullification) of the marriage.

Thus, ironically, the many Catholics whose interpretive autonomy empow-ers them to disagree with Church teaching or to advocate for changes in the Church—such as on divorce and remarriage, or same-sex relationships—want the imprimatur of the Church and to be in full communion with their fellow Catholics even as they contest and selectively disregard Church teachings. This coupling of autonomy and solidarity (communal inclusivity) embodies the postsecular task entailed in negotiating the crosscutting pull of the secular and of faith. It is not just individual Catholics who live this tension. So, too, does the Church hierarchy. How the Church manages the interpretive diver-sity of its increasingly secularized faithful, and the various tensions encoun-tered in balancing the forces of tradition and change, is an ongoing process whose dynamics will be further illuminated in subsequent chapters.

Is Interpretive Autonomy a Trojan Horse?

Catholics who disagree with various aspects of Church teaching—whether activists for doctrinal change or the typical Catholic interviewed in national surveys or in local parish settings—are often referred to as dissenting, disaffected, or cafeteria-style, pick-and-choose Catholics. In this view, Catholics simply suit themselves and take from the Church only those elements that suit them or that make them feel good, thus serving their own narcissistic or therapeutic purposes.[49]

A contrary view, however, is that many such Catholics might more accurately be referred to as *nonassenting* Catholics. To assent to something is to give active agreement to it. A nonassenting Catholic, therefore, is one who is unable, in conscience, to give deliberate assent to a particular moral teaching. Thinking of Catholics as nonassenting is especially fitting in terms of the postsecular turn and its accent on the importance of both religious and secular reflexive dialogue. As Francis A. Sullivan explains, assent to Church teaching is not an automatic or mechanical response. It is, rather, the outcome of a deliberative, cognitive process.[50] Being a good Catholic is not about obedience, as used to be taught by the (old) Catechism, but about discerning the appropriate moral action in a given set of circumstances.

The response that Catholics give to Church teachings and papal and hierarchical decisions is expected to derive from a process of "sincere assent."[51] Sincere assent cannot be coerced. It must be grounded, instead, in individuals' sincere evaluation and acceptance of the claims put forward. This deliberative process requires much more than a superficial consideration of the teaching. It calls for the dutiful examination of both the Church's claims and the individual's own biases and desires. It also requires an honest and sustained effort to overcome any contrary opinion the person holds. If, as a result of this process, Catholics discern that a specific Church teaching fails to make reasonable sense, they should be regarded as *conscientiously* dissenting, or as nonassenting. In sum, if a Catholic's disagreement with official Church teaching is not coming from some manipulative purpose or some self-absorbed desire, but from lingering doubts about the truth of a particular teaching after having made "an honest and sustained effort to achieve internal assent" to it, then this nonassent is not disobedience or disrespect.[52]

That Catholics' interpretive autonomy might be seen as a conscientious position of nonassent is indirectly supported by the fact that it is college-educated Catholics who are the most engaged in the Church. College education tends to foster critical thinking and a certain cognitive complexity that discourages individuals from seeing things in simple black-and-white or either-or terms.[53] This may help explain why, compared to those without a college degree, college-educated Catholics have higher weekly Mass attendance rates and higher rates of Communion participation. It is not that they are necessarily less "sinful"; rather, their moral discernment may allow them to be more fully engaged Catholics. Moreover, Catholics who have been educated at Catholic schools or colleges are among the most active in advocating for changes in the Church. These findings suggest perhaps that those who are better trained in critiquing and evaluating situational scenarios and/or who have the deepest immersion within Catholicism are at ease in discerning what, in good conscience, is both morally acceptable and in tune with the larger Catholic tradition.[54]

Another framing, one from a culture-war perspective, might suggest that Catholics who either publicly disregard Church teaching or advocate for changes in the Church simply want to politicize doctrine or to undermine Catholicism in the pursuit of a secular agenda. This may well be true of some Catholics. But if these are motivating forces, it would probably be more fruitful for such Catholics to drop their religious identity and detach from the Church rather than propping it up both numerically and in public culture. By the same token, it would likely be more productive to pursue a secular agenda through public policy and legislative arenas rather than through the Church. In any event, the claim that Catholic interpretive autonomy is driven by a secular agenda does not jibe with the evidence. As I have discussed, American Catholics embody the postsecular entwining of the religious and the secular. While their faith is uneven, its pull persists, and the Church's doctrinal and sacramental resources nurture their commitment even as they live out a Catholicism that is variously at odds with Church teachings.

Catholic Political Community

The Catholic Church's tradition of social justice makes it well disposed to postsecular expectations that it can mobilize collective action against economic inequality and related ills. Principles of solidarity and concern for the poor are central to its teaching and its public engagement, evident for example in the social services provided by Catholic Charities.[55] Long before it became elevated as a top priority by Pope Francis, American Catholics embraced the importance of helping the poor.[56] Indeed, despite the extensiveness of the Church's abortion activism, Catholics tend to see its social justice work as an equally if not more important policy priority. When pollsters ask Catholics to choose between social justice and abortion/pro-life advocacy, social justice narrowly eclipses abortion. In other words, a majority of self-identified Catholics in general (60 percent) and of weekly churchgoers (51 percent) say that the Church's public policy statements should focus more on social justice and the obligation to help the poor, even if it means focusing less on its advocacy against abortion.[57]

Can Solidarity Be Stoked Amid Political Partisanship?

The collective motivation to remedy economic inequality and other problems is constrained by shifting currents in Catholics' political ideology and by a new ethnic and generational divide. In their secular activity as political citizens and voters, white Catholics show increased support for the Republican Party. A majority of white Catholics has voted for the Republican nominee in every presidential election since 2000. In the two most recent elections, 59 percent voted for Mitt Romney (in 2012) and 60 percent for Donald Trump (in 2016).[58] White Catholics' long-term drift toward the Republican Party, whose policies favor a reduced role for government in dealing with economic inequality, puts them at odds with some of the Church's social justice priorities. This trend is part of a larger current in America. Since the Great Recession (2007–2008), there has been an intensification both in political partisanship and in antipathy toward the role of government in social welfare.[59]

As one would expect, white Catholic Republicans and Democrats differ in their policy priorities. Republicans are more likely than Democrats to favor cutbacks in welfare programs, and less likely to favor more government funds for health care for poor children. They also assign greater importance to the Church's teaching on abortion, and are more likely than Democrats to affirm the Church hierarchy's authority on sexual morality. Despite these and other political differences (e.g., on climate change; see chapter 3), there are some grounds for solidarity. White Catholic Democrats and Republicans have similar levels of weekly Mass attendance, and they express similar views on the importance of the Church in their lives. Moreover, on the hot-button issue of immigration, both are equally supportive of the U.S. bishops' advocacy of an inclusive immigration policy. Being Catholic may not be strong enough to override partisan views on many issues, but its relevance in shaping bipartisan support for specific policy outcomes—such as on immigration—should not be overlooked.[60]

Worlds Apart: Young Hispanic and White Catholics

The support among white Catholics for immigration reform would seem to portend well for the bridging of communal ties between white Catholics and the growing number of Hispanic Catholics. Underscoring the current demographic transformation, 54 percent of young adult (18–35 years old) American Catholics are Hispanic.[61] This ethnically divided millennial generation is the new face of Catholicism and its vanguard. Its potential to forge communal solidarity around inequality, however, is challenged by its socioeconomic and political divisions. Young Hispanic Catholics are much less educated and much poorer than whites. Over a third (35 percent) of young white Catholics have a college degree, but fewer than one in ten (9 percent) Hispanics do; and while a majority (52 percent) of young Hispanics have an income of $25,000 or less, this is true of only 15 percent of young white Catholics. Young Hispanic Catholics are also more likely to be in nonmarital, cohabiting relationships, which in turn tend to be less economically stable than marriage.[62]

The socioeconomic circumstances of young Hispanic Catholics sharpen attention on the Church's pastoral challenges and its public policy priorities. The prospects for Hispanic economic mobility, unlike those of earlier generations of immigrant Catholics, are hindered by the high level of poverty among Hispanic children and the cycle of intergenerational disadvantage it propels.[63] Their upward mobility is also hindered by the current weakness of the Catholic parish-school infrastructure that was historically so crucial to the mobility of previous immigrant groups.[64]

The very different socioeconomic circumstances of young white and Hispanic Catholics are stoking an intragenerational political divide. Especially striking is the large gap between them on issues that are central both to the Church's social justice commitments and to those of a contrite modernity. Young Hispanics are three times more likely than young whites to support immigration reform (65 versus 21 percent), and more than twice as likely as whites to favor increased government funds for poor children's health care (66 versus 30 percent). They are also much more likely to say that the Church's concern for the poor is a meaningful element of Catholicism for them (70 versus 56 percent).[65]

The assumption that membership in a religious community may strengthen collective mobilization against economic and social exclusion seems more optimistic, therefore, than perhaps warranted by the changing ethnic and generational dynamics of contemporary American Catholicism. The findings highlighted here show that Catholics need look no further than within their own religious community to see the prevalence of socioeconomic inequality, the policy challenges it poses, and the polarities that fracture the solidarity that may be necessary to ameliorate it. Catholic community is fractured to some extent by disagreements among Catholics on sexual morality. Though the majority of American Catholics favor changes in Church teachings on contraception, divorce and remarriage, and same-sex relationships, the differences of opinion that do exist point to the importance of intra-Church and religious–secular dialogue on these issues.[66] The greater challenge to Catholic solidarity comes from political partisanship, and especially from the stark contrast in the socioeconomic status and priorities of young Hispanic and white Catholics. Such inequality accentuates the pressure on the U.S. bishops to pursue public policies that would ameliorate the socioeconomic circumstances of Hispanics and other disadvantaged Americans. This focus would align well with the postsecular expectation of religion as a remedial political force against inequality. It would also mirror Pope Francis's prioritization of economic inequality and social inclusion, the subject of the next chapter.

3

The Church's Postsecular Moment

ECONOMIC INEQUALITY AND global warming are major concerns today. They are also issues of particular concern to Pope Francis. The Church's participation in the public sphere from the late nineteenth century onward reflects its longstanding engagement with social, economic, and political issues.[1] What is new today is acute public awareness of the problems of modernity, and the postsecular recognition that moderate religious actors can help reframe how we think and what we might do about them. Thus, postsecular expectations open up space for the Church to step in (anew) and articulate an ethical path for contemporary society. And, opportunistically for the Church, it does so amid increasing secularization in society and in the Church.

Church leaders may or may not envision a postsecular role for the Church. It is nonetheless apparent that Francis and Benedict, too, are attuned to the importance of public conversation between the religious and the secular—a necessary dialogue noted by John XXIII and Vatican II.[2] Indeed, Benedict's own public dialogue with Habermas (see chapter 1) models this idea. Befitting postsecular expectations, all three of Benedict's encyclicals focused on modernity and social justice. In particular, *Caritas in Veritate* (*CV*) intentionally reengages with the ethical challenges of economic overdevelopment and underdevelopment, first outlined by Paul VI's *Populorum Progressio*. Issued in 1967, that encyclical emphasized the inequality fostered by economic underdevelopment and it foreshadowed many of the global economic issues confronting society today.

In revisiting these issues, Benedict notes that the Church has a public responsibility, "a public role over and above her charitable and educational activities" to be "at the service of the world in terms of love and truth"

(*CV* #11). In line with the postsecular expectation that religious voices can and should inform political responses to societal ills, he states:

> In today's complex situation, not least because of the growth of a glo-
> balized economy, the church's social doctrine has become a set of fun-
> damental guidelines offering approaches that are valid even beyond
> the confines of the church: In the face of ongoing development these
> guidelines need to be addressed in the context of dialogue with all
> those seriously concerned for humanity and for the world in which we
> live. (*Deus Caritas Est* [*DC*] #27)

Further, while affirming the role of the state, Benedict argues that it is the Church's duty "not to remain on the sidelines in the fight for justice." As he elaborates:

> The church cannot and must not take upon herself the political battle
> to bring about the most just society possible. She cannot and must not
> replace the state. Yet at the same time she cannot and must not remain
> on the sidelines in the fight for justice. She has to play her part through
> rational argument, and she has to reawaken the spiritual energy with-
> out which justice, which always demands sacrifice, cannot prevail and
> prosper. A just society must be the achievement of politics, not of the
> church. Yet the promotion of justice through efforts to bring about
> openness of mind and will to the demands of the common good is
> something which concerns the church deeply. (*DC* #28)

He echoes the postsecular expectation of fruitful religious–secular dialogue in crafting a more egalitarian society. And further in tune with postsecular thinking, he denounces the extremes of both secular and religious fundamen-talism, stating:

> The exclusion of religion from the public square—and, at the other
> extreme, religious fundamentalism—hinders an encounter between
> persons and their collaboration for the progress of humanity. . . .
> Secularism and fundamentalism exclude the possibility of fruitful dia-
> logue and effective cooperation between reason and religious faith.
> Reason always stands in need of being purified by faith: this also holds
> true for political reason, which must not consider itself omnipotent.
> For its part, religion always needs to be purified by reason in order

to show its authentically human face. . . [*CV* #56]. Fruitful dialogue between faith and reason . . . constitutes the most appropriate framework for promoting fraternal collaboration between believers and non-believers in their shared commitment to working for justice and the peace of the human family. (*CV* #57)

Like Benedict, the notion of a public Church that Francis advocates fits well with the postsecular moment. He argues: "It is no longer possible to claim that religion should be restricted to the private sphere and that it exists only to prepare souls for heaven" (*JG* #182). Rather, evangelization means "going out into the world," and requires the Church to be in the vanguard, showing "concern for the building of a better world" (#183). He too articulates the postsecular expectation of reciprocal religious–secular dialogue. Reminding secular citizens (and religious believers) that religion has a central place in secular discourse, *Laudato Si' (LS)*, his encyclical on the environment, states:

in the areas of politics and philosophy there are those who firmly reject the idea of a Creator or consider it irrelevant and consequently dismiss as irrational the rich contribution that religions can make toward an integral ecology and the full development of humanity. Others view religions simply as a subculture to be tolerated. Nonetheless, science and religion, with their distinctive approaches to understanding reality, can enter into an intense dialogue fruitful for both. (*LS* #62)

And, by the same token, Francis reminds religious believers (and secular citizens) that faith is inherently public, demanding a commitment to building a just society. As he argues in *The Joy of the Gospel* (*JG*):

no one can demand that religion should be relegated to the inner sanctum of personal life, without influence on societal and national life, without concern for the soundness of civil institutions, without a right to offer an opinion on events affecting society. . . . An authentic faith— which is never comfortable or completely personal—always involves a deep desire to change the world, to transmit values, to leave this earth somehow better than we found it. (*JG* #183)

Both Benedict and Francis thus share an understanding of Catholicism as a public Church not only well suited but also required to fruitfully engage with the secular. Yet, Francis is better able to translate this into practice. The

following pages show how he accomplishes this, and how by doing so he amplifies the Church's postsecular relevance, whether intended as such or not.
I argue that Francis's positive affirmation of secular reality, his communicative
openness, his prioritization of economic inequality and climate change, and
the secular vocabulary in which he presents his critique bolster the Church as
a postsecular actor.

Encountering God in the Secular

In September 2013, in his first lengthy interview as pope, Francis unequivocally asserted that God dwells in the secular. He stated:

> God is in history [and] in [its] processes. . . . God is certainly in the
> past, because we can see his footprints. And God is also in the future
> as a promise. But the "concrete" God, so to speak, is today. For this
> reason, complaining never helps us find God. The complaints of today
> about how barbaric the world is—these complaints sometimes end up
> giving birth within the church to desires to establish order in the sense
> of pure conservation, as a defense. No: God is to be encountered in the
> world of today.[3]

He frequently repeats this, reminding Catholics and others that God is present in "everyday affairs" and "concrete activities." These remarks are important because they reposition the Church as affirming of secular society and
not simply its critic. Postsecular reciprocity requires religious actors to not
just talk *about* the secular but also to talk *with* it (see chapter 1). This is what
Francis does. He meets secular society as it is, and engages with its realities
and expectations.

The presence of God in the everyday world—incarnation and imma-
nence—are core principles of Catholic theology. They are at the heart of the
Catholic imagination that, as Andrew Greeley elaborates, sees God and other
elements of the Catholic faith (e.g., Jesus, Mary, the Trinity) "lurking in the
[ordinary everyday] objects, events and people of creation."[4] Yet at the macro
level, the Church often looks anxiously at secular society. Modernization,
which expanded scientific thinking and accelerated industrialization and
urbanization, prompted Church leaders at the turn of the twentieth century
to take a dim view of social change. Seeing a threat to the Church's moral and
institutional dominance, Pope Leo XIII's statement on Americanism (1899)
and Pope Pius X's on Modernism (1907) were critical of pluralism, equality, and

scientific reasoning. John XXIII's papacy (1958–1963) and Vatican II (1962–1965) marked a major change in orientation, consciously forging a bridge to secular society. For example, Vatican II affirmed the Church as a "historical reality" that positively influences and benefits from the modern world and the "development of humanity." And, as I noted in chapter 2, it committed itself to having relevance in the modern world and thus being open and responsive to societal change.[5]

Paul VI succeeded John XXIII, who died in June 1963, less than a year after Vatican II began. He continued its agenda, and in his address at its final general meeting (in December 1965), he clearly summarized the Church's changing orientation:

> we cannot pass over one important consideration in our analysis of the religious meaning of the council [Vatican II]: it has been deeply committed to the study of the modern world. Never before perhaps, so much as on this occasion, has the Church felt the need to know, to draw near to, to understand, to penetrate, serve and evangelize the society in which she lives; and to get to grips with it, almost to run after it, in its rapid and continuous change. This attitude, a response to the distances and divisions we have witnessed over recent centuries, in the last century and in our own especially, between the Church and secular society—this attitude has been strongly and unceasingly at work in the council."[6]

Getting to grips with secular society is not easy. Part of the challenge for the Church lies in the gap between Catholic teaching—on marriage, social justice, or abortion, for example—and contemporary culture. Additionally, the tension between tradition and change in the Church complicates its secular disposition. Paul VI was keenly aware of these tensions and of their presence during Vatican II's deliberations. He noted that the need for the Church to "run after" societal change—to be open to ideas of lay competence, pluralism, and religious freedom, for example—was so strongly present that it led to talk that the Church was being unfaithful to tradition. He rejected this allegation, stating:

> some have been inclined to suspect that an easy-going and excessive responsiveness to the outside world, to passing events, cultural fashions, temporary needs, an alien way of thinking . . . may have swayed persons and acts of [Vatican II's] ecumenical synod, at the expense of

the fidelity which is due to tradition. . . . We do not believe that this shortcoming should be imputed to it, to its real and deep intentions, to its authentic manifestations.[7]

Yet similar suspicions have continued during the more than fifty years since Vatican II. And they persist even as papal decisions, such as Paul VI's rejection of contraception (see chapter 2), suggest that the Church's openness to social change is always tempered by deference to its moral tradition.

John Paul II's papacy strongly reasserted Church doctrine in the face of secular currents. He framed his critique in terms of a starkly dichotomized culture of life and culture of death. His 1995 encyclical *The Gospel of Life* (*GL*), which elaborated Church teaching on abortion, euthanasia, and the death penalty, was especially forceful. It drew a portrait of society "character-ized by the emergence of a culture which denies solidarity and in many cases takes the form of a veritable culture of death." It further argued that "powerful cultural, economic and political currents" foster "a kind of conspiracy against life" and that "the value of life has undergone a kind of 'eclipse.'"[8]

This sharp dichotomy reinforces rather than bridges the Church–secular divide. In John Paul's framing, the Church and its moral truths stand for a culture of life. And secular society, which manifests the "eclipse of the sense of God" (*GL* #24), embodies a culture of death. For Benedict, the dichotomy was more abstract, but it was given voice in his frequent critique of what he saw as the tyranny of secularism and relativism versus the unchanging, univer-sal truth of the Church. As he elaborated in his homily (as dean of the College of Cardinals) prior to the papal conclave that would elect him pope:

> Today, having a clear faith based on the Creed of the Church is often labeled as fundamentalism. Whereas relativism, that is, letting oneself be "tossed here and there, carried about by every wind of doctrine," seems the only attitude that can cope with modern times. We are building a dictatorship of relativism that does not recognize anything as definitive and whose ultimate goal consists solely of one's own ego and desires.[9]

Francis's insistence, then, just a few months into his papacy that "God is to be encountered in the world of today" is a turning point in the Church's con-strual of the secular. Whether or not he intends to, he conveys a postsecu-lar sensibility. He explicitly recognizes that the secular and the religious are mutually entwined rather than polarized. His emphasis on God in the secular changes the tenor of the Church's approach; it projects a desire to deal with the realities of secular society in a way that is proactively constructive. The postsecular task of talking *with* secular society requires that it should not be seen primarily as an object of denunciation. Francis recognizes this. As he acknowledges in *Amoris Laetitia* (*AL*),

> We have often been on the defensive, wasting pastoral energy on denouncing a decadent world without being proactive in proposing ways of finding true happiness [*AL* #38].... We should not be trapped into wasting energy in doleful laments. (*AL* #57)

Thus, giving practical realization to his frequently reiterated argument that "realities are greater than ideas" and that ideas and realities must be in continuous dialogue (*JG* #231–233), he is deliberately forging a new role for the Church in dealing with societal realities.

Evangelization—or outreach—is a central part of the Church's mission. And a "new evangelization" program was already under way in the Church before Benedict resigned. It is seeking new ways to convey the relevance of the gospel to increasingly secularized Catholics, as well as to lapsed and ex-Catholics. Francis, however, brings a different accent to this mission; he is self-consciously leading the Church on "new paths" (*JG* #1). His intent in charting a new direction is demonstrated in several ways, most visibly by his choice not to live in the Vatican's apostolic palace and in everyday, humble gestures that are extraordinary for a pope. It is also evident discursively. For example, the apostolic exhortation he wrote—*The Joy of the Gospel* (*JG*)—was an outgrowth of the Synod of Bishops that convened in October 2012 (under Benedict) to discuss evangelization. Francis, however, declined to use the bishops' report that summarized their recommendations. Instead, he used the opportunity—his first fully single-authored document as pope—to outline what he called "a new chapter . . . for the church's journey in years to come" (*JG* #1).[10]

Postsecular Communicative Openness

The Church's new chapter fits well with postsecular expectations. This is true not only of these issues highlighted by Francis—economic inequality and climate change—but also of his communicative openness. In tune with a postsecular sensibility, he emphasizes the importance of reciprocal dialogue with and amid differences (*JG* #227–228), and that such dialogue is not to avoid conflict or to dilute differences. Conflict, rather, is to be negotiated. Thus, Francis is clear that a consensus-building process is not a "facile syncretism" or a "diplomatic openness that says yes to everything in order to avoid problems" (*JG* #251). Rather, as Habermas also argues (see chapter 1), it entails sincere reciprocal dialogue with, and openness to understanding the convictions of, the other party; it not about diluting one's convictions but, rather, reflexively examining them in light of alternative views (*JG* #251).

Communicative openness also entails the relinquishing of preemptive, hierarchical authority. As such, postsecular expectations fit well with American Catholics' and Vatican II's expectations of the Church as an interpretive community in which lay opinions and experiences matter (see chapter 2). The pope and other church officials are thus expected to be open to a range of arguments and to refrain from unilateral, declaratory statements that preemptively shut down dialogue on any given religious or secular issue.

A postsecular sensibility is well conveyed by Francis's communicative openness. He tends to refrain from claiming magisterial authority as legitimation for the validity of his arguments. To the contrary, he specifically points out that "neither the pope nor the church have a monopoly on the interpretation of social realities or the proposal of solutions to contemporary problems" (*JG* #184). Echoing Vatican II's affirmation of interpretive pluralism, he further states: "Nor do I believe that the papal magisterium should be expected to offer a definitive or complete word on every question that affects the church and the world" (*JG* #16; see also *JG* #3). Similarly, in *Laudato Si'* he emphasizes the importance of honest debate, saying:

> On many concrete questions, the church has no reason to offer a definitive opinion; she knows that honest debate must be encouraged among experts, while respecting divergent views . . . [*LS* #61]. . . . I am concerned to encourage an honest and open debate so that particular interests or ideologies will not prejudice the common good." (*LS* #188)

This communicative openness contrasts especially with John Paul II, who frequently invoked magisterial authority. He insisted that doctrinal debates, including those among academic theologians, should defer to the authority of the magisterium.[11] Benedict acknowledged the collaborative nature of the relationship of the pope and the bishops. Nonetheless, he gave primacy to the pope as the unifying personification of the Church, notwithstanding his concession that "Everyone knows that the Pope is not an absolute monarch."[12]

Francis's communicative style is explicitly open to wide-ranging discussion of societal and doctrinal issues, something highlighted by the Synod on the Family (see chapter 6). His openness also reflects and extends his push for greater decentralization in the Church. Thus, in line with Vatican II and postsecular principles of interpretive community, he tends to look inclusively to the arguments offered by others whose situational expertise is pertinent to the subject being addressed, including national bishops' conferences, other religious leaders, theologians, and scientists, among others. In *Joy of the Gospel*, for example, he makes several references to the statement issued by the General Conference of Latin American and Caribbean Bishops' meeting in Aparecida, Brazil, in 2007; and he also variously cites documents from the bishops' conferences in the United States, India, France, Brazil, Congo, and the Philippines. In *Laudato Si'*, he references documents from seventeen geographically diverse bishops' conferences encompassing North America, Latin America, Africa, Asia, Oceania, and Europe. He thus conveys that he is not looking to privilege the interpretive authority of the Vatican, but that he values the standpoint of others, including the nonordained. A noteworthy exception is the question of women's ordination, which, Francis reiterated, is settled and closed to discussion. (I leave this aside for the moment but discuss it in chapter 4.) Throughout the rest of this chapter, I focus on his societal critique, turning first to his analysis of economic inequality and its reception, and then to his discourse on climate change and public response to it.

Francis's Critique of Economic Inequality
An Economy of Exclusion

In *The Joy of the Gospel* (*JG*), issued in November 2013, Francis identifies "an economy of exclusion and inequality" (*JG* #53), as a fundamental societal ill. He argues that "the inclusion of the poor in society" is "fundamental at this time in history" and to shaping "the future of humanity" (*JG* #185). Social inclusion is deeply embedded in the Catholic understanding of the common good. As summarized by Jesuit theologian David Hollenbach, its "understanding of justice . . . calls for action that goes beyond exclusion to active support for inclusion. . . . The preservation of human dignity requires positive action in support of those who are vulnerable to de facto conditions of unequal and non-reciprocal interdependence."[13]

The obligation toward the poor, Francis argues, is grounded squarely in scripture; and he extensively quotes from a range of gospel passages to support his assertion that "there is an inseparable bond between our faith and the poor" (*JG* #48). He is forthright that "the rich must help, respect and promote the poor." This is an obligation, he argues, that requires a "generous solidarity and a return of economics and finance to an ethical approach that favors human beings" (*JG* #58). This argument echoes Benedict and other popes who, too, stressed the need for economic and social policies that respect the "integral development" of individuals and communities. Thus, in framing the social inclusion of the poor as a command imposed by the principle of solidarity, Francis appeals to a value substantiated by the gospel and at the heart of Catholic social teaching. It is also a salient secular value based on the foundational democratic principle that all citizens should be able to actively participate in social and political life.

Secular Framing of Solidarity

The solidarity required for the full inclusion of the poor in the riches of society necessitates, Francis argues, both structural and ideological transformation. This task requires a "new mindset." It entails a shift in worldview away from belief in the invisible hand of the market, trickle-down economics, the idolatry of money, and the overvaluing of consumption and profit (*JG* #202, 204). He thus outlines his understanding of solidarity not solely in the vocabulary of "integral human development," which may seem abstract to audiences unfamiliar with Catholic ethics, but also in highly secular language. His critique is discomfiting. This is not because being well grounded in scripture it might appear irrational to nonreligious, secular citizens. Rather, it is because it uses a secular vocabulary that is highly critical of contemporary economic and financial practices (e.g., profit accumulation) and our deeply embedded assumptions that such practices and the inequality they cause are normal and unproblematic. He is highly specific and concrete in elaborating his claim that attentiveness to the cry of the poor and the oppressed requires a commitment to enacting structural changes. For him, the remediation of the ills of modernity:

> means working to eliminate the structural causes of poverty and to promote the integral development of the poor as well as small daily acts of solidarity in meeting the real needs we encounter. The word solidarity is a little worn and at times poorly understood, but it refers to something more than a few sporadic acts of generosity. It presumes the creation of a new mindset that thinks in terms of community and

the priority of the life of all over the appropriation of goods by a few [*JG* #188]. Solidarity is a spontaneous reaction by those who recognize that the social function of property and the universal destination of goods are realities that come before private property. The private ownership of goods is justified by the need to protect and increase them, so that they can better serve the common good; for this reason, solidarity must be lived as the decision to restore to the poor what belongs to them. These convictions and habits of solidarity, when they are put into practice, open the way to other structural transformations and make them possible. Changing structures without generating new convictions and attitudes will only ensure that those same structures will become, sooner or later, corrupt, oppressive and ineffectual. (*JG* #189)

In this framing, a contrite modernity—one whose problems require the forging of a new solidarity—must embrace the radicalness and the urgency of structural and cultural transformation.

The postsecular resonance of Francis's economic critique

The postsecular expectation is that religious actors should translate their religious-based arguments into a secular idiom. Francis clearly accomplishes this. His critique is anchored in Christian faith—literally, in the joy of the gospel (the title of his exhortation), and a "mission focused on Jesus Christ and . . . commitment to the poor" (*JG* #97). These faith principles have long been translated into Catholic social teaching (e.g., solidarity, just wages). Francis takes an additional step and translates these values into a highly secular and plain-spoken vocabulary.

Such translation, however, is not the endpoint of public religious engagement. Its reception also matters. Addressed to Catholics and Christians more generally, Francis's critique received extensive media coverage and public secular commentary. Such coverage reflects and reinforces the fact that the Church is a public Church, and when it speaks on any issue, it garners public attention. Additionally, the political salience of economic inequality accentuates public interest in Francis's critique.

The Cloud of Marxism

The Economist, the internationally renowned newsmagazine strongly committed to free-market economics (and whose tagline affirms "intelligence" over "timid ignorance"), commended Francis. It noted that while he may not be "getting the diagnosis exactly right . . . he is asking the right questions."[14] Overall, however, Francis's critique was negatively received by high-profile conservatives in the United States. Rather than conveying postsecular appreciation for religious voices in public debates, their remarks instead reflected a secular bias. Some challenged his authority to discuss such issues, arguing that he lacks economic expertise and, in any case, should stick to religious issues, a critique reminiscent of the conservative response in the 1980s to well-publicized pastoral letters by the U.S. bishops on economic justice and on nuclear deterrence.[15] Thematically, a prevalent response to Francis was the charge of Marxism, a label which received extensive publicity in the U.S. and global media.[16] Additionally, his American critics discredited his arguments as distorted by the fact that, as a South American, he was familiar only with "crony capitalism," not free-market (implicitly benign) American capitalism. Those who made this case included the prominent Catholic Republican Congressman Paul Ryan (the 2012 Republican vice-presidential nominee, and current Speaker of the House of Representatives).[17] Intertwined here, Francis's South American perspective on capitalism—and his well-publicized pastoral work on the streets of poor Buenos Aires neighborhoods— conveyed that his critique was shaped by the region's Marxist-tinted liberation theology.

Liberation theology is mostly a post-Vatican II development in line with the view that the Church and Catholics should not be "lifeless spectators"— in John XXIII's words (see chapter 2)—but actively engaged in society. It draws on Christianity to argue against the ideas and practices (including those of the Church itself) that perpetuate economic and social inequality. It is primarily associated with Latin American Catholicism and politics in the 1970s and 1980s. Its principles, however, also inform a more generally shared Catholic vision of a Church that emphasizes giving priority to the situation of the poor and other marginalized groups. Because of its focus on socioeconomic inequality, liberation theology is politically controversial. John Paul II was especially critical, concerned that its Marxist-inspired, materialist focus distracted from spiritual truths. Benedict was somewhat less wary, though he too denounced its political-secularizing force.[18] Francis, by contrast, is more explicitly disposed to its theological principles, and has publicly embraced one of its central figures, the Peruvian theologian Gustavo Gutierrez.[19]

Irrespective of the motivating context for the accusation, a "cloud of Marxism" hovers over Francis's critique. It is so pervasive that he himself felt compelled to point out that he is not a Marxist (though he was also quick to say that he knows good people who are!).[20] The label persists nonetheless, and the media's framing of him as "a hard pope for capitalists to love" shadows coverage of his routine activities, even by mainstream, liberal-leaning newspapers such as the *New York Times*.[21]

Given Marx's critique of religion's alleged role in perpetuating blindness to economic inequality, there is some irony in calling the leader of one of the world's largest religious groups a Marxist. And it would be easy to dismiss the charge against Francis as simply a reflection, as Marx would predict, of the inevitable pushback from political elites against any serious criticism of capitalism. However, a sharp denunciation of capitalism is not in itself sufficient to warrant this label. Moreover, Benedict also argued against what he called "reckless capitalism," the "worship of profit," and the "scandal of glaring inequalities," and he was highly critical of capitalism's "pernicious" effects and deeper causes.[22] He, too, denounced "global economic dysfunction" and spoke of the "urgent need to eliminate its structural causes . . . and to correct models of growth" that damage society's "most vulnerable populations."[23] Indeed, one month prior to his resignation, Benedict firmly asserted, "If justice is to be achieved, good economic models, however necessary, are not sufficient."[24] Yet his remarks did not draw a Marxist charge.

What, then, in the actual content of Francis's critique might fuel the Marxist label? We hear an echo of Marxist language in Francis's discussion of work and social exclusion. In Catholic social teaching, employment and "just wages" are critical to human dignity. As Francis explains, referencing John XXIII,

> We are not simply talking about ensuring nourishment or a "dignified sustenance" for all people but also their "general temporal welfare and prosperity." This means education, access to health care and above all employment, for it is through free, creative, participatory and mutually supportive labor that human beings express and enhance the dignity of their lives. A just wage enables them to have adequate access to all the other goods destined for our common use. (*JG* #192)

The view of labor as, in principle, an engaging and creative activity is also shared by Marx. Under capitalism, however, as Marx argued and as Francis intimates, work dehumanizes. This is because it treats workers simply as cogs in the production and accumulation of profit. In other words, human value is defined solely by the amount of profit a worker can produce for the capitalist. As such, workers are commodities: they are used (exploited) and disposed of (fired) when no longer useful in generating profit.

Francis extends the metaphor of commodification beyond workers to society as a whole. He argues that it is not merely commodification and exploitation but also social exclusion that has become the defining product of contemporary society. He argues:

> Today everything comes under the laws of competition and the survival of the fittest, where the powerful feed upon the powerless. As a consequence, masses of people find themselves excluded and marginalized: without work, without possibilities, without any means of escape. Human beings are themselves considered consumer goods to be used and then discarded. We have created a "disposable" culture that is now spreading. It is no longer simply about exploitation and oppression but something new. Exclusion ultimately has to do with what it means to be a part of the society in which we live; those excluded are no longer society's underside or its fringes or its disenfranchised—they are no longer even a part of it. The excluded are not the "exploited" but the outcast, the "leftovers." [JG #53] . . . This leads to a kind of alienation at every level, for [quoting John Paul II] "a society becomes alienated when its forms of social organization, production and consumption make it more difficult to offer the gift of self and to establish solidarity between people." (JG #196)

The solidarity that Francis sees necessary for our time is, therefore, a generous solidarity in accord with the gospel exhortation to love one's neighbor. This, he argues, can only be achieved if society can remedy the structures and everyday culture that impede it. Such restructuring is necessary to reverse "the processes of dehumanization" (JG #51). Otherwise, the expansion of the "leftovers" is likely to occur if the excesses of the financial system and the high levels of economic inequality and social exclusion remain unchecked.

Contra Marx

Yet, despite this linguistic resonance with Marx, Francis explicitly contravenes Marxist thinking on several important points. Unlike Marx, he does not advocate the abolition of capitalism, or of private property, or of the profit-and-wage structure. Instead, he calls for a restructuring of economic relations such that the financial system will serve rather than rule society (JG #55–57), and thus ensure human flourishing (JG #192). In short, Francis believes that inequality can be remedied without dismantling capitalism because he, unlike Marx, sees it as a *result* of, rather than *inherent* in, capitalist structures.

The Emancipatory Power of Democracy

For Francis, the incorporation of the excluded back into society can be achieved by existing democratic political processes. He expresses confidence that the state and political and business elites have the capacity to set in motion the kind of necessary structural and ideological changes that can lead to a society in which economic growth and growth in social justice go hand in hand (*JG* #203–204). Therefore, again unlike Marx, he does not see the state and political leaders as serving only the economic interests of corporations and business. He is optimistically confident, rather, in their willingness and ability to enact policies that can serve the common good (*JG* #205, 240). This is why he exhorts them—as did Benedict—to use their moral leadership to negotiate more socially just global trade and climate change agreements. And he points to their obligation to care for the many vulnerable groups whose plight is worsened by the financial forces driving political priorities and socio-economic inequality (*JG* #57, 58). His confidence in democracy fully extends to the grassroots. He conveys that political and social change is the obligation not alone of elites and institutions (e.g., government) but also of ordinary individuals and local communities. His positive views of the state and of political dialogue and action fully accord with the principles of democratic civil society, and also with Vatican II's emphasis on individuals as the collective authors of their culture (see chapter 2). He thus blends a forceful critique of economic inequality and social exclusion with an equally forceful articulation of the power of democratic engagement to restructure the economy in ways that make economic growth and social justice compatible. Thus,

> In a culture that privileges dialogue as a form of encounter, it is time to devise a means for building consensus and agreement while seeking the goal of a just, responsive and inclusive society. The principal author . . . is the people as a whole and their culture, and not a single class, minority, group or elite. We do not need plans drawn up by a few for the few, or an enlightened or outspoken minority that claims to speak for everyone. It is about agreeing to live together, a social and cultural pact. (*JG* #239)

What accounts for the negative reception of Francis's economic critique?

While the negative reception of Francis's critique may have been stoked by elements in its vocabulary faintly resonating with Marxism, this does not explain why other elements were largely silenced. Of particular note is the disregard of his highly positive view of civil society and his trust in the ability of political and business leaders to articulate new societal paths. In the next few pages I argue that cultural ideology, as well as the *perception* of Francis's moral authority, pushed its negative reception.

Cultural Ideology

Ideologically, Francis's critique unearthed the longstanding but generally unspoken tension between politics and markets. He voiced a core democratic assumption that political processes are supposed to control markets, not the inverse. In other words, he conveys that the values of democracy—equality and societal participation, not social exclusion—have to be proactively balanced with capitalist principles of economic competition.[25] The pointed nature of his critique shocks the common view, held by elites and ordinary individuals alike, that capitalism is a highly successful system whose problems can be remedied by welfare reforms and income redistribution programs alone.

The hold of capitalism in everyday consumer culture means that even when its most negative excesses are highlighted, such criticism is treated defensively. Francis's critique was deflected by critics' dismissal of the message (as Marxist), and the messenger (as someone lacking economic expertise, and biased by Latin American capitalism and liberation theology). It was easy for Benedict's economic critique to be tuned out. He was less forceful in his criticism of capitalism and though sincere, did not give it sustained attention. But even if he had, it is unlikely it would have evoked the same level of media coverage and the same response Francis's did. The relative lack of interest in Benedict's arguments was because, fairly or unfairly, his reserved personal style and intellectualism conveyed a pope out of touch with everyday currents (a perception generated during his previous role enforcing doctrinal conservatism as head of the Vatican's Congregation for the Doctrine of the Faith).

The perception of Francis's moral authority

By contrast, the evening Francis was elected pope and humbly greeted the crowds gathered in anticipation in Saint Peter's Square, he became a public celebrity, celebrated not only by Catholics but also in the secular media. This affirmation has included "Person of the Year" accolades and front-cover stories in several magazines including *Rolling Stone, The New Yorker*, and *Time*. His appeal is not based solely on his charisma. His moral credibility is also bolstered by the evident consistency between his modest behavior and the inclusive ethics he espouses. He projects postsecular authority, an ability to be listened to and taken seriously by religious and secular audiences alike. I have argued that papal popularity should not be conflated with papal authority (see chapter 2). The *perception*—really, the misperception—of papal authority, however, is highly salient. The (mis)perception of Francis's moral authority, and the political context further accentuating it, have contributed to the undermining of his critique.

Perceptions of Francis's authority are intensified by the interwoven religious–secular identities of voters and politicians, including a congressional leadership with publicly self-identified Catholics (e.g., Paul Ryan).[26] His popularity among Catholics and non-Catholics may have fed politicians' concern that his charisma and (perceived) moral-religious authority would nudge voters to push for greater attention to redressing income inequality. And, independent of local constituents, politicians may have anticipated pressure from the U.S. bishops, who have a history of advocating for economic redistribution. In 2012, for example, the bishops issued a public statement denouncing the budget cuts to social programs outlined by Paul Ryan, then chairman of the House Budget Committee. Additionally, several other Catholic figures publicly rejected Ryan's claim that the cuts were inspired by Catholic teaching.[27] This public denunciation was particularly significant because Ryan's political views closely align with the moral conservatism of the U.S. bishops (e.g., on abortion and same-sex marriage), and he is seen as a close ally of New York Cardinal Timothy Dolan and other conservative clerics. The anticipation of religious-based pressure related to Francis's critique may thus have stoked the motivation of conservative Catholic politicians like Ryan to proactively dismiss his arguments.

The timing of Francis's critique is also salient. His discourse on exclusion—coming in late 2013—fed into political elites' wariness of the growing anti-establishment activism spurred by the 2008 financial crisis and the Great Recession. The Occupy Wall Street protests in 2011 and the economic populism evident in the 2012 presidential election accentuated political awareness of economic discontent. Given this context, political elites may have been further motivated to push back rhetorically against any traction Francis's arguments might garner. Such pushback, and politicians' silence in response to the moral leadership Francis asks of them in economic restructuring, is reinforced by their close ties to finance. Strategically, they thus resist his call to action simply by invalidating his diagnosis of economic and social exclusion.

Secular pushback against postsecular expectations

Irrespective of the motivations and concerns of his critics, the dismissal of Francis's economic critique detracts from the potential persuasiveness of its arguments. It may be that the Church's social justice principles are unpersuasive, in any case, in a capitalist culture. Yet, an unanticipated consequence of postsecularity is that when the Church employs a highly secular vocabulary, it opens itself to dismissal. Postsecular expectations require secular citizens to take seriously the religious-based secular claims of religious actors. They also assume that when religious actors use secular arguments, they will be evaluated on rational grounds.

Ironically, despite the Catholic or other religious ties of many of Francis's critics, their response to his economic critique reflected a more secular than postsecular sensibility. The response conveyed secularistic presumptions that as a religious leader Francis is out of his depth, that he lacks the background experience and expertise to understand capitalism, and that he is inappropriately encroaching on a sphere in which religion has, and ought to have, nothing to say—hence the frequency of such dismissive statements as "the pope should stick to religion and avoid economics."[28] Had Francis used a less culturally accessible and more explicitly religious, faith-based discourse, perhaps his arguments would have garnered a different reception. Perhaps they would have received a more subtle rejection. The dismissal of his critique indicates that while religious language may restrict the Church's public relevance, a secular vocabulary also has persuasive limits. Such limits will vary depending on the sociopolitical and cultural context and the issue being addressed.

Nevertheless, Francis's economic discourse itself shows that the Church is solidifying its role as a postsecular religious actor, whether intended as such or not. It is actively contributing to the articulation of complex social problems and their possible amelioration. Even if Church discourse does not directly impact political and policy outcomes, its presence impacts civil society. It has to be taken account of, however minimally, by secular and secular-religious elites and by ordinary Catholics. Importantly, too, the Vatican—and national bishops' conferences if they so choose—also has the agenda-setting power and the resources to focus continued political attention on specific issues and principles. Church officials are not easily cowered. And the postsecular turn gives them an expanded opportunity. The response to *The Joy of the Gospel* has not deterred Francis from continuing to focus attention on economic inequality. His commitment to engaging with pressing societal issues is further underscored by his second major official document, his encyclical on the environment, to which I now turn.

Francis's Critique of Global Warming

From a postsecular perspective, debate about the problem of climate change is again the sort that can benefit from the ethical steering offered by moderate religion.[29] Whether or not intended as a postsecular contribution, Francis's groundbreaking encyclical *Laudato Si'* (On Care for our Common Home) takes on this task. Issued in June 2015, the encyclical marks the Vatican's first extensive discussion of environmental issues, though previous popes frequently noted the negative consequences of climate change.

In 1971, Paul VI warned of the potential for "ecological catastrophe" owing to accelerated industrialization and "unchecked human activity."[30] John Paul II, at the outset of his papacy in 1979, identified "exploitation of the earth" as a serious moral issue. Across several subsequent statements he criticized the "irrational destruction of the natural environment" and emphasized the need to "safeguard the moral conditions for an authentic human ecology."[31] Benedict frequently highlighted environmental protection in his public statements, including to the United Nations General Assembly in 2008. He initiated "green-friendly" programs at the Vatican, and in *Caritas in Veritate* further argued against an economic expansionism that denigrates the natural environment.[32] *Laudato Si'* (*LS*), however, with its focus on environmental issues, squarely places the problem of climate change on the public agenda.

The Natural Environment as a Common Good

Francis forthrightly states that he is appealing "for a new dialogue about how we are shaping the future of our planet" (*LS* 14). Arguing for "a new and universal solidarity" (*LS* 14), and extending the Church's long-held ethical emphasis on the "common good," he articulates the relatively novel idea that the "natural environment" and "climate" are a common good. Thus,

> The climate is a common good, belonging to all and meant for all. At the global level, it is a complex system linked to many of the essential conditions for human life [*LS* 23]. . . . The natural environment is a collective good, the patrimony of all humanity and the responsibility of everyone. If we make something our own, it is only to administer it for the good of all. If we do not, we burden our consciences with the weight of having denied the existence of others. (*LS* 95)

Addressing "every person living on this planet" (*LS* #3), humanity, he states, "is called to recognize the need for changes of lifestyle, production and consumption in order to combat . . . [global] warming or at least the human causes that produce or aggravate it" (*LS* #23). In outlining this obligation, he translates the biblical story of the Creation and other scriptural passages into the secular language of environmental stewardship. Making extensive reference to biblical passages, he emphasizes that "dominion" over the earth means to "till it and keep it," not to exploit it. He explains:

> Tilling refers to cultivating, plowing or working, while keeping means caring, protecting, overseeing and preserving. This implies a relationship of mutual responsibility between human beings and nature. Each community can take from the bounty of the earth whatever it needs for subsistence, but it also has the duty to protect the earth and to ensure its fruitfulness for coming generations. (*LS* #67)

Francis argues that the elevated uniqueness of humans in God's creation does not mean that human mastery of the world permits either environmental exploitation or, consistent with his economic critique, exploitation of other people. Rather, he states, "our 'dominion' over the universe should be understood more properly in the sense of responsible stewardship" (*LS* #116). Responsible stewardship maintains a balance between human activity and respect for the environment, and deviations from this balance, he argues, are risky. On the one hand, they risk a distorted anthropocentrism, an excessive focus on human ability counterpoised against God and guided only by utilitarian motives (*LS* #68, 69, 116, 122). And on the other, they risk a "biocentrism" that fails to recognize the uniqueness of human dignity and personhood relative to other creatures (*LS* #118).

Confronting Empirical Realities

Climate change is a highly politicized issue, and denial of global warming and its human causes is prevalent among politically conservative Americans.[33] Engaging this reality, Francis invokes a central theme of his papacy—namely, that ideas need to be in continuous dialogue with empirical realities (*JG* #231–233), a point consistent also with postsecularity.[34] He is critical of those who deny the scientific reality of global warming or who are indifferent to it (*LS* #14, 92, 115). Further, he calls for "an ethics of ecology" that fosters "ecological equilibrium" and an "ecological citizenship" rooted in recognition of the "covenant between humanity and the environment" (*LS* #209–211). Throughout the encyclical, he ties the ethical responsibility of care for the planet to the accumulating scientific data on climate change. He states, for example,

> A very solid scientific consensus indicates that we are presently witnessing a disturbing warming of the climatic system. In recent decades this warming has been accompanied by a constant rise in the sea level and, it would appear, by an increase of extreme weather events, even if a scientifically determinable cause cannot be assigned to each particular phenomenon. (*LS* #23)

Amplifying his focus on the structural causes of poverty and inequality (*JG* #202), he makes a strong case that there is "an intimate relationship between the poor and the fragility of the planet" (*LS* #16). Thus,

> The human environment and the natural environment deteriorate together; we cannot adequately combat environmental degradation unless we attend to causes related to human and social degradation. In fact, the deterioration of the environment and of society affects the most vulnerable people on the planet: Both everyday experience and scientific research show that the gravest effects of all attacks on the environment are suffered by the poorest. (*LS* #48)

Supporting this claim, he provides several empirical examples showing how the poverty of individuals, as well as of whole communities, countries, and geopolitical regions, correlates with environmental degradation.

Francis is especially critical of the ways in which global economic interests and transnational corporations undermine both the poor and the environment (*LS* #38). He also highlights the relationship of economic dependency and inequity between the economically developed Global North (e.g., North America and Europe) and the financially poor, but ecologically rich Global South (e.g., South America, Southeast Asia; *LS* #48–52). He states:

> The land of the Southern poor is rich and mostly unpolluted, yet access to ownership of goods and resources for meeting vital needs is inhibited by a system of commercial relations and ownership that is structurally perverse. The developed countries ought to help pay this debt by significantly limiting their consumption of nonrenewable energy

and by assisting poorer countries to support policies and programs of
sustainable development. (*LS* #52)

He thus argues that given the many diverse ways in which human economic
activity and the environment interact, poverty and environmental degradation constitute one and the same societal crisis:

> We are faced not with two separate crises, one environmental and
> the other social, but rather with one complex crisis that is both social
> and environmental. Strategies for a solution demand an integrated
> approach to combating poverty, restoring dignity to the excluded and
> at the same time protecting nature. (*LS* #139)

The Juggernaut of Technology and Consumerism

In addition to reiterating several elements of his critique of economic inequality, Francis elaborates on the fusion between financial interests and technological progress. He refers to this as the dominance of "the techno-economic
paradigm" (*LS* #53). By using this phrase, he engages with the political view
that advances in technology invariably entail economic growth and human
progress. Individuals who embrace this view would tend to argue, for example, that global warming can be ignored because new technologies will emerge
that will remedy its effects. Francis rejects this paradigm, arguing instead that
it stunts the political leadership and creativity necessary to remedy global
societal-environmental ills. It also, he argues, undermines the principles of
justice and freedom demanded by an ethical commitment to the common
good (*LS* #53). While praising the wide-ranging ways in which technology
improves society, he warns nonetheless, as has Benedict, that "our immense
technological development has not been accompanied by a development in
human responsibility, values and conscience" (*LS* #105). Thus, he states:

> Some circles maintain that current economics and technology will
> solve all environmental problems and argue in popular and nontech-
> nical terms that the problems of global hunger and poverty will be
> resolved simply by market growth. . . . Yet by itself the market cannot
> guarantee integral human development and social inclusion. (*LS* #109)

Relatedly, and in line with his broader critique of contemporary capitalism,
he is highly critical of "compulsive" consumerism (*LS* #203). He denounces

a "throwaway culture" that prioritizes short-term gain and quick profits, and that significantly impacts pollution and "despoils nature" (*LS* #20–22, 184, 192). In short, he argues:

> a sober look at our world shows that the degree of human interven-
> tion, often in the service of business interests and consumerism, is actu-
> ally making our earth less rich and beautiful, ever more limited and
> gray even as technological advances and consumer goods continue to
> abound limitlessly. We seem to think that we can substitute an irre-
> placeable and irretrievable beauty with something that we have created
> ourselves. (*LS* #34)

Consequently, he argues (*LS* #206), quoting Benedict, because "[p]urchasing is always a moral—and not simply economic—act ... environmental degradation challenges us to examine our lifestyle."[35]

Despite Francis's sober analysis of climate change and its effects especially on the poor, he is optimistic that political and cultural changes can occur.[36] As in his analysis of economic inequality (discussed earlier), he praises the societal ability to craft positive changes. He states:

> Human beings, while capable of the worst, are also capable of rising
> above themselves, choosing again what is good and making a new start,
> despite their mental and social conditioning. We are able to take an
> honest look at ourselves, to acknowledge our deep dissatisfaction and
> to embark on new paths to authentic freedom. No system can com-
> pletely suppress our openness to what is good, true and beautiful, or
> our God-given ability to respond to his grace at work deep in our
> hearts. (*LS* #205)

He thus exhorts society to "move forward in a bold cultural revolution" so that "sustainable progress" can be achieved (*LS* #114). Among other strat-
egies, he stresses the importance of renewed attentiveness to individuals' lifestyle choices (e.g., *LS* #206). Additionally, as on economic inequality, he envisions a broad spectrum of democratic political engagement. He thus looks to individuals, communities, social movements, civic organizations, nation-states, and transnational organizations and alliances to effect change. He is realistic about the prospects for change, noting how politicians are motivated by short-term gains and consumer-driven pressures (*LS* #178). Yet, amid such impediments, he appreciates the importance of transitional

measures prior to the formulation and enactment of more sweeping policy changes (*LS* #180).

The Reception of *Laudato Si'*

The publication of *Laudato Si'* received extensive media publicity.[37] Much of its reception was highly positive. It earned praise from President Obama, scientists, environmentalists, and a broad range of Catholic and non-Catholic religious and political leaders. *The Economist*, too, praised it, commenting:

> As religious statements go, the one by Pope Francis on the environment is readable and in places, beautiful. . . . [I]t affirms that carbon emitted by humans is the main reason why Earth is warming, and urges rapid action, especially by rich countries, to curb it. . . . Many of its 190 pages or so could have come from a secular NGO; but there are tender and lyrical passages which call for a "change of heart" among consumers and decision-makers.[38]

In light of postsecularity, *The Economist*'s explicit categorization of Francis's encyclical as a "religious statement" is noteworthy. It points to the challenge confronting the postsecular expectation that religious statements should be considered on a par with secular statements. The secularization of culture and social institutions is such that notwithstanding calls for a postsecular consciousness—recognizing religion's public relevance amid secularism—the public arguments of moderate religious actors are eyed warily. Even though *LS* uses secular reasoning and extensively draws on the scientific consensus, *The Economist* still saw Francis's arguments as religious; and though "readable" and "lyrical," perhaps not as legitimate as its own secular reasoning.

Given the conservative politicization of climate change there was, not surprisingly, pushback against the authority of Francis's claims. Similar to his exhortation on economic inequality, his legitimacy in weighing in on climate change was questioned. Even though he openly acknowledges that "the church does not presume to settle scientific questions or to replace politics" (*LS* #188), a frequent retort was that he "should leave science to the scientists." Underscoring the pervasiveness of politicization, including within the Church hierarchy, this view was conveyed, for example, by the high-ranking Australian Cardinal George Pell. He noted that the Church has neither the scientific expertise nor the "mandate from the Lord to pronounce on scientific matters."[39]

Relatedly, some critics dismissed the encyclical by arguing that Francis is naively taken in by the scientific consensus, and that in any case, the science is faulty (i.e., liberally biased). Ironically, this is a charge usually made by nonscientists who nonetheless assume they have the expertise to make this judgment. They do so, moreover, even as they reject the lack of expertise and authority of others such as Francis to have an alternative judgment. Again pointing to the interweaving of individuals' religious and secular identities, those who make such claims include conservative Catholic politicians.[40] The rejection of the Church's scientific reasoning on climate change appears to be driven by political bias on this particular issue itself, rather than by a more general belief that the Church should not use empirical reasoning. This inference is supported by the fact that when Catholic bishops use scientific findings in their public arguments against abortion or divorce, for example, their expertise to do so is not similarly questioned.[41]

Conveying the encyclical's postsecular potential, Francis addresses it (as noted earlier) to "every person living on this planet" (*LS* #3). The intentional breadth of its audience, and Francis's confidence in the power of ordinary individuals to impact change, beg attention to its impact. Is there evidence that his discourse on the environment is steering public opinion and views of political action on global warming? This is a complicated question to address even with the most comprehensive and rigorous research design. I have not set myself this task. Instead, in the following pages, I discuss how Francis's relevance on climate change is being publicly construed. To do so, I draw on survey data from national opinion polls, some conducted prior to the encyclical's release and others subsequently.

I argue that there is little evidence Francis's discourse is changing how people think about climate change, even if they may be thinking about the issue more often now than a few years ago. In making sense of *LS*'s reception, I highlight what might be considered the liberal politicization of Francis's authority. The conservative politicization of climate change is well documented, and as already highlighted in this chapter, conservatives respond to Francis's arguments on economic inequality and on climate change by denying his authority in these domains. By contrast, the liberal appropriation of his perceived moral authority is an unexpected effect of his climate change intervention. It is also one I suggest that, contrary to Francis's goal, undermines the advancement of communication on climate change.

Before turning to the survey data, I want to acknowledge some general evidence of Francis's influence on climate change. Some observers point to his moral influence in helping push approval of the Paris Agreement (in

December 2015), committing 195 countries to reduce greenhouse gas emissions. The Vatican also organizes ongoing conferences on specific environmental issues. Additionally, the Vatican and several Catholic dioceses and parishes in the United States and around the globe have instigated or expanded environmental awareness policies. Importantly, too, many Catholics in the United States and elsewhere who are personally involved in environmental activism cite the importance of Francis's moral leadership on the issue.[42] In the United States, the work of Catholic Climate Covenant, an environmental advocacy organization established in 2006 and composed of several Catholic partner organizations, has been energized by Francis's prioritization of climate change issues.[43] Similarly, Francis's support for the Pan-Amazonian Church Network in Latin America, established in 2014, strengthens the political and religious legitimacy of its environmental advocacy.[44]

The construal of a "Francis effect" on attitudes toward climate change

At the aggregate level of public opinion, however, the evidence is more ambiguous. Like Americans as a whole, Catholics are divided in their environmental views. In June 2015, immediately prior to the release of *LS*, over two-thirds (71 percent) of Catholics in a Pew Forum survey said there is solid evidence that the earth is warming, and almost half (48 percent) said that global warming is a "very serious problem." More people today than in 2013 see global warming as a very serious problem. This increase, however, is not necessarily indicative of a linear change in attitudes. Rather, opinions on the environment, as on other issues, are responsive to the immediate sociopolitical context. In 2009, President Obama's first year in office, slightly more Americans (51 percent) said climate change was a very serious problem than did so in 2015 (48 percent). There are partisan political differences on climate change among Americans, and they find parallel expression among Catholics. Thus, whereas 62 percent of Catholic Democrats believe that global warming is caused by human activity, only 24 percent of Catholic Republicans think so.[45]

What I am calling the liberal politicization of Francis's attentiveness to climate change is evident, I will show, in the tendency to overstate or misrecognize a "Francis effect." An illustrative example is provided by a report jointly issued in November 2015 by research centers on climate change communication at Yale and George Mason universities. The report, based on panel data from pre- and post-encyclical surveys is called *The Francis Effect: How Pope Francis Changed the Conversation About Global Warming.* Its authors state:

We conclude that, over the past six months, Americans—especially Catholic Americans—became more engaged in and concerned about global warming. Furthermore, our findings suggest that the Pope's teachings about global warming contributed to an increase in public engagement on the issue, and influenced the conversation about global warming in America; we refer to this as *The Francis Effect*.[46]

A review of the study's findings, however, and of other polls suggests a less definitive "Francis Effect."

The extensive media coverage surrounding the publication of Francis's encyclical is captured in the increased proportion of Americans who report having heard more about climate change in the media. In the pre- and post-*LS* surveys conducted by Yale and George Mason researchers, the proportion of individuals who reported "hearing more about global warming in the news" increased from 20 percent in March 2015 to 27 percent in October 2015. Among Catholics, the increase was slightly larger, from 18 percent to 27 percent.[47] However, though it is in keeping with a more general pattern of limited lay Catholic awareness of well-publicized Church statements, only one in ten Catholics (11 percent) said they had heard "a lot" in the media about the pope's views on global warming, and close to half (46 percent) said they had heard "some" or "a little." Remarkably, four in ten said they had not heard anything (26 percent) or were unsure (17 percent).[48] By the fall of 2015, 24 percent of Catholics were "aware" of the encyclical, and 18 percent said it had been discussed at their church—but not much: 2 percent said it was discussed "a lot," 8 percent "some," and 8 percent "a little."[49]

Pointing to the postsecular, transreligious relevance of the encyclical, evangelicals were as likely as Catholics to say it had been discussed a lot at their churches. And mainline Protestants were twice as likely as Catholics (and evangelicals) to say they had discussed it a lot.[50] These findings simultaneously highlight the comparatively limited amount of interest among local Catholic churches, including pastors, in discussing it. Further, a separate survey conducted in fall 2014 (several months prior to the release of *LS*), shows that church-based discussion of climate change then was relatively similar to that reported in October 2015, three months after *LS*'s publication.[51] These findings thus underscore the challenge in mobilizing conversation (not to mention action) on climate change. They also point, at best, to a very limited impact of *LS* in igniting new or different conversations about it.

Trust in Francis's authority on climate change

The liberal co-opting of Francis is also seen in the claims made by self-identified, politically liberal Catholics that Francis has moral authority on climate change. John Gehring, for example, the Catholic Program Director at the Washington, D.C.–based Faith in Public Life center, argues that:

> Prominent Catholic politicians who are climate change skeptics now find themselves in the unenviable position of not only disputing the overwhelming scientific consensus on this issue, but also standing on the opposing side of the world's most influential moral leader. . . . [I]f anyone can help begin to break the political stalemate over climate change and reach an audience far beyond the progressive choir, it's a global leader with approval ratings most politicians crave and the moral gravitas they usually lack.[52]

As I have argued, however, papal popularity does not necessarily translate into deference or adherence to what the pope says (see chapter 2). And this extends to Francis's arguments on the environment. In fact, following *LS*'s publication, there was a decrease in the proportion of Catholics who say they "strongly trust" Francis on climate change: from 25 percent (in spring 2015) to 20 percent (in fall 2015).[53] This decrease may be understood, in part, as being related to the broader politicization of climate change, including the dismissal by conservative religious and political figures of both Francis's authority to speak about it and of the scientific findings informing his stance.

The politicization of science poses a challenge to secular and postsecular assumptions about the cultural accessibility of scientific reasoning. Today, public trust in science cannot be assumed. For example, while three in four Americans trust scientists for information about climate change, this is true of only six in ten of those who are politically conservative.[54] In any case, invoking scientific findings does not guarantee public trust in the authority of the speaker and/or in what is being said. It is apparent that many Catholics (and others) withhold trust in the pope as an authoritative voice on climate change, even though he uses scientific argumentation. This does not mean that the pope lacks moral or persuasive authority. But it does mean that his authority needs to be weighed against the political biases of Catholics, as well as more generally the interpretive autonomy they demonstrate toward the Vatican and Church teachings as a whole (see chapter 2). Notwithstanding the different questions at issue, it is evident that this autonomy extends to climate change.

Only 4 percent of Catholics in the Yale/George Mason study said they had changed their opinion on global warming in the past year. Six percent said that the "pope's position on global warming" has influenced their own views "a lot," and an additional 29 percent said it has "some" (6 percent) or "a little" (23 percent) influence. Respondents were not probed as to what specifically they understood to be the pope's position. We know from other surveys, however, that respondents tend to think that their attitude on an issue aligns with the official position on that issue.[55] Among those who say they were influenced, 19 percent said they are now "much more concerned" about global warming. There were also increases in the proportion of Catholics who say they are "very worried" about global warming (from 6 percent to 13 percent), and more certain that global warming is happening (from 31 percent to 44 percent).

It is uncertain whether these perceptions of influence and/or of increased worry or concern are due to the encyclical. The views expressed may be due to social desirability, such as the desire to indicate awareness of the encyclical and/or to identify one's views with a popular religious and celebrity public figure. They may also be related to several other factors, including personal experience of extreme weather events.[56] Regardless, despite an increase in environmental concern, and despite Francis's emphasis on the importance of political action, the data show no post-encyclical change in this domain. As the report authors themselves note, there is no change in the proportions of Catholics who think that Congress, the President, corporations and industry, or citizens themselves should take more action on global warming. Nor is there an increase in support for specific, environmentally friendly policies.[57] Beyond these data, Francis's limited impact on the American public conversation is also suggested by national politics. Environmental issues were largely ignored during the 2016 presidential campaign debates, and global warming was ranked last in importance as a voting issue. Further, a majority of white Catholics (and others) voted for a president whose candidacy mocked climate science and vowed to cancel the Paris Agreement (campaign rhetoric subsequently translated into the Trump administration's environmental policies).[58]

Climate Change Frames

The encyclical's limited impact is further illuminated by opinion on its substantive content. There is essentially no change in Catholics' views on central themes such as it is "Humankind's responsibility to care for the earth" (from 80 percent to 81 percent), and that global warming is caused by human activity (a 1 percent decrease from 57 percent to 56 percent). There is a 2 percent increase in the proportion who say that global warming is important to them personally (from 55 percent to 57 percent), and a notably bigger increase in the view that climate change will harm the world's poor "a great deal"—from 22 percent to 32 percent.[59] But, given that only 24 percent of Catholics were aware of the encyclical in the months after its release, it is an open question whether this opinion change is a result of the encyclical and the publicity it garnered. Indeed, in a separate survey conducted in the fall of 2014, several months before the encyclical's release, a majority of Americans (54 percent) said that climate change would do a great deal of harm to poorer, developing countries.[60] Thus, the twinning of climate change and economic underdevelopment, explicitly elaborated in the encyclical, appears to have already taken hold in the public's understanding prior to Francis's intervention.

The encyclical emphasizes the interrelation between climate change and poverty and inequality. Yet, there has been no change in the small minority who agree that climate change is a major social justice issue (13 percent). There is a very slight increase in seeing it as a major poverty issue (from 14 to 16 percent), and a small increase in the minority who agree it is a major moral issue (from 18 to 23 percent). There is a noticeably larger increase (from 35 to 44 percent) in those agreeing it is a major lifestyle issue—as also emphasized by Francis. It is particularly striking that despite the extensive media attention given to the encyclical and to Vatican and other Church events surrounding its release, very few Catholics (or others) think of climate change as a religious (5 percent) or a spiritual issue (7 percent). Most people, in fact, think of it as an environmental (75 percent) and a scientific (67 percent) issue.[61]

Reframing Climate Change

The hesitancy among Catholics (and other religiously affiliated Americans) to think of climate change as a religious or spiritual issue may be a disappointment to environmental activists and educators who search for new ways to mobilize the public to the urgency of the cause. Given the extensive political resistance to the reality of climate change, it is understandable that those engaged in communications about climate change would seek new strategies and frames that might help persuade a larger sector of the public. They find in Francis a highly popular and media-friendly figure, but they misrecognize the limits to his moral and religious authority. It is then not surprising, perhaps, that they seek to impose his mantle on their agenda. In a subsequent report, Yale and George Mason researchers state:

global warming is being reframed as a moral and spiritual issue by religious leaders—most notably by Pope Francis. . . . A moral framing of climate change may have particular resonance in the U.S., as Americans tend to be more religious than citizens in many other industrialized nations. . . . Dispassionate statements by climate scientists couched in cautious, neutral language and supported by charts, figures and statistics, may resonate less than admonitions from religious leaders to respond to the ethical and moral implications of a changing climate.[62]

However, given that so few Americans, in fact, think of climate change as a religious or spiritual issue, the recourse to religion-related frames may not be a very productive strategy. Additional grounds for this caution lie in increased secularization conveyed by the growth in religious disaffiliation. Religious and spiritual motifs may be especially limiting among young Americans who, while they have the most at stake in the regulation of global warming, are also the least religious (see chapter 1). Moreover, just because someone self-identifies as religious does not mean that the individual defers to religious-based moral claims or to religious-based authority; Catholics, in particular, have long defied papal admonitions (see chapter 2). Further, as underscored by the public opinion data on climate change, political affiliation is more significant than religious identity in predicting an individual's views. This does not mean that appeals to religious figures or to spiritual themes have no resonance for Catholics or others. But other arguments may be more persuasive.

Indeed it may be counterproductive to tie communication strategies on climate change to religious figures such as Francis, or to incorporate moral, religious, and spiritual themes in the campaigns. This caution is suggested when one specifically looks at religiously unaffiliated individuals. Many studies indicate that the religiously unaffiliated are more positively attuned than other Americans to global warming. They are more likely than Catholics and other religiously affiliated Americans to say that global warming is a "very serious problem" and is caused by human activity.[63] A solid majority of the unaffiliated (68 percent) also have a favorable opinion of Francis.[64] Might their positive disposition toward both climate change and Francis enhance the salience of a "Francis frame" for them? Despite their growing numbers, and despite the fact that there are as many religiously unaffiliated Americans as there are Catholics, religiously unaffiliated individuals were not included in the Yale/George Mason panel survey.[65]

We can look, however, to a separate survey conducted in May 2016, a year after *LS*'s release. It shows that the unaffiliated (17 percent) are only half as likely as Catholics (35 percent) to "think they generally agree with Pope Francis about the environment and climate change."[66] Therefore, even though there is an objective affinity between the unaffiliated and Francis on climate change, it is not perceived as such by them. This gap is likely due to several factors, but one reason may be cognitive bias. Politically conservative Americans are more likely to look to and to trust conservative sources on climate change and other issues.[67] By the same token, many religiously unaffiliated Americans may be hesitant to give credibility to religious figures, regardless of the public nature of the societal issue, the secular reasoning used, or the moderate position articulated.

Postsecular Implications

From a postsecular perspective, the relative lack of salience of religious (e.g., religious, spiritual, moral) and religious-based secular (e.g., social justice) idioms in opinion on climate change is interesting in a number of ways. First, it suggests that even when a high-profile religious figure engages the public on an issue such as climate change, the issue retains its established secular framing. In other words, a large majority still sees it, essentially and predominantly, as an environmental and a scientific issue (as noted earlier). In accord with postsecular expectations, then, the reasoned (secular) authority of the arguments is more important than the (religious) authority of the speaker. Therefore, just because a well-regarded religious leader engages with a secular issue in the public sphere, this does not necessarily make the issue religious or moral.

Second, Francis's engagement on climate change highlights the normalcy of public religion in contemporary society. This is indicated in several ways. Most basically, it is by the simple fact that the pope and other religious individuals are entitled to participate in public debate and to embark on various environmental initiatives; that they evidently feel at home in doing so; that they receive extensive media coverage for their forays; and that their intervention is taken note of by political and scientific elites, and to some extent, by ordinary religious and secular citizens. The societal acceptance of religious engagement is further reinforced by the fact that the issue being addressed is not necessarily religious, spiritual, or moral (though it is for some) but, rather, is one that is mundanely secular and pertinent to a contrite modernity: what to do about climate change.

Third, although I highlight the limited impact of Francis's arguments on public opinion, I reaffirm the postsecular rhetorical power of his environmental reasoning. The fluency he shows in integrating scientific data and a secular critique of consumer lifestyles may reinforce or contribute to the apparent increase in Catholics' (and others') framing of climate change in such secular terms. This is noteworthy given that individuals' experiences and views are deeply embedded in an everyday existence defined by consumer habits, making it hard to be open to changing those habits (as Francis encourages). Nonetheless, as noted earlier, Americans are now more likely to consider climate change as a major lifestyle issue than they were prior to the release of *LS* (whether related or not to its influence).

Secular reasoning, therefore, may indeed be far more effective—as postsecular theorizing assumes—than recourse to specifically religious themes or specifically religious authority. At the same time, at least in American society, the civil religious discourse of covenant language and stewardship, for example, means there is a blurred line between a religious and a secular idiom.[68] A vocabulary of environmental stewardship, therefore, may have an intensified secular and religious salience in bridging partisan divisions over climate change. Thus, in and amid the secular, a certain civil religious literacy can be a useful cultural resource in advancing public debate about complex policy issues.

Conclusion

Increasingly today there is awareness that the human community is a global community. There is recognition that everyday local and national societal experiences are impacted by globalizing economic, political, and cultural forces. Notwithstanding resurgent appeals to nationalism, ethicists and social scientists emphasize the need for public policies that can serve a global common good.[69] This is not new territory for the Catholic Church. With its universal presence—a "church without frontiers" (*JG* #210)—it has long been a transnational actor. It has also long appreciated the ethics of global citizenship. And as a member of the United Nations and as a diplomatic power in its own right, it has long engaged in dialogue with nations and with other transnational institutions.[70]

This chapter has focused on the Church's renewed relevance in dealing with the problems of contemporary society. Francis's focus on economic inequality and climate change and the culturally accessible, secular reasoning he employs illuminate the postsecular relevance of religion. He is carving out a new space for the Church in secular society. He shows greater appreciation than his predecessors for the secular—for God's presence in secular realities—and greater attunement to secular expectations, evident in his issue focus, his vocabulary, and his general communicative openness. These characteristics fit well with postsecular expectations.

Although my interest is anchored in the American context, Francis shows a very clear understanding of the sociological realities of globalization. He frequently highlights how globalization impacts the causes and consequences of economic and social inequality and climate change, and the local and regional contexts in which they are experienced. This multifaceted sensitivity is not a surprise, given his own lived experiences within the Global South, where the crosscutting pressures of underdevelopment and overdevelopment accentuate political tensions concerning economic resources. These socio-geographical realities are indeed different, as some of his critics point out, from the Western or American context. They are nonetheless illuminative of how capitalism intertwines economic growth, inequality, and environmental degradation. As a Jesuit, moreover, Francis is virtually by definition a global citizen, given the geographical breadth of the Jesuits and their historical expansion in tandem with capitalism's global development.[71] He is thus particularly well suited to amplifying the Church's public presence and its articulation of the economic, political, and moral stakes at issue amid globalization.

Whether Francis's critique is dismissed or its effects overstated, its politicization means that the actual realities of contemporary society (e.g., economic inequality, global warming, public opinion) are not encountered as they are. This response is contrary to Francis's own insistence on attentiveness to actual empirical realities (*JG* #231–233), and does little to advance the evidence-based dialogue a contrite modernity needs in order to deal with its problems. Tension between ideas and realities is not uncommon. In the next chapter, I focus on how tension between doctrinal ideas and secular realities permeates Church teaching on sex and gender.

4

The Church's Dilemma

SEX AND GENDER

SEX AND GENDER occupy a central place in the Church's teaching on "faith and morals." They are also publicly defined markers of personal and social identity, and are central to how people understand themselves and others.[1] Hence, how the Church frames these issues impacts individuals, personal and social relationships, and public culture in ways beyond their theological significance.

The Order of Sex

The Church's inquisitive interest in the sexual longings and sexual acts of Catholics has long been recounted in cultural histories and works of fiction. Pre-Vatican II moral theology focused primarily on a legalistic categorization of sexual sins.[2] These were vividly documented in the Church's *moral manuals*, the seminary texts with which all priests were trained. Dating to the late sixteenth century, the manuals were periodically revised, but they remained largely unchanged until the mid-twentieth century. Across the Catholic world, these handbooks not only taught priests how to categorize sins and assign penance but also guided them "to learn how to discover the source of sin in the individual penitent."[3] The probing incision of such inquiry— "He had to confess, to speak out in words what he had done and thought, sin after sin"—is well captured in the confession prompted from sixteen-year-old Stephen Dedalus in James Joyce's *A Portrait of the Artist as a Young Man*.

— How long is it since your last confession, my child?
— A long time, father.
— A month, my child?

— Longer, father.

— Three months, my child?

— Longer, father.

— Six months?

— Eight months, father.

He had begun. The priest asked:

— And what do you remember since that time?

He began to confess his sins: masses missed, prayers not said, lies.

— Anything else, my child?

Sins of anger, envy of others, gluttony, vanity, disobedience.

— Anything else, my child?

There was no help. He murmured:

— I ... committed sins of impurity, father.

The priest did not turn his head.

— With yourself, my child?

— And ... with others.

— With women, my child?

— Yes, father.

— Were they married women, my child?

He did not know. His sins trickled from his lips, one by one, trickled in shameful drops from his soul, festering and oozing like a sore, a squalid stream of vice. The last sins oozed forth, sluggish, filthy. There was no more to tell. He bowed his head, overcome.

The priest was silent. Then he asked:

— How old are you, my child?

— Sixteen, father.

The priest passed his hand several times over his face. Then, resting his forehead against his hand, he leaned towards the grating and, with eyes still averted, spoke slowly. His voice was weary and old.

— You are very young, my child, he said, and let me implore of you to give up that sin. It's a terrible sin. It kills the body and it kills the soul. ... As long as you commit that sin ... you will never be worth one farthing to God.[4]

Perhaps Pope Francis had this scene in mind when he wrote: "I want to remind priests that the confessional must not be a torture chamber but rather an encounter with the Lord's mercy that spurs us on to do our best" (*JG* #44).

It is easy to treat Joyce's account, written in 1916, as a narrative of a previous time when many social things, including the Church, were different. Vatican II's affirmation of personal conscience and religious freedom significantly reframed Catholic understanding of sexual morality (see chapter 2). More generally, post-Vatican II moral theology takes a person-centered and relationship approach. It tends to emphasize the virtues of living an ethical life, in contrast to a narrow focus on the sinfulness of specific sexual acts.[5]

Vatican II's doctrinal developments fostered expectations of a Church that would be less intrusive about sexual behavior. This, however, has not fully eventuated. And it is largely due to the Church's construal of sexual morality. As part of its modern compromise with political liberalism, the Church ceded authority to the state and secular society on sociopolitical issues, while insisting on its institutional authority over matters of "faith and morals."[6] This distinction is not as straightforward as it might seem. Although the Church affirms the legitimacy of the separation of church and state, and of civil law from Catholic morality, it defines sexual morality as a societal and not solely a religious issue. The Church's teachings on sexual morality are grounded in natural law, which essentially argues that ethics and moral principles derive from, are inherent in, and are discerned through "natural" human reason. Natural law understands certain things, by nature, to be inherently and objectively good in and of themselves— for example, human life, everyday practical reason, the beauty of art and nature, and importantly, the natural structure of human sexual differences and of female–male complementarity.[7] With this understanding, therefore, the Church claims sexual behavior as not simply a religious or a faith-based matter but, more so, one of universal, fundamental morality. Sexual morality thus assumes moral and sociopolitical significance beyond Catholicism.

From a postsecular perspective, the Church's adherence to natural law is interesting. It projects the Church's self-understanding that it has an institutional obligation to articulate not a specifically Catholic but, rather, a transreligious, secular morality. Its (self-defined) task is to articulate an objectively reasoned *public* morality. This is so, notwithstanding the differentiation of church and state—and of religious morality and civil law—at the core of political liberalism and as affirmed by the Church itself at Vatican II. Because natural law is, in principle, a universally accessible discourse, the Church's embrace of natural law positions it well, theoretically, as a postsecular actor with access to a culturally accessible idiom. In practice, however, the Church struggles both to translate its natural law reasoning and to rein in the sexual habits of Catholics and the larger culture.

Since the 1970s, there has been a rapid liberalization in Western society of contraception, abortion, divorce, remarriage, and more recently, same-sex marriage. It is thus not surprising that sexual morality is a persistent topic on the Church's agenda. This focus was further motivated by Vatican concerns that the changes instituted by Vatican II—and Catholic attitudes and behavior—were undermining the authority of the Church's specific moral teachings, as well as respect for magisterial authority in general.[8] Since Vatican II, therefore, there has been a reassertion of Vatican authority on sexual morality, with an authority-consolidating, "moral magisterium" especially evident during John Paul II's papacy.[9] The issues of abortion and gay sexuality were heavily targeted. And the Vatican also reiterated its opposition to women's ordination.

Abortion Pre-Francis

During his long tenure, John Paul II issued several important and lengthy statements on sex-related issues. Notable among these, his 1995 encyclical *The Gospel of Life* (*GL*), forcefully tackles abortion. It reaffirms that:

> procured abortion is the deliberate and direct killing, by whatever means it is carried out, of a human being in the initial phase of his or her existence, extending from conception to birth . . . and is always gravely immoral . . . reasons . . . however serious and tragic, can never justify the deliberate killing of an innocent human being. (*GL* #58)

GL thus unequivocally asserts the Church's opposition to abortion. Yet it also situates it as one of a number of "crimes committed against life." It thus contextualizes abortion within the framework of Church opposition to the death penalty (*GL* #56–57) and euthanasia (*GL* #64–65).

The Postsecular Strands in John Paul II's Abortion Discourse

While emphasizing that abortion is "particularly serious and deplorable" (*GL* #58) and a "grave moral disorder" (*GL* #62), the life ethic elaborated by John Paul opens up the discourse beyond abortion. He does not solely reassert longstanding Church teaching on the grave sinfulness of abortion, which would phrase it within a familiar Catholic vocabulary. Rather, he partially frames abortion within a constellation of human rights (e.g., *GL* #18, 19, 87,

88) and sociopolitical issues (e.g., violence against life as a result of poverty and hunger and the unjust distribution of resources, *GL* #10). This broader approach places the values at issue as secular, not solely religious. It imposes an ethical standard obliging not just Catholics but citizens in general to see— and to act in response to—the life issues that thread through the life course from birth to death. In this framing, one cannot be "pro-life" on abortion but in favor of the death penalty, and one cannot be opposed to capital punishment but in favor of abortion. This broader ethical framing, I suggest, is evidence of the compatibility of the Church's reasoning with a secular idiom.

A second way in which Church discourse on abortion resonates with a postsecular sensibility is its appreciation for the larger sociological context of abortion. Church officials insist that abortion can never be morally justified. Because the Church teaches that human life begins at conception, it opposes abortion in all circumstances; it thus rejects the broadly accepted view that abortion should be legal in cases such as rape, incest, the health of the mother, or fetal abnormality. Nevertheless, John Paul acknowledges the personal and social circumstances that can lead some women to have an abortion. He states:

> the decision to have an abortion is often tragic and painful for the mother insofar as the decision . . . is not made for purely selfish reasons or out of convenience, but out of a desire to protect certain important values such as her own health or a decent standard of living for the other members of the family. Sometimes it is feared that the child to be born would live in such conditions that it would be better if the birth did not take place. (*GL* #58)

He also notes the pressures variously exerted by "existential and interpersonal difficulties" (*GL* #11), "acute poverty" (*GL* #11), violence against women (*GL* #11), fathers, either directly or by abandoning the mother, and pressure from other family members and friends (*GL* #59).

The Church certainly regards abortion and its cultural acceptance as a dangerous moral crisis (*GL* #58). However, its recognition of it also as a social problem related to difficult personal, economic, and family circumstances bolsters the public relevance of its anti-abortion discourse. It allows the Church to engage, however thinly, with secular audiences who may or may not agree with its opposition to abortion, but who might nonetheless appreciate its recognition of the social circumstances in which abortion decisions are made.[10] Further, and independent of abortion, it can find resonance with secular citizens who might appreciate the Church's pushing of society to be attentive to poverty and family violence, for example, and their amelioration. Thus, abortion becomes or is not solely a moral-religious problem of particular concern to the Church but also one that is related to other societal ills (e.g., poverty, interpersonal violence).

John Paul was succeeded by Benedict who, as Cardinal Ratzinger, worked closely with him for twenty-five years as prefect of the Congregation for the Doctrine of the Faith (CDF), the Vatican office in charge of clarifying doctrine. Benedict gave abortion much less attention than was anticipated, given his CDF role. Only one of his three encyclicals, *Caritas in Veritate (CV)*, highlights abortion, and does so very briefly. Benedict stresses abortion's moral gravity, but he too encases it in a broader societal, life-issues frame that includes euthanasia and eugenics (*CV* #28). Also like John Paul, he explicitly links abortion to other societal ills, notably poverty and economic underdevelopment (*CV* #28); further fitting with postsecular accessibility, he also invokes human rights. He argues, for example, that:

> The building of peace always comes about by the protection of human beings and their fundamental rights. . . . Foremost among these is respect for human life at every stage. . . . Direct abortion, that is to say willed as an end or as a means, is gravely contrary to the moral law. In affirming this, the Catholic Church is not lacking in understanding and mercy, also towards the mother involved. Rather, it is a question of being vigilant lest the law unjustly alter the balance between the right to life of the mother and that of the unborn child, a right belonging equally to both.[11]

The Secular Limits of John Paul II's Discourse

Other elements in the Church's abortion discourse are in sharp tension with a postsecular sensibility. This is particularly apparent in John Paul's dichotomized contrast of a culture of life and a culture of death (noted in chapter 3). Seeing current societal forces as conspiring against life, he highlights abortion as crystallizing the dominance of a "culture of death." Some scholars see this phrasing as reflective of John Paul's flair for dramatic rhetoric, owing to his having been an actor for many years.[12] The sharp contrast, however—a culture of life versus a culture of death—pits the religious against the secular, and detracts from the moral and sociological nuance that is otherwise present in his arguments. It also distracts from the ethical complexity in his interlinking of abortion to other life and societal issues (e.g., the death penalty, poverty). Relatedly, it may preemptively close off the openness of Catholic and secular audiences to more fully consider the Church's abortion discourse as a whole. That this is, in fact, the case is suggested by the ongoing evidence of the limited salience of the Church's anti-abortion arguments among Catholics and other Americans.[13]

The Gospel of Life's postsecular potential is also undermined by its grouping together of abortion and contraception. John Paul argues that the "conspiracy against life" (*GL* #12) is most apparent with respect to the prevalence of abortion. But he is clear that abortion and contraception are rooted in the same cultural mentality. He states:

> the negative values inherent in the "contraceptive mentality"— which is very different from responsible parenthood, lived in respect for the full truth of the conjugal act—are such that they in fact strengthen this temptation when an unwanted life is conceived. Indeed, the pro-abortion culture is especially strong precisely where the Church's teaching on contraception is rejected. Certainly from the moral point of view, contraception and abortion are *specifically different* evils. . . . But despite their differences of nature and moral gravity, contraception and abortion are often closely connected, as fruits of the same tree. . . . The close connection which exists, in mentality, between the practice of contraception and that of abortion is becoming increasingly obvious. (*GL* #13, emphasis in original)

By aligning abortion and contraception, he collapses the distinction that many Catholics, including theologians, have long made.[14] The rhetorical conflation of the two as constituting the same mentality may strike some as an unreasonable moral and empirical claim, at odds with the lived experience of many highly committed Catholics (and others) who use contraception and who define abortion as categorically very different.[15] John Paul's framing here thus limits the postsecular reach of his discourse as one deserving attention from Catholics and non-Catholics alike. Of further postsecular consequence, it may be difficult for individuals to thoughtfully engage with Church teaching on abortion—and on other societal issues— if the Church is perceived as being morally fundamentalist on account of its wholesale rejection of contraception and its categorization as "intrinsically evil."[16]

A third way in which John Paul's abortion discourse contravenes post-secular expectations is its declaratory use of religious-grounded authority. Substantiating the Church's anti-abortion position, he states:

> By the authority which Christ conferred upon Peter and his successors, and in communion with the Bishops of the Catholic Church . . . *I confirm that the direct and voluntary killing of an innocent human being is always gravely immoral.* This doctrine, based upon that unwritten law which man, in the light of reason, finds in his own heart (cf. Romans 2:14–15), is reaffirmed by Scripture, transmitted by the Tradition of the Church and taught by the ordinary and universal Magisterium. (*GL* #57, emphasis in original)

As clearly demonstrated in this quote, John Paul invokes his unilateral authority as pope to articulate the Church's teaching. Moreover, he firmly grounds papal authority in the equally imposing, intersecting authorities of scripture, apostolic succession, and Church hierarchy. Additionally, he grounds the teaching itself in natural law, scripture, tradition, and his own magisterial authority and that of his fellow bishops. He thus conveys that there is no doubt about his interpretive authority on abortion, nor any ambiguity in the authoritative validity of the teaching. Hence, there is little room for a postsecular dialogue that might engage with abortion as a moral and social problem. Nor is there room, more ambitiously, for the probing of an alternate consensus on the issue.

In sum, the absolute and definitive nature of the Church's teaching on abortion, John Paul's dichotomization of a culture of life versus a culture of death, and the specifically religious sources of authority he forcefully invokes in outlining these arguments circumscribe the discursive reach and potential impact of the discourse. Yet, it still warrants attention that Church officials talk about abortion not simply as a moral sin but also as a social problem, and one related to other social problems (e.g., poverty). Thus, the Church challenges modernity and uses the secular language of modernity to do so. By connecting abortion to socio-economic and other interpersonal, family, and societal problems, and couching the ethical issues at stake in the vocabulary of human rights, the Church invokes language that is not only familiar to but also respected by secular society.

For a contrite modernity for whom abortion is indeed a social problem, and one closely related to poverty, racial and ethnic inequality, and family problems, the Church's discourse has postsecular relevance.[17] It emphasizes the sanctity of life but also the sanctity of interpersonal and social relations and the ethic of care they require. Its life ethic thus obliges attentiveness not only to diverse problems (e.g., abortion and the death penalty) but also to the social conditions that contribute to their prevalence, and thus nudges their mending.

Sexuality Pre-Francis

The Church's discourse on same-sex relationships is far more narrowly construed. This may come as a surprise to contemporary secular and Catholic audiences for whom the questions at stake may appear less inherently complicated than those at issue over abortion (e.g., the right to life). The Vatican's official statements on gay sexuality use a highly restricted secular idiom. There is partial recourse to a vocabulary of human rights. Across its statements, the Vatican emphasizes that "homosexuals" should never be subject to discrimination and that they deserve full respect and acceptance.

The cultural resonance of this anti-discrimination motif, however, is attenuated by the Church's core teaching on sexuality and its condemnation of same-sex relationships. This teaching is couched in a highly technical vocabulary. It refers to gays as "individuals of homosexual orientation"—a deviation from the natural order of heterosexuality—and elaborates its natural-law reasoning using an essentialist, physical, and act-centered language. In its declaration on sexual ethics in 1975 (with Paul VI as pope), the Congregation for the Doctrine of the Faith (CDF) stated that "homosexual acts are intrinsically disordered and can in no case be approved of."

A subsequent declaration, issued eleven years later (in 1986), used particularly strong language. It pushed back against what Church officials saw as a culture of increased political and theological acceptance of "homosexuality" and "grave disregard" for its denunciation of it. The 1975 statement had distinguished between "constitutional" and "transitory homosexuality." Church officials subsequently acknowledged their view that this distinction had contributed to an "overly benign interpretation" among Catholics, including theologians. The naming of this as an *interpretive* problem reflects the Vatican's deep concern about secularism's undermining of Church authority. Of particular alarm to the hierarchy, it is not merely secular citizens but also its own laity and theologians who are misconstruing and misrepresenting Church teaching.

The 1986 statement therefore clarified that a "homosexual inclination" is "a more or less strong tendency ordered toward an intrinsic moral evil and thus the inclination itself must be seen as an objective disorder." It further emphasized that "homosexual activity" is sinful. It is objectively sinful because it "is not a complementary union able to transmit life." Therefore, while a "homosexual inclination" in itself is not sinful (though disordered), "when persons engage in homosexual activity they confirm within themselves a disordered sexual inclination which is essentially self-indulgent." Several subsequent Vatican statements reiterated similar, act-centered language. In 2003, for example, it stated:

> Sacred Scripture condemns homosexual acts "as a serious deprav-ity." . . . This judgment of Scripture does not of course permit us to conclude that all those who suffer from this anomaly are personally responsible for it, but it does attest to the fact that homosexual acts are intrinsically disordered.[18]

Same-sex Marriage

This 2003 statement, and others coinciding with the then newly growing cultural momentum in favor of legalizing gay civil unions and gay marriage, also outlined the Church's objections to gay marriage. The reasoning used is grounded in the Church's moral framework of natural law, a discourse that, in principle, as I noted earlier, is secular insofar as its ethical reasoning is derived from "natural" human reason. Projecting a certain postsecular consciousness, the U.S. bishops themselves emphasize the persuasive value they see encased in the rationality of their moral claims. They state, for example:

> Given such strong [hedonistic & consumeristic] influences in our cul-ture, it is not surprising that there are a number of groups active in our society that not only deny the existence of objective moral norms but also aggressively seek public approval for homosexual behavior. The message of such groups misleads many people and causes considerable harm. In the face of this challenge the church must continue her efforts to persuade people through rational argument, the witness of her life and the proclamation of the Gospel of Jesus Christ.[19]

What counts as legitimate rational argument, however, has to accord with social and cultural expectations of reasonableness, of what makes sense given everyday experience.[20] The Church's reasoning is grounded in a belief in the objective order of sexual complementarity. In other words, it believes in the natural, physical complementarity of the duality of male and female sexual differences.[21] In contemporary society, complementarity is a difficult thesis to defend. It challenges the widely shared view that sex or gender roles are socially defined, and that their characteristics, as well as the opportunities for their realization, vary across sociohistorical contexts. Further complicating its translation today is the increased everyday normality of same-sex couples and same-sex marriage.

In Church teaching, marriage is a sacrament, but it is also, essentially, a "natural institution" and as such an "irreplaceable good for society and all people."[22] Same-sex marriage, the Church argues, is therefore contrary to God's law and natural law. It contravenes God's creation of male and female (as complementary, heterosexual partners), and contravenes the sanctity of marriage as a male–female union based on sexual difference. Consequently—the Vatican's 2003 statement argues—same-sex marriage is harmful to society and the common good because it gives legal approval to "gravely immoral" private behavior, and is thus equivalent to public "toleration of evil." And, as Benedict states:

> the marriage of a man and a woman . . . is not a simple social convention, but rather the fundamental cell of every society. Consequently, policies which undermine the family threaten human dignity and the future of humanity itself.[23]

By extension, the Church opposes the adoption of children by same-sex couples, and, additionally, family formation based on in vitro fertilization, whether by gay or straight couples. In general, it regards families headed by same-sex couples as being "detrimental to children." It grounds this claim in "experience," and in reference to the U.N.'s articulation of children's rights— two sources that would seem to bring secular validity. Thus:

> As experience has shown, the absence of sexual complementarity in these unions creates obstacles in the normal development of children who would be placed in the care of such persons. They would be deprived of the experience of either fatherhood or motherhood. Allowing children to be adopted by persons living in such unions would actually mean doing violence to these children, in the sense that their condition of dependency would be used to place them in an environment that is not conducive to their full human development. This is gravely immoral and in open contradiction to the principle recognized also in the U.N. Convention on the Rights of the Child that the best interests of the child, as the weaker and more vulnerable party, are to be the paramount consideration in every case.[24]

Human experience is a well-recognized, legitimate source of Catholic moral theology.[25] The "experience" alluded to in the statement, however, is ambiguous. While the Vatican appears to be making an empirical claim to bolster its religious (moral) teaching, its assertion is presented independent of supporting studies. It thus falls short of the postsecular expectation that religious actors should draw on empirical reasoning. Additionally, the U.N. reference is used to imply that children would be especially vulnerable in same-sex families, even though the language of vulnerability was used by the U.N. in a far more general way.

Taken as a whole, the Church's framing of gay sexuality and behavior as unnatural lacks secular resonance. For example, only one-third (35 percent) of American Catholics say it is a sin to "engage in homosexual behavior," and two-thirds (66 percent) approve of gay parents raising children.[26] The Vatican does not knit its teaching into a secular vocabulary that might garner the attention of audiences who are skeptical or lack understanding of natural law. Nor does it make allowance for those who are wary of a vocabulary that talks of "objectively disordered" individuals and of objectively disordered and gravely immoral sexual acts.[27] Its argument that same-sex behavior is essentially "self-indulgent" is a strand that has some fit with the secular critique of contemporary culture as narcissistic.[28] However, this claim may be increasingly difficult to reconcile with the accumulating evidence of the commitment of LGBT individuals to long-term couple relationships and family formation.[29]

As I noted, the Church denounces discrimination against LGBT individuals. Yet, for some, this may be difficult to reconcile with its categorization of gays as "disordered" or its denunciation of the objective immorality of same-sex relationships.[30] In sum, the Church's official discourse on gays does not accomplish the secular bridging it does on abortion. It does not, for example, engage with the scientific and social scientific research on the "origins" or the developmental context of same-sex attraction. Nor has it issued any formal statement in which it deletes or rephrases the language used in earlier declarations. Specifically, it has not retracted the "objectively disordered" vocabulary of its 1986 declaration. In short, despite a lot of change in the scientific, theological, and cultural understanding of gay sexuality over the past thirty years, there has been no revision in official Church language. This is so notwithstanding the Church's own emphasis at Vatican II on the relevance of empirical sciences in informing theology, pastoral care, and the understanding of individual development.[31] It also contrasts with its use of scientific studies in public debates on abortion and divorce.[32] Clearly, the Church tends to employ empirical reasoning only when it is consonant with its moral agenda.

Francis's Postsecular Tilt on Abortion and Sexuality

So far I have focused on the doctrine articulated prior to Francis's election. There is good reason to do so. His papacy provided early indication that Church discourse on abortion and sexuality was likely to change. In his widely publicized September 2013 interview, Francis named what he called the Church's obsession, and called for a new balance in its priorities. He stated:

> We cannot insist only on issues related to abortion, gay marriage and the use of contraceptive methods. This is not possible . . . when we speak about these issues, we have to talk about them in a context. The teaching of the church is clear, for that matter, and I am a son of the church, but it is not necessary to talk about these things all the time. The dogmatic and moral teachings of the church are not all equivalent. The church's pastoral ministry cannot be obsessed with the transmission of a disjointed multitude of doctrines to be imposed insistently. Proclamation in a missionary style focuses on the essentials, on the necessary things. . . . We have to find a new balance; otherwise even the moral edifice of the church is likely to fall like a house of cards, losing the freshness and fragrance of the Gospel. . . . [T]he proclamation of the saving love of God comes before moral and religious imperatives. Today sometimes it seems that the opposite order is prevailing. [33]

Francis's decentering of the importance of abortion was stunning and unexpected. It has long had primacy as the Church's top moral and public policy priority. Further, given the Church's unwavering emphasis on its grave immorality, to speak of it in this manner—as an obsession—seemed to question its pastoral and even its moral-theological salience.

Decentering Abortion

Francis has changed the conversation on abortion. He has done so not by changing Church teaching—which, as he notes, is impossible given the sanctity of life (*JG* #214)—but by giving it less attention and less priority. He stands out for his public prioritization of other issues. It is poverty and other concerns such as the environment that he returns to time and again in his formal and informal statements (see chapter 3). For him, neither abortion nor gay sexuality are the imposing societal threats identified by his predecessors. John Paul II defined abortion as an "immense threat . . . to the life of individuals but also to that of civilization itself" (*GL* #59). And Benedict regarded same-sex marriage as undermining the family and thus threatening "human dignity and the future of humanity itself."[34] Francis, by contrast, defines the amelioration of poverty and social exclusion as fundamental to shaping the future of humanity (*JG* #185).

Nevertheless, as Francis himself frequently states, he is "a son of the church" and fully endorses its teaching on abortion.[35] In several important statements, including *Joy of the Gospel*, he strongly emphasizes the imperative of protecting unborn life (*JG* #213, 214). Similarly, in his widely publicized encyclical on climate change (*Laudato Si'*), he locates the prevalence of abortion as part of the throwaway culture of consumerism and environmental degradation. Like his predecessors, he also links abortion to human rights and social justice concerns. He asks:

> Since everything is interrelated, concern for the protection of nature is also incompatible with the justification of abortion. How can we genuinely teach the importance of concern for other vulnerable beings, however troublesome or inconvenient they may be, if we fail to protect a human embryo, even when its presence is uncomfortable and creates difficulties? (*LS* #120)

He also discusses the interpersonal and socioeconomic context in which abortion occurs. Yet he goes a step further than his predecessors, noting the relative inattentiveness of the Church to helping women in difficult situations. He states:

> it is also true that we have done little to adequately accompany women in very difficult situations, where abortion appears as a quick solution to their profound anguish, especially when the life developing within them is the result of rape or a situation of extreme poverty. (*JG* #214)

Another way in which Francis has nuanced the conversation on abortion is by expanding the Church's emphasis on forgiveness. He presents confession as a welcoming situation for women who have had an abortion. In keeping with his stress on the need for a continuous dialogue between realities and ideas (*JG* #231)—a theme compatible with postsecular expectations—he places attention on women and their actual circumstances. He gives less focus to the sinfulness of abortion itself, couching confession more in terms of forgiveness than penance. Thus, his approach strikes a more pastoral-therapeutic tone than a legalistic one. For example, when he discusses abortion he does not mention canon law or excommunication. In the context of Church teaching, this is a significant silence, because John Paul, by contrast, explicitly elaborated on canon law and its automatic excommunication provision for abortion.[36]

Like his predecessors, Francis stresses the importance of repentance and reconciliation for women who have had an abortion. In honor of the Extraordinary Jubilee Year of Mercy (December 8, 2015, to November 20, 2016) he explicitly allowed all priests (not solely bishops) the discretion to absolve and forgive women who have had an abortion.[37] And he specifically exhorted priests to express "words of genuine welcome" in confession to such women. For the 1983 Holy Year, John Paul similarly affirmed the sacramental power of all priests to aid in the remission of sins.[38] He stressed the importance of their reaching out to give special attention to the sick, the imprisoned, the old, and all those suffering. But unlike Francis, he did not explicitly mention women who have had an abortion. Francis's overall approach, therefore, of forgiveness and explicit outreach to women suggests closer attunement to their situation and to secular realities than is true of the excommunication–repentance frame that tends to place forgiveness in a more religious-legalistic context.

In sum, Francis has changed the Church's abortion discourse and has done so in ways that strengthen the Church's postsecular relevance. Of particular significance is the decentering of the singular primacy of abortion from the Church's public agenda and its displacement with attentiveness to a broader set of societal problems (e.g., economic inequality and climate change). Further, Francis seeks greater mutuality between women's secular realities and the Church's religious-sacramental resources. This is shown by attentiveness to what the Church can do to accompany women in their actual circumstances, and by expanding the sacramental accessibility of forgiveness. As such, this increased postsecular attunement may nudge Catholics and others to take a second look at the Church's abortion discourse as a whole and, perhaps, find new appreciation for the broader ethical agenda it sets for a contrite modernity.

Francis's Disruptive Discourse on Gays

Francis's discourse on gays is particularly striking in its postsecular openness. His words and gestures stand in remarkable contrast with the Vatican's pattern of condemnation of same-sex relationships and its advocacy against same-sex marriage. Although many priests are accepting of LGBT individuals in various pastoral situations, Francis's public, nonjudgmental acknowledgment of the desires and lived realities of LGBT individuals is a clear departure from official Church discourse. Early in his papacy, he infamously stated: "If someone is gay and he searches for the Lord and has good will, who am I to judge?" He subsequently elaborated:

> A person once asked me, in a provocative manner, if I approved of homosexuality. I replied with another question: "Tell me: when God looks at a gay person, does he endorse the existence of this person with love, or reject, and condemn this person?" We must always consider the person. Here we enter into the mystery of the human being. In life, God accompanies persons, and we must accompany them, starting with their situation.[39]

In addition to the nonjudgmental and person-centered attitude conveyed, Francis's use of the very word *gay* marks a significant change in Church discourse. *Homosexuality* is the word that, until Francis publicly invoked *gay*, is the term always used in official Church statements referencing the topic. For him to use the preferred vocabulary of LGBT individuals—the language that has paramount everyday relevance for them—is symbolically disruptive of official Church discourse. It is also in tune with the everyday language used by politically and religiously moderate Catholics and other citizens.

The discourse is also being changed—as with abortion—by the Church's relative displacement of gay issues from its public agenda. This is part of Francis's intentional decentering of the Church's obsession with sexual matters. In this regard, as on abortion, what is *not* said is as important as what is said. In his historic speech to the joint houses of Congress during his trip to the United States in September 2015, Francis spoke of the contemporary challenges to the institution of marriage. He framed these largely in terms of the economic problems that couples and families confront. Notably, he did not mention the increased legal and cultural acceptance of same-sex marriage as one such challenge. In *Joy of the Gospel*, he is similarly critical of the cultural forces undermining the sanctity of marriage. He sees it threatened by the influence of the entertainment and media industries (*JG* #62), and by what he calls a postmodern individualism—that is, the valuing of transitory emotional satisfaction over the obligations associated with marriage and the family as "the fundamental cell of society" (*JG* #66, 67). Yet here again, he does not identify the increased cultural acceptance of same-sex relationships or same-sex marriage as a negative cultural force.

These are symbolically important shifts. Additionally, even though Francis frequently affirms Church teaching that "marriage is between a man and a woman," he also formally acknowledges the stability that same-sex unions can offer (*AL #52*). Further, he has not contradicted the influential German Cardinal Reinhard Marx's publicly stated view that the Church should not oppose structures in society that respect gay rights, including civil unions. Additionally, echoing another of Cardinal Marx's opinions, Francis has stated that the Church should seek forgiveness from gay people for how it has treated them.[40] All of these gay-friendly nods matter. They become critical moments in the institutionalization of the Church's acceptance of LGBT individuals, and in forging new paths between the Church and secular society. They convey that same-sex relationships are an everyday reality whose existence may not be as disordered or as sinful as its (still) official but somewhat silenced vocabulary maintains.[41]

The Perception of Change

Against the backdrop of increased acceptance of gay relationships among Catholics (two-thirds of whom support gay marriage) and in public culture more generally, there is a positive association between Francis's positive disposition toward gays and Catholics' *perceptions* of Church teaching. In 2003, 65 percent of American Catholics said that gay marriage was against their religion's beliefs. In December 2013—a few months after Francis's well-publicized "Who am I to judge" remark—53 percent said so. And in August 2016—a few months after *Amoris Laetitia* affirmed same-sex unions while also reaffirming the Church's opposition to same sex marriage—only 45 percent said support for gay marriage was against their religion's beliefs. Moreover, nearly half (49 percent) of all Catholics who support same-sex marriage also believe the pope does.[42]

Once such perceptions take hold, it is difficult to turn them back to what is, in fact, the official teaching. Rather, they create a new generalized expectation of the accepted morality and normality of the behavior in question. When people act on what they believe to be true—that, for instance, the Church approves of gay sexual behavior—the ensuing behavior contributes to creating and reinforcing the new reality—underscored by the steadily increasing acceptance and prevalence of same-sex relationships and gay marriage. These changes in turn contribute to further normalizing the reality of LGBT individuals in society and in the Church. Normalization is additionally accelerated by cultural or cognitive biases that dispose people to both see and to accept evidence that confirms the validity of their assumed beliefs.[43] In short, the ongoing normalization of gays can be credited among other influences to Francis's papacy.

Toward a Rebalanced Church

In sum, Francis is bolstering the Church's postsecular relevance by decentering it from a preoccupation with abortion and gay sexuality—issues on which it is out of step with many Catholics and non-Catholics. For him, unlike his predecessors, these are not the defining issues threatening humanity. He is committed to preserving the sanctity of life, and has reaffirmed the Church's opposition to abortion, frequently doing so in the context of economic inequality. Further, in keeping with his keen attentiveness to everyday lived realities, he has spoken of the Church's responsibility to do more to alleviate the circumstances that may motivate recourse to abortion. By the same token, he has expanded the Church's message of mercy and forgiveness to women who have had an abortion, and has made a welcoming confession more accessible to them. Thus, he is nuancing the Church's framing of abortion while also nudging attentiveness to the societal relevance of its broader ethics.

Francis is also disrupting what the Church says about gays and how it says it. His culturally resonant vocabulary, his welcoming gestures toward gays, his silences in identifying gay relationships as a threat to marriage, and his affirmation of the stability offered by same-sex unions all convey a Church increasingly attuned to secular society, while also telegraphing the ethical importance of committed relationships (even as it withholds moral and sacramental approval of gay marriage). This attunement feeds Catholics' perceptions—and misperceptions—of a changing Church. I now turn to an area of Church teaching that notably defies postsecular expectations: women's ordination.

Women's Ordination

Sexual complementarity not only informs the Church's opposition to gay sexual behavior and gay marriage, it also informs its opposition to women's ordination. While the Church affirms women's equality with men, it also insists on their difference. This difference is pivotal to the Vatican's prohibition of the possibility of women priests, a teaching that the Church defines as "belonging to the deposit of faith."[44] As such, in the Church's construal, women's ordination is principally an internal matter of Church doctrine and institutional practice; it is not a public issue of fundamental, universal morality like abortion or gay sexual behavior. Sociologically, however, it is a public issue. Many Catholic theologians, and a majority of Catholics in the United States, Western Europe, and some South American countries favor women's ordination.[45] Its prohibition shapes the public identity of the Church and, more generally, it bears upon broader secular conversations about women's equality and the understanding of gender in society.

The Vatican's reasoning on women's ordination is summarized in three straightforward arguments, two grounded in scripture and the third in tradition. First, it argues that ordaining women would contravene the will and intention of Jesus who called only men to be apostles. Second, because women do not physically mimic the male Christ, they cannot mimic him in the sacramental consecration of the bread and wine during the Eucharist (Communion), which is done in memory of Christ at the Last Supper and his command "Do this in memory of me." The third reason is that an exclusively male priesthood is part of the Church's constant and essential hierarchical tradition.

Postsecular Tensions in the Vatican's Arguments Against the Ordination of Women

The Vatican's reasoning on women's ordination is in tension with postsecular expectations. This is not because of the difficulty of translating a faith-based belief or scriptural pronouncement. One tension derives, rather, from the interpretive frame deployed. Ironically, Church officials relinquish their hierarchical authority. But they do so, not in deference to Catholic interpretive community (as would accord with postsecular and Vatican II expectations), but to the higher authority of the Church's founding narrative. The Vatican argues that the exclusion of women from the priesthood is a settled matter because even if the pope wanted to ordain women, he cannot. In this view, the approval of women's ordination would contradict Jesus's actions—specifically, his action in not calling women to be apostles.

Many Catholic theologians, church historians, and lay Catholics contest this claim. They argue that scripture is replete with stories of Jesus's positive actions toward and interactions with women. Women are highly visible, for example, in all the major redemptive events in Jesus's life, including his death and resurrection, and during significant miracle-situations such as the wedding feast of Cana. In this line of reasoning, the argument is that if one focuses, as the Vatican does, on the founding narrative of Jesus's actions, a gender-inclusive Jesus is in fact portrayed. Further, this makes it hard to fathom the Vatican's focus on what Jesus did *not* do. Church officials counterargue, however, that given Jesus's inclusivity it is "all the more remarkable" that he did not call women as disciples. Consequently, they insist, "the Church has no power over the substance of the sacraments." It is "bound by Christ's manner of acting"—that is, his action in not calling women as disciples, rather than his many inclusive actions toward women.[46]

A second postsecular tension is the gender essentialism in the Vatican's reasoning. This is conveyed by the argument that women are physically unable to mimic the "iconic maleness" of Jesus and his manner of acting.[47] Such essentialism reflects a view of sex as physically or biologically definitive and determinative of behavior. Essentialist thinking is not confined to the Church. It still manifests in the secular spheres of work and family, even as gender equality is more fully realized.[48] It has long been challenged, however, especially by feminists, who reject the notion that biology is destiny. And more broadly, it is contrary to the sociological recognition that all social roles, including family and church roles, are socially and historically contingent.

Additionally, the Church's focus on women's inability to physically mimic Christ's maleness presents a concreteness and literalism that Catholicism has long eschewed. It also sits uneasily with the Catholic imagination and its affinity for metaphor. This sensibility sees things as analogous, rather than different, to other things. In this analogical view, as Andrew Greeley explains, the sacramental imagination would sense "that a woman's body is as much a sacrament of God's love as a man's body," and hence equally well suited to mimic Christ's actions.[49]

Dialogue with Tradition

The third reason for women's exclusion from ordination—the force of "constant tradition"—is also in tension with postsecular expectations. Any living tradition, and Catholicism in particular, has multiple strands.[50] Postsecularity requires reflexive dialogue with tradition in order to discern which elements might be reworked in ways that, in light of current secular realities, serve the Church's mission and a larger common good. This task is, in principle, well suited to Catholicism given its moderation, its reflexivity, and its doctrinal and interpretive pluralism.

In the case of women's ordination, the Church's tradition of an exclusively male priesthood might possibly be reinterpreted in the context of social change in women's roles and women's equality. And, more explicitly related to the Church's theology and institutional identity, it might be evaluated in light of the practical reality imposed by the shortage of priests in the United States and in other Western countries. The celebration of the Eucharist in the Mass is foundational to Catholicism, both to its theology and its lived communal practices; it is, as the *Catechism* states, "the source and summit of the Christian life . . . the efficacious sign . . . by which the Church is kept in being . . . the sum and summary of our faith."[51]

Because only ordained priests can consecrate the Eucharist, the shortage of priests directly impacts the Church's theological and communal identity. This dilemma thus places in sharp relief the question of what is "essential" to the Catholic tradition: Is it more Catholic to ordain women priests, or to forgo the Eucharist? The tension lies in whether the defense of a constant tradition—an exclusively male priesthood—may mean the depletion of another constant tradition (the Eucharist) and the specific command of Jesus at the Last Supper to "Do this in memory of me." In interpreting the narrative of Jesus's actions, therefore, which action is more critical to Catholicism—his not calling women apostles, or his words and actions at the Last Supper?

The Vatican's Ban on Dialogue About Women's Ordination

Postsecular expectations would require a probing, reflexive engagement with this question and its various complications and implications. The Vatican, however, has definitively closed off the possibility of such dialogue. In current Church teaching, women's ordination is a matter not "open to debate." As stated by John Paul II, writing in 1994:

> in order that all doubt may be removed regarding a matter of grave importance, a matter which pertains to the church's divine constitution itself . . . I declare that the church has no authority whatsoever to confer priestly ordination on women and that this judgment is to be definitively held by all the church's faithful.[52]

Further clarified by the Vatican's Congregation for the Doctrine of the Faith, an exclusively male priesthood "is a matter of full definitive assent, that is to say, irrevocable, to a doctrine taught infallibly by the church. . . . It is to be held always, everywhere, and by all, as belonging to the deposit of faith."[53] And, Francis, too, departing from his general openness to dialogue and contravening his emphasis on the need for a continuous conversation between ideas and realities, has reaffirmed the settled definitiveness of the Church's exclusion of women priests: "The reservation of the priesthood to males, as a sign of Christ the Spouse who gives himself in the Eucharist, is not a question open to discussion" (JG #104).[54]

The prohibition on discussing women's ordination is clearly at odds with the postsecular expectation of dialogue between the religious and the secular. It also contravenes the Church's own understanding of Catholicism as an interpretive community in which legitimate divergent opinions should be honestly and respectfully discussed.[55] Moreover, even though Church officials define the impossibility of women priests as part of the "deposit of faith," the deposit of faith and the manner in which it is formulated are not beyond reflexive engagement in light of current realities. Again, as Vatican II stated: "Theological inquiry should seek a profound understanding of revealed truth without neglecting close contact with its own times." Further, the new knowledge and understandings that such inquiry yields are to assist in the development of a more theologically and pastorally mature church.[56]

This recognition would seem to have urgent relevance for a contrite Church committed to a path of renewal (see chapter 1). In the wake of the priest sex-abuse crisis, reflexive consideration of the question of women priests might be elevated to a broader discussion engaging both Church officials and the laity about what sort of priesthood and what qualities of priesthood are necessary for today's Church. This has not happened. Nonetheless, the ban on dialogue has not silenced Catholic activism for change and nor has it dampened lay Catholics' support for women priests. Two-thirds of Catholics, including similar majorities of women and men, favor women's ordination.[57] Catholic women were significantly more involved in the Church than men for much of the twentieth century. They were, for example, far more likely to attend weekly Mass and to say that the Church is among the most important parts of their life. Today, that gender gap has disappeared owing to women's decreased commitment (especially evident among young white women). Among the contributory factors are women's growing impatience with Church teachings on sex and gender issues, including ordination. Also salient is the negative attitude toward women conveyed by the hierarchy's investigation of the social justice and other routine activities of American nuns, and its criticism of some feminist theologians (e.g., Margaret Farley and Elizabeth Johnson).[58]

Gender Equality and Difference

Complicating the tension over women's place in the Church is the fact that Church teaching emphasizes gender equality. It maintains that the natural differences between women and men are complementary but not hierarchical. Thus, Church officials emphasize that women and men are fundamentally equal *and* different. Further, since the late 1980s, the Church has condemned sexism as a sin.[59] Francis moreover has affirmed the positive contributions of "feminine emancipation" and the women's movement. He denounces the "excesses of patriarchal cultures that considered women inferior" (*AL* #54), and the chauvinism that tries to control women or blame them for various societal problems.[60] He has also argued that femininity and masculinity are not rigid categories and should not be accentuated, for example, in the division of family household chores (*AL* #286). Similarly, he has argued that women and men should receive equal pay for equal work, and he calls such earnings disparities a "pure scandal."[61]

It is difficult for many Catholics and others to square the Church's emphasis on equality with its opposition to women priests. In the Vatican's reasoning, however, the aspiration to priestly office is not simply another domain of gender equality or human rights. Rather, it is of a different order, and hence "priestly office cannot become the goal of social advancement."[62] From a postsecular perspective, this "different order" framing is particularly significant. It means that even if dialogue on women's ordination were allowed, a secular discourse on equal rights or social equality would be of little use. Nor would the Church's own vocabulary of either social or theological equality be useful to Church officials or to others in evaluating the theological and practical questions raised. Because the question of women's ordination is of a different order, it transcends language claims. It is beyond secular reasoning. It is also beyond religious reasoning; in the Vatican's construal as outlined here, even the pope, in his magisterial and doctrinal authority, cannot contravene the inferred will of Christ.

Feminine Genius and Church Functions

The postsecular translation of Church teaching on women's equality is further impeded by its emphasis on female-specific difference. Building on sexual-gender essentialism, Church leaders from John Paul to Francis laud women's special "feminine genius," and they emphasize how essential it is to the Church (*JG* #103) and to the common good of society (*AL* #173–174).[63]

Yet, women's roles and place in the Church, as stated by Francis, should not be reduced to their functions within the Church. Function, he has argued, should not be confused with dignity. In this vein, he denounces what he sees as "female machismo," stating:

> It is necessary to broaden the opportunities for a stronger presence of women in the church. I am wary of a solution that can be reduced to a kind of "female machismo" because a woman has a different make-up than a man. But what I hear about the role of women is often inspired by an ideology of machismo.[64]

Francis conveys that to talk of functions is to think of women in secular terms. For him, such secular thinking denies women's natural sexual difference (their different makeup and feminine genius). It also fosters the construal of priesthood in terms of occupational and leadership roles and social advancement, a framing the Vatican rejects. His understanding, however, misrecognizes how many Catholics see the issue. Advocates of women's ordination tend not to make their case on grounds of social advancement, nor do they use a secular, individual rights vocabulary. Rather than projecting a "female machismo," they show an affinity for doctrinal reasoning. They reflexively engage with Catholic doctrine—with scriptural accounts of Jesus's life and ministry, the documents of Vatican II, and the Church's social justice and liturgical tradition. They draw on these thoroughly Catholic resources and argue that women priests would be in accord with Catholic theological values of pluralism, inclusivity, communion, and ministry.[65]

Church Functions and Power

Regardless of how either the Vatican or supporters of women's ordination frame the issue, the sociological reality is that functions matter. They matter in all domains of life, including the Church. Indeed, function and hierarchy of function are central to the Church's structure and culture. While rejecting women's ordination, Francis argues that women's presence should be guaranteed in "settings where important decisions are made, both in the Church and in social structures" (*JG* #103). In this line of reasoning, as Church officials frequently aver, one doesn't need a clerical collar to have a leadership role in the Church. Yet, in the Church, the important decision-making settings are populated by, and the important decision makers are, the ordained—those who have the imprimatur to wear a cleric's collar. Hence, ordination and func-tion are not only positively associated but also deeply entangled.

In the context of rejecting women's ordination, Francis says that "it can prove especially divisive if sacramental power is too closely aligned with power in general" (*JG* #104). However, the reality in the Church today (and historically in the Church's "constant tradition") is that the ordained are the power elite. And as Francis has noted many times, the Church itself, including the Vatican, reproduces a power-driven and elitist clerical culture through its everyday practices. He strongly denounces clericalism and its related "curial diseases," including narcissism, and he seeks to disincentivize clericalism.[66] He states, for example, that "[i]t is good for us to remember that the Church is not an elite of priests, of consecrated people, of bishops—but that everyone forms the Holy Faithful People of God."[67]

Yet, there seems little recognition of the possibility that precisely because priests and bishops are a consecrated elite, this may—consciously or unconsciously—infuse a male bias in the Vatican's reasoning on its exclusion of women from ordination. Interpreting and translating "the essentials" of Catholic doctrine is a human endeavor. Incorporating a standpoint analysis would require that Church teachings be interrogated for how they advance the interests and power of the hierarchy. In particular, it would require the all-male, celibate hierarchy of Church officials to scrutinize how their maleness and their vow of sexual abstinence may lead them (whether consciously or not) to advance particular biased understandings of gender and of sexuality. More generally, it pushes for attention to what elements of a doctrinal tra-dition get elevated and what are given secondary emphasis, and how those different emphases may be related to the standpoint of those doing the cat-egorizing. Such inquiry would also benefit from openness to the ultimately *arbitrary* way in which doctrines are classified even as those categorical dis-tinctions may seem quite natural and reasonable to those in power. On wom-en's ordination, in any case, Church reasoning actively contributes to women's subordination in and by the Church.[68]

Many Catholics share Francis's negative view of clerical elitism, and they are sympathetic to the challenge he encounters in trying to change it. For example, over two-thirds of the respondents in my survey of liberal (Call to Action) Catholics say that reducing clericalism (69 percent) and increasing the presence of women in visible leadership roles in the Vatican (71 percent) should be top priorities for change in the Church. And even among conser-vative (Catholic League) Catholics, close to half identify reducing clerical-ism (45 percent) and placing women in visible leadership roles in the Vatican

(49 percent) as priorities.[69] Indeed, many contend that clericalism will not be attenuated until women are admitted to priesthood. For them, women's ordination is not seen as a pathway to clerical power but, rather, to eliminating clericalism. It is thus construed as a bedrock issue on which other desired institutional changes hinge.

A Theology of Woman

In what might seem like an emancipatory gesture toward women, Francis says that in recognition of women's feminine genius the Church needs, in fact, to "work harder to develop a profound theology of the woman."[70] However, this claim is also fraught with tension. On the one hand, this concession can be read as a reflection of the Church's postsecular openness to developments in secular reasoning. Specifically, it might be seen as supporting the feminist stance that "the ruling texts" in the Church—scriptural narratives, the liturgy, Canon Law, encyclicals and pastoral letters, and the documents of Vatican II and of the Congregation for the Doctrine of the Faith—were and are written by and for men. As such, they are therefore exclusionary of women's lived experiences and blind to the relations of power that symbolically silence women in the Church (and elsewhere).[71] A corollary of this insight, then, might be to articulate a new theology that would be inclusive of women's diverse realities. This new theology would need to be sensitive to diverse standpoints, including (but not limited to) the aspirations of those who discern a call to priesthood. Yet, the task of writing a new theology from the standpoint of women seems to lack communicative sincerity. This is because the Vatican, simultaneously, has definitively closed off the possibility that women can be priests.

An alternative reading also falls short of a postsecular sensibility that values gender equality and women's contributions to ongoing historical processes. Church officials' articulation of the need to develop a "theology of woman" may (unintentionally) convey that women present a problem for the universal (male) Church. Notably, despite the Church's embrace of sexual complementarity, Church officials do not talk of a male genius—only a feminine genius. It is women, not men, who are different. Women present as a complication to a Church whose theology of sin and redemption was assumed to apply to men and women. But if a theology of woman is now needed, it may suggest that women are, and have been, interlopers—or even misfits—trying to find sense (and power) in a male theology designed by and only for a male Church.

These concerns aside, a papal commission on the possibility of women deacons, and a symposium convened by the Congregation for the Doctrine of the Faith on women's roles are rethinking women's value to the Church.[72] Such inquiries are not addressing women's ordination, and they may or may not lead to a change in the Vatican's understanding of women (either of their "feminine essence" or of their roles). But as postsecular expectations convey, conversation *with* difference is a more emancipatory path than either no conversation or conversation *about* difference. Talking *with* opens the possibility of forging a new synthesis, and one that might more fully integrate the mutual pull exerted by secular expectations of equality and the religious draw of the sacraments.

Conclusion: The Tension in Postsecularity

Not surprisingly, because of their status as matters of "faith and morals," the Church's discourse on abortion, same-sex relations, and women's ordination is more constrained and narrowly drawn than its arguments on economic inequality and climate change. Nonetheless, Church arguments on abortion and same-sex relations show varying degrees of postsecular attunement. Francis's papacy, I have argued, is giving them a further postsecular tilt. His notably reduced public prioritization of abortion and gay sexuality is symbolically disruptive. Additionally, he is injecting greater nuance into the Church's framing of abortion and, more so, gay relationships. Notwithstanding the Church's opposition to same-sex marriage, Francis's acknowledgment of the stability offered by gay civil unions, as well as his vocabulary and meaningful silences regarding gays, conveys a more gay-friendly Church, and one that is increasingly seen as such. Church discourse on women's ordination, by contrast, largely defies postsecular expectations. Francis has reinforced the definitiveness of the Church's opposition to women priests, even as he is opening a conversation on the possibility of women deacons.

The postsecular limits in the Church's discourse are well illustrated by sexual difference and complementarity, a principle informing its arguments on both women's ordination and same-sex relationships. Complementarity ties physical and biological differences to a natural hierarchical order: a gender hierarchy in which only men can be (physically natural) priests, and a sexuality hierarchy in which heterosexuality is the natural, complementary orientation. It is difficult to translate the Church's natural-law reasoning on sexual difference into a secular idiom that would resonate with current cohorts. Such reasoning is, in principle, universally accessible, but even Church officials including Benedict acknowledge its contemporary cultural and intellectual limitations.[73]

Another limit in the Church's postsecular voice on sex and gender is its communicative stance. When the Church speaks on issues of morality (abortion and same-sex relationships) and faith (women's ordination), it retreats from the communicative openness that the postsecular requires. In particular, when it grounds its claims in the unilateral authority of the magisterium, it forecloses the possibility of mutual dialogue with and amid interpretive differences, and stifles the conversation between ideas and realities. It also departs from the Church's own commitment both to institutional self-critique and renewal and to the dialogical integration of faith and reason. It may detract, too, from episcopal collegiality, given that some bishops quietly raise alternative views on same-sex relationships and women's ordination.[74]

It is understandable, nonetheless, that the Church does not want to yield ground on "faith and morals." On abortion, for example, because the Church teaches that human life begins at conception and is inherently valuable, it will not entertain exceptions to its opposition to abortion. Its valuing of life is the same ethic articulated in its other social justice commitments (e.g., the death penalty) and its critique of economic inequality and global warming (though on these issues it acknowledges the reasonableness of alternative opinions notwithstanding its advocacy of remedial action).

Women's ordination and gay sexuality do not encompass the complex moral questions at issue on abortion. Hovering over them, however, (and independent of standpoint analysis) is the ever-present tension in Catholicism between tradition and change; it shadows doctrinal debates and the Church's identity. It also unveils a tension in postsecularity. In looking to moderate religion for the ethics that might reorient modernity, part of the draw is religion's longevity and constancy, its preservation over millennia of those beliefs and values, and "intuitions about error and redemption," that provide meaning notwithstanding societal change.[75]

The tension in the postsecular expectation of religion is that it wants religion to be open to modernity and, at the same time, to act as a bulwark against its erroneous tracks. Yet, this is something Catholicism can do if, by and large, as Church officials believe, it maintains fidelity to what it considers its long-preserved, "fundamental moral truths." In this view, the Church cannot rescue modernity from its ills if, in its openness to secular currents, it itself goes off-track. Church officials therefore push back hard against what they perceive as attempts to entrap the Church in the cultural relativism and other ideological ills of modernity. These are forces perceived as contradicting the Church's moral truths, and ultimately undermining its relevance.[76]

The tension between openness to secular influences and ethical constancy despite and amid the secular is exacerbated in the case of Catholicism by its intellectual reliance on natural law. As Benedict has argued:

> Natural law—especially in the Catholic Church—remains the topos [the typical frame] with which the Church, in conversations with secular society as well as with other communities of faith, appeals to a shared reason and searches for the foundations of a communication about the ethical principles of the law in a secular, pluralistic society.[77]

Church officials themselves recognize that advancements in biological science and current cultural understandings require the translation of natural law into a more persuasive vocabulary (see chapter 6). In light of current knowledge and realities, the Church's discourse on natural sexual difference might well be considered in need of revision. However, this would require the Church not only to reframe its vocabulary but also to rethink the grounds for its reasoning on sexual difference and, by extension, the truths it maintains about marriage, gender roles, same-sex attraction and relationships, and women's ordination. Clearly, such rethinking would open up the possibility of changes in Church teachings on a host of issues that Church officials have said cannot be changed.

The additional dilemma posed by such rethinking is that it may disturb the Church's understanding of other societal issues, including economic inequality and related problems. The Church's understanding of natural sex (and gender) differences, and the limits imposed by those differences, derives from natural reason. This is the same natural reason that underpins its understanding of inherent natural rights and, relatedly, of the duties and obligations they impose. In short, for the Church, natural law provides the objective moral norms that impose *limits* on what is morally permissible and *obligations* on what is morally required.[78] These objective norms extend to a whole range of issues—hence, the Church's opposition to abortion, euthanasia, in vitro fertilization, stem-cell research, and same-sex relationships. And by the same token, they extend to its advocacy of social justice and its articulation of the moral limits to profit accumulation and climate degradation.

In sum, in the Church's view, it would neither be ethically sound nor in keeping with its intellectual tradition to revise its doctrine on natural rights—and natural limits—in response to secular currents on sex and gender. Nor,

moreover, might it be culturally productive, a point sharpened by the comparative decline of moderate Protestantism despite its openness to secular
understandings of sex and gender. Hence, there is pressure on the Church
both from itself and implicitly from and in tension with postsecular expectations to maintain its teachings on sexual difference. Their constancy amid and
despite societal change reinforces its more broadly based ethical authority in
the public sphere, even as they simultaneously undermine its openness to secular influences and its authority among Catholics and in society at large. The
next chapter will show how secular principles and postsecular expectations
entwine to give the Church an unexpected opportunity not only to resist but
also to attempt to reorient secularism.

5

Religious Freedom

THE U.S. BISHOPS AND THE SHOCK OF THE SECULAR

ON JANUARY 28, 2014, the Catholic bishops told the U.S. Supreme Court that:

> A Catholic cannot in good conscience "profess . . . beliefs in church on Sunday, and then during the week . . . promote business practices or medical procedures contrary to those beliefs." He cannot claim to respect the teachings of the Church, and then operate his business in a way that "ignore[s] or exploit[s] the poor and the marginalized . . . [or] promote[s] sexual behavior contrary to Catholic moral teaching.". . . [F]or Catholics . . . faith is not something to be checked at the door of their businesses or ignored when determining how to conduct their corporation's affairs.[1]

Religious freedom is a major tenet of liberal democracy. It is complicated globally by political tensions surrounding the rights and cultural acceptance of religious minorities.[2] In the context of American society, it is further complicated by postsecular expectations. Because postsecularity requires mutual respect for religious and secular claims in the public sphere, it nuances the secular understanding of religion as a narrowly defined domain relatively compartmentalized from nonreligious activities. The bishops' argument that being Catholic cannot be confined to Sunday but, rather, extends across the work week appears on the surface as a postsecular claim for recognition of the mutuality of the religious and the secular. The bishops' religious freedom campaign, however, pushes back against secular currents and highlights the limits of both the bishops' understanding of religious freedom and that of secular society. Before discussing the bishops' turn to religious freedom, I first provide some background on the political context precipitating it.

The Contraception Mandate in the Affordable Care Act

Contraception has been a relatively moot issue in the Church since the 1970s, when Catholics by and large decided for themselves that one can be a good Catholic and use contraception (see chapter 2). It was a surprise, then, when contraception became newly energizing for the U.S. bishops in late 2011. And—notwithstanding Francis's rebalancing of the Church's priorities away from sexual issues—it has been stoking much of their public activism since then. It was precipitated by the Affordable Care Act (ACA). Signed into law by President Obama in March 2010, the Act subsequently (August 2011) added contraception to the preventative services that would be mandatorily covered by insurance.

The initial publication of the mandate did not specify that religious organizations such as Catholic parishes would be exempt from providing coverage for their employees. Thus, by default, this meant that all religious employers would be required to provide contraception coverage as part of their employees' insurance policy. This contravened the religious-exemption clause in other legislative mandates (e.g., on abortion), and was heavily criticized by the bishops and an array of Catholic health, educational, and business and civic organizations.[3] In response, the government amended the policy so that the insurance companies, and not the Catholic employer institutions, would pay for and administer the contraception coverage.

These changes were unsatisfactory to the bishops and to some Catholic employer organizations. They claimed that, as Catholics morally opposed to contraception, having to sign the exemption form was an imposition on their conscience and thus a violation of religious freedom. Underscoring the diversity of views and of voices within Catholicism, several other major Catholic employer organizations—in health care, education, and social services—who had initially opposed the government mandate were satisfied with the amended policy.[4] Nevertheless, bishops and others who rejected the compromise filed a lawsuit (in May 2012) challenging the mandate's legality, notwithstanding its amended exemption. And, with a broader mix of conservative religious groups involved, the issue expanded to the claim that owners of selected privately held, for-profit businesses should also be exempt on grounds of conscience from having to pay for or administer contraception coverage.[5]

Subsequently, the U.S. Supreme Court (in *Burwell v. Hobby Lobby*, June 2014) ruled in favor of such an exemption. The court invoked the principle that "government cannot substantially burden a person's exercise of religion" when alternatives to the government-mandated service provision exist. This accords with the Religious Freedom Restoration Act (1993), which itself was enacted in response to a previous Supreme Court decision (in 1990) widely seen as unfriendly to religious freedom. In May 2016, the U.S. Supreme Court remanded the bishops' and related cases to the lower courts. It instructed the government and the religious defendants to find a compromise that would allow for contraception coverage for all employees independent of requiring any action (e.g., a signature) by the religious employer. Such compromise has to reconcile the bishops' core argument that:

> [T]he contraception mandate forces [Catholic employers] to do what their religion tells them they must not do. [They] sincerely believe that taking the required actions would make them complicit in an immoral act. . . . That is a religious judgment, based on Catholic moral principles regarding the permissible degree of cooperation with wrongdoing.[6]

The Shock of the Secular: The Erosion of the Moral Law

From a postsecular perspective, the bishops' elevation of contraception as a religious freedom issue is interesting because it illuminates both the secular openness of the Church and the limits to that openness. The post-*Humanae Vitae* consensus among Catholic laity that one can be a good Catholic and use contraception is more or less tacitly accepted by the Church. Priests, for example, give contraception little or no attention during Mass homilies, and pre-ACA, Church statements did not put much stress on contraception. John Paul affirmed the Church's moral condemnation of contraception in the *Gospel of Life* and in other encyclicals (see chapter 4). And a statement from the U.S. bishops' Committee for Pro-Life Activities in 2006—"Married love and the gift of life"—emphasized that "every act of intercourse must remain open to life" and that contraception is "objectively immoral."

Nevertheless, relative to the bishops' public activism on abortion, contraception did not warrant much attention pre-ACA. Since the legalization of abortion in 1973, the U.S. bishops have issued three major pastoral plans for pro-life activities (1975, 1985, 2001), and are heavily engaged in ongoing activism at the state and federal levels. In testifying to Congress and filing friend-of-the-court briefs on proposed policy and legal changes on abortion, the bishops tend to explicitly demarcate the Church's view of the far greater moral and societal significance of abortion, and to downplay contraception. Their most recent *Pastoral Plan for Pro-Life Activities* (issued in November 2001), for example, briefly acknowledges the links between the use of contraception and abortion. But it notes that while contraception is evil, it is specifically different from abortion; and most of the plan's substance focuses on abortion. Further indicative of contraception's marginality, the bishops do not list it among the many topics highlighted in their "faithful citizenship" statements issued to coincide with U.S. presidential election campaigns.

Moral Fundamentalism

Yet, despite its relative marginalization, opposition to contraception is central to the Church's moral agenda and its anxiety about secularism. I am not discounting the sincerity of the bishops' commitment to protecting religious freedom, nor ignoring the immediate policy context of the ACA. But in the following pages I argue that the bishops' turn to religious freedom was abetted by their long-festering concern over the shifting moral landscape in the United States and its accelerating secularism.

A major reason why Paul VI declined to change Church teaching on contraception was a fear it would undermine the Church's moral tradition. Paradoxically, of course, by not changing it, he accelerated the decline both in papal authority and in acceptance of Church teachings on sexual morality in general (see chapter 2). The fact remains, nevertheless, that official Church teaching has not changed. And this anti-secular stand in the face of increased secularization in society and in Catholicism underpins the hierarchy's resistance to formal changes in Church teaching on contraception and the complexity of debate on other sexual issues (including same-sex relationships and divorce and remarriage; see chapter 6).

The ACA contraception mandate gave the Church a new opening in its resistance to secularism, increasingly evident in public acceptance of same-sex marriage.[7] Rather than tacitly conceding the reality of secular change, the bishops chose to fight back. After a decade in which their relative contrition over the sex-abuse scandals had a somewhat tempering effect on the intensity of their public activism, and with their revised guidelines for the protection of minors in place, the ACA provided the opportunity for resurgent activism.[8] The bishops were eager to publicly reassert Church teachings on marriage and sexual morality. Such eagerness, moreover, was accompanied by their self-acknowledged belief that their silence in the face of Catholic dissent on sexual issues has contributed to the secularization of Catholicism. Archbishop Lori, chairman of the Bishops' Committee for Religious Liberty, argued:

> As fewer people practice the faith, the culture becomes more secular and as the culture becomes more secular still fewer people are inclined to practice their faith . . . religious freedom begins to take a back seat to other so-called freedoms. . . . Among the most significant . . . sexual freedom. When people lose interest in the Church or claim to have issues with the Church, it oftentimes has to do with the Church's teachings on sex and marriage: contraception, sterilization, abortion, same-sex marriage, LGBT issues. Some have walked away in protest but many have just faded away without a real understanding of what the Church actually teaches and why. In such matters, silence has not been golden.[9]

The steadily expanding cultural and legal approval of same-sex relationships, and especially gay marriage, was particularly troubling to the bishops. In a 2009 pastoral letter on marriage, they identified same-sex unions, contraception, divorce, and cohabitation as the four *fundamental* challenges to the meaning and purpose of marriage.[10] Between 2004, when Massachusetts became the first state to legalize gay marriage as a result of its State Supreme Court's ruling, and 2012 when the contraception mandate took effect, nine states had approved the legalization of same-sex marriage. Further, in an important symbolic victory for gay rights, the California Supreme Court had struck down the constitutionality of California's ban on same-sex marriage. The trend in favor of same-sex marriage presented the bishops with clear evidence of the declining relevance of Catholic (natural law) morality in shaping civil laws and public policies, not seen since *Roe v. Wade* legalized abortion in 1973.

In this larger context, the ACA mandate gave the bishops the legal and the political opportunity to act on the moral shock presented by what they saw as the increasing erosion of fundamental truths from civil law.[11] Religious freedom thus became the mobilizing force fusing the political-legal opportunity and the bishops' moral vision. It became a highly useful and culturally salient moral frame by which to reassert Catholic teaching and the Church's (religious and secular) authority to articulate that teaching. From a postsecular perspective, moreover, it is highly strategic. The appeal to religious freedom allows the Church to pursue its religious interests in a way that seems to be less about any specific teaching and more about the larger, politically shared, secular value of religious freedom. In the United States, against the backdrop of a long tradition of religious pluralism, there is a strong consensus that individuals should be free to practice their religion. Notwithstanding complexities in its legal and practical translation, this principle is supported by very large majorities both for whom religion is personally important (89 percent) and for whom it is less important (79 percent).[12] Religious freedom, therefore, is a far more culturally resonant idiom than denouncing the objective immorality of same-sex relationships or contraception.

The Emerging Prominence of Religious Freedom in Church Discourse

Religious freedom has had only minimal presence in the bishops' ongoing statements on abortion, intermittently recurring alongside other themes.[13] And it was slow in emerging in Church discourse on same-sex relationships; in the Vatican's major statements on homosexuality, the focus is on sexual disorder (see chapter 4). Religious freedom was mentioned only once for example, in a letter on "Family, marriage and 'de facto' unions" issued by the Vatican's Pontifical Council for the Family in 2001. Nor was it a recurring theme in the collective statements of the U.S. bishops or in statements by individual bishops responding to changes in their respective states regarding the legalization of same-sex civil unions.[14]

The theme got more play in the bishops' 2009 pastoral letter on marriage; it was mentioned briefly (twice) and specifically in the context of same-sex marriage. The bishops stated:

> The legal recognition of same-sex unions poses a multifaceted threat to the very fabric of society, striking at the source from which society

and culture come and which they are meant to serve. Such recognition affects all people, married and nonmarried . . . [and] also . . . religious freedom. . . . Basic human rights must be afforded to all people. This can and should be done without sacrificing the bedrock of society that is marriage and the family and without violating the religious liberty of persons and institutions.

By June 2011, however, religious freedom had achieved prominence in the bishops' agenda. Of particular note, the bishops emphasized that they were using religious freedom as part of an intentional communicative strategy. It was one of "four messaging themes" explicitly identified in a new initiative against same-sex marriage introduced by their Subcommittee for the Promotion and Defense of Marriage. Committee chairman Archbishop Cordileone explained to his fellow bishops that "strategies of language are crucial here." And he elaborated that they were necessary in part to push back against the "manipulation of language" that he noted was prevalent in same-sex marriage and abortion debates. In light of the postsecular expectation that religious-based beliefs should be translated into an accessible secular vocabulary, the bishops' intentional attentiveness to language and messaging conveys a certain postsecular sensibility, whether intended as such or not. The archbishop was optimistic about the persuasive value of the new initiative, saying he saw "signs of hope" against same-sex marriage based on the resistance apparent in a few states. Indeed, he confidently declared: "The myth of the inevitability of same-sex 'marriage' remains just that—a myth."[15]

The U.S. Bishops' Freedom Project

Notwithstanding Archbishop Cordileone's optimism, the specter of change was sufficiently urgent that a couple of months later (September 2011), the bishops had established a new committee dedicated to defending and advocating religious liberty.[16] This organizational response was, in the words of Cardinal Dolan (then president of the U.S. Catholic bishops), historic. It would be, he said, "one element" in what he expected "to be a new moment in the history" of the bishops' conference. Stressing the urgency of concerted action to safeguard religious liberty, he defined it in highly accessible cultural terms. He emphasized that religious freedom is "inherent in the dignity of the human person" and—invoking thoroughly American motifs—a "foundational principle of our country . . . enshrined in the U.S. Constitution, further enumerated in the First Amendment and explicitly extended to all U.S. citizens."

From the outset, the bishops underscored their own "strongly unified and intensely focused" opposition to threats to religious freedom, and their "resolve ... to act strongly, in concert with our fellow citizens" in its defense.[17] It thus became the anchoring theme in several public actions taken by the bishops, including letters to President Obama outlining what they saw as various federal threats to religious liberty, testimony to congressional committees and to the Courts, and letters to members of Congress advocating conscience protections in health-care provision.[18]

Additionally, too, for the first time in their history, the bishops issued a lengthy statement on religious freedom ("Our First, Most Cherished Liberty," April 2012) and committed the Church to a public campaign specifically dedicated to religious freedom. Again the bishops emphasized their unity—a gesture underscoring the certainty of their resolve but also implicitly acknowledging that they are not always in agreement on various initiatives and strategies.[19] They designated the project a "Fortnight for Freedom." In a move that captures the postsecular mutuality of the religious and the secular, the scheduling of the Fortnight deftly resonates with both the liturgical and the cultural calendars. It starts on the feast day of two Catholic martyrs, St. Thomas More and St. John Fisher, executed for defying the self-proclaimed religious supremacy of Henry VIII; and it ends on the politically and culturally symbolic Fourth of July, U.S. Independence Day. The campaign committed not just the bishops' conference but also all dioceses and local parishes to a "special period of prayer, study, catechesis and public action [which] would emphasize both our Christian and American heritage of liberty ... [to] constitute a great national campaign of teaching and witness for religious liberty."[20]

The first Fortnight for Freedom took place in summer 2012, and the campaign has occurred annually since then (see Table 5.1). Notwithstanding Pope Francis's rebalancing of the Church's priorities toward economic justice and away from sexual issues, the bishops continue to reaffirm their ongoing commitment to the campaign. Moreover, in June 2017 they voted (though not unanimously) to make the ad hoc religious freedom committee a regular standing committee, thus signaling its elevated prioritization relative to other pressing political issues (such as immigration). Additionally, religious freedom is one of five strategic priorities outlined in the bishops' 2017–2020 strategic plan.[21]

Table 5.1 Timeline of U.S. Bishops' Activism on Religious Freedom

2003: Massachusetts State Supreme Court rules in favor of same-sex marriage; it becomes law in May 2004

2004: U.S. bishops announce National Pastoral Initiative for Marriage

November 2009: U.S. bishops issue Pastoral Letter, "Marriage: Love and Life in the Divine Plan"

March 2010: President Obama signs the Affordable Care Act (ACA)

June 2011: U.S. bishops' Subcommittee for the Promotion and Defense of Marriage announces new initiative against same-sex marriage

August 2011: Contraception pills added to the list of prescription medicine to be mandatorily covered by insurance under the ACA; takes effect in 2012

September 2011: U.S. bishops announce the formation of an Ad Hoc Committee for Religious Liberty

October 2011: U.S. bishops give congressional testimony on religious liberty

November 2011: Archbishop Lori addresses the U.S. bishops on religious liberty

December 21, 2011: Bishops and representatives of various Catholic institutions and organizations sponsor a full-page statement in the *New York Times* on their response to the HHS (the U.S. Health and Human Services Department) "preventive services" mandate

February 2012: U.S. bishops give testimony before the Committee on the Judiciary, U.S. House of Representatives

February 2012: U.S. bishops and some Catholic organizations reject compromise offered by President Obama to shift the contraception insurance burden from Catholic employers to insurance companies

March 14, 2012: U.S. bishops issue Statement on Religious Freedom and HHS Mandate

April 2012: U.S. bishops issue formal, foundational statement on religious liberty, "Our first, most cherished liberty," including announcement of Fortnight for Freedom campaign

May 2012: Individual bishops and dioceses and various Catholic institutions file 12 lawsuits in various federal courts contesting the contraception mandate

June 21–July 4, 2012: U.S. bishops hold first Fortnight for Freedom

July 17, 2012: U.S. bishops' Secretariat of Pro-Life Activities sends letter to members of the House Subcommittee on Labor/HHS

(*continued*)

Table 5.1 Continued

August 3, 2012: U.S. bishops' Secretariat of Pro-Life Activities sends letter to members of Congress

November 2012: President Obama is reelected

February 2013: Pope Benedict resigns

February 15, 2013: U.S. bishops issue statement urging Congress to include conscience provision in funding bills

March 2013: Pope Francis is elected

June 21–July 4, 2013: U.S. bishops hold second Fortnight for Freedom

November 2013: Publication of Pope Francis's exhortation, *The Joy of the Gospel*

December 31, 2013: U.S. bishops send a letter to President Obama regarding the ACA

June 2014: U.S. bishops unanimously decide to continue its committee for religious liberty for another three-year term

June 2014: The U.S. Supreme Court's *Burwell v. Hobby Lobby* decision rules in favor of religious conscience exemptions for family and other for-profit businesses

June 21–July 4, 2014: U.S. bishops hold third Fortnight for Freedom

November 17, 2014: U.S. bishops send letter to members of Congress regarding protection of conscience rights

February 12, 2015: U.S. bishops issue statement on health-care conscience rights

February 13, 2015: U.S. bishops send letter to members of Congress regarding protection of conscience rights

June 2015: U.S. Supreme Court rules that there is a constitutional right to same-sex marriage

June 2015: Publication of Pope Francis's encyclical, *Laudato Si'*

June 21—July 4, 2015: U.S. bishops hold fourth Fortnight for Freedom

September 8, 2015: U.S. bishops send letter to U.S. senators regarding protection of conscience rights

November 2015: U.S. bishops commit to continue their advocacy of religious liberty

May 2016: U.S. Supreme Court issues its *Zubik v. Burwell* decision (remanding the case to the lower courts) and requiring the federal government, the bishops, and relevant parties to work out an alternative approach to the contraception insurance mandate

Table 5.1 Continued

June 21–July 4, 2016: U.S. bishops hold fifth Fortnight for Freedom

July 7, 2016: U.S. bishops send letter to Congress supporting enactment of the Conscience Protection Act of 2016, which would allow individuals and organizations to opt out of providing health and related services that they deem contrary to their conscience

July 12, 2016: U.S. bishops urge support for the First Amendment Defense Act, as it would provide a measure of protection for religious freedom at the federal level

November 15, 2016: U.S. bishops approve their 2017–2020 Strategic Plan, which includes the defense and promotion of religious freedom as one of five strategic priorities

January 27, 2017: President Trump bans admission to the U.S. of all refugees and of all individuals from seven Muslim-majority countries

January 31, 2017: In a joint statement with two other committees, the U.S. bishops' religious liberty committee notes the rights of all religious minorities

February 16, 2017: U.S. bishops issue statement asking President Trump to protect religious freedom in the U.S. ("to restore basic protections" eroded by ACA and other federal rules)

June 2017: U.S. bishops vote (by 132 to 53) to make their Ad Hoc Committee for Religious Liberty a permanent standing committee

June 21–July 4, 2017: U.S. bishops hold sixth Fortnight for Freedom

September 2017: U.S. bishops submit brief to the U.S. Supreme Court in support of Masterpiece Cakeshop's right to deny business service to same-sex couple

October 6, 2017: The Trump administration/HHS announces new rules giving employers a broad exemption from the ACA contraception mandate

October 6, 2017: In a joint statement, the president of the USCCB and the chairman of the bishops' religious liberty committee praise the HHS for expanding the contraception exemption

Arguing for Religious Freedom

The arguments advanced by the bishops are forcefully grounded in the twin vocabularies of secular and religious claims. This is the case across the themes elaborated in the bishops' April 2012 foundational statement, in homilies at the

Masses officially opening and closing the annual Fortnight activities, and in the bishops' congressional testimony and letters to government officials. Drawing on the language of political citizenship and American culture, they invoke, for example, the American nation "conceived in liberty," the words of various founding fathers and presidents, the First Amendment, and more recent figures such as Martin Luther King Jr. They simultaneously reference the Church's multiple sources of teaching and, implicitly, its teaching authority. Scripture, papal statements and encyclicals, the documents of Vatican II, and the actions of saints and martyrs who resisted government tyranny (especially St. Thomas More and St. John Fisher) are all invoked to elaborate and contextualize the Church's position. Thus, the bishops graft the secular-cultural reasonableness of their arguments onto both their religious authority and their legitimate right as religious and secular citizens to "defend our religious freedoms."[22]

This is not a new communicative strategy for the bishops. The mixing of religious and secular themes has long characterized their public engagement, and it well befits Catholicism as a public religion.[23] What is new is the elevation of the subject of religious freedom and its targeting as a societal issue. Further, in this project, the bishops show their keen sensitivity to the strategic importance of messaging (as outlined by Archbishop Cordileone in 2011 in adopting religious freedom as a language strategy in opposing same-sex marriage). Paying heed to Francis's popularity, they have folded photos of him and excerpts from his statements into their campaign documents and videos. These include images of him meeting with the Little Sisters of the Poor, the plaintiffs contesting the ACA contraception mandate exemption, when he was in Washington, D.C. (in September 2015). This deft appropriation of Francis and his assumed moral authority helps to frame the bishops' agenda as one that enjoys his imprimatur. However, not unlike how advocates of climate-change education invoke Francis (see chapter 3), the bishops' adoption of his mantle is somewhat manipulative. The origins of the bishops' campaign preceded his election. More to the point, their tactical use of religious freedom to advance their opposition to same-sex marriage contrasts with his explicit prioritization of economic inequality and social exclusion. It is clear, nonetheless, as noted here, that they have a long-term commitment to this strategy.

The bishops' messaging strategy also makes effective use of St. Thomas More and St. John Fisher. Providing a good illustration of how a religious argument can be translated into a compelling secular claim, the bishops use More and Fisher to emphasize the secular assumption that religious freedom is a central tenet of democracy. They talk of these martyrs in the context of Henry VIII's repudiation of Rome, his assumption of religious supremacy, and their refusal to comply with the Oath of Supremacy—and they link them to religiously conscientious employees today. Archbishop Lori, in his homily at the Mass opening the first Fortnight for Freedom (in 2012), for example, states:

> St. Thomas More [who was Henry VIII's Councilor and the Lord Chancellor] could be said to represent that conscientious private employer or employee who seeks to avoid doing or facilitating moral evil in the course of daily work while striving to live and work in accord with the demands of social justice. He stands for those who go about their daily work in accord with their faith . . . and those who understand how dangerous it is to the common good to separate faith from life, the Gospel from culture.

The bishops' framing of this argument has notably evolved. In 2016, for the first time in the series of annual Fortnight homilies, Bishop Lori invoked the precipitating circumstances for Henry VIII's repudiation of papal authority—namely, his divorce and remarriage. Building on this historically momentous rupture with Church teaching on marriage, Lori emphasizes: "Both Fisher and More died not merely for freedom of conscience in the abstract but for freedom of conscience in defending marriage and the rights of the Church."[24] Thus, for the bishops, as I argue, the religious freedom campaign is not solely about defending a secular democratic right. It is simultaneously a campaign to reassert the Church's teachings on sexual morality and marriage. They thus execute a push against secularism through the framework provided by the secular value of religious freedom. In short, the bishops use their authority as religious and secular citizens to try to steer modernity away from the secular paths undermining the Church's (uneven and contested) moral authority.

The Common Good Amid the Pluralism of Religious and Secular Claims

The normative value of postsecularity is that it requires recognition of the mutual relevance of moderate religious and secular convictions in articulating the common good amid pluralism. In practice, however, the public priorities of both religious and secular actors lean toward a selective construal of what the common good entails. I use the next few pages to illustrate how the U.S. bishops' religious freedom campaign unveils these limitations. I first discuss how the bishops translate what appears on the surface as a postsecular claim into a more narrowly circumscribed, religious position. I then note the limits in the secular construal of religious accommodation.

The U.S. Bishops' Construal of Civil Society

The bishops argue that religious freedom is not alone the right to worship. It also includes, they maintain, the right of religious individuals, groups, and institutions to act on their religious beliefs across multiple arenas—including business and the workplace (as noted in this chapter's initial quotation). At first glance, this claim seems to accord with a postsecular consciousness recognizing religion's relevance in the public domain amid, and notwithstanding, the settled empirical reality of secularization. As the bishops argue:

> To be Catholic and American should mean not having to choose one over the other. Our allegiances are distinct, but they need not be contradictory and should instead be complementary. That is the teaching of our Catholic faith, which obliges us to work together with fellow citizens for the common good of all who live in this land. . . . Religious liberty is not only about our ability to go to Mass on Sunday or pray the rosary at home. It is about whether we can make our contribution to the common good of all Americans. Can we do the good works our faith calls us to do without having to compromise that very same faith?[25]

This aspiration recognizes that religious and secular roles and activities intersect, and that such continuities enrich civil society. For the Church, a robust civil society is essential to democracy. Sociologists share this view. They argue that the resources and institutions of civil society, such as public media, social movements, nonprofit groups, and political organizations, bring attention to various problems of economic and social inequality and help remedy them.[26] Additionally for the Church, the civil sphere is the arena where it can legitimately counter what it identifies as "radical," "aggressive," and "reductive" secularism.[27] The bishops are explicit about this. In his homily at the opening Mass for the first Fortnight, Archbishop Lori stated:

> Some would even say that the Catholic Church is a primary obstacle that stands in the way of creating a completely secular culture in the United States. Let us remain united with our ecumenical and interfaith partners in being that obstacle![28]

Similarly, Cardinal Wuerl, at the Fortnight's closing Mass in 2013, highlighted the necessary relevance of the Church as a bulwark against the expanding secularism of politics and culture. And he specifically exhorted lay Catholics to push back against its particular embodiment in threats to religious freedom. Quoting Pope Benedict, he reiterated the significance of "an engaged, articulate and well-formed Catholic laity [who are] endowed with a strong critical sense vis-à-vis the dominant culture and with the courage to counter a reductive secularism."[29]

In principle, the countering of a reductive or aggressive secularism has an affinity with the postsecular rejection of a secular fundamentalism that would exclude religion from the public sphere. And this goal is entwined in the bishops' view of religious liberty as being more than simply the freedom to worship. Their expansive definition assumes that they and other religious citizens should be free to act on their religious-moral conscience across diverse settings. The bishops state:

> What is at stake is whether America will continue to have a free, creative and robust civil society—or whether the state alone will determine who gets to contribute to the common good and how they get to do it. Religious believers are part of American civil society, which includes neighbors helping each other, community associations, fraternal service clubs, sports leagues and youth groups. All these Americans make their contribution to our common life. . . . Restrictions on religious liberty are an attack on civil society and the American genius for voluntary associations.[30]

They thus oppose restrictions that infringe on the religious beliefs of individuals and groups as they go about their everyday routines. And this includes the economic sphere. As the bishops have elaborated, "Religion is not something that can or should be divorced from the commercial sphere. Indeed, it is religion that often serves to direct that sphere toward the common good."[31]

However, despite their expansive view, the bishops are selective in what they identify as threats to religious liberty. Their campaign conveys that an aggressive secularism is that which undermines Church teachings on sexual morality. Because for the Church the common good rests on marriage as the natural, fundamental cell of society (see chapter 4), many of the threats identified by the bishops center not on economic inequality, for example, but on same-sex marriage. Thus, in responding to the U.S. Supreme Court's June 2015 decision legalizing gay marriage, the bishops called its redefinition of marriage "profoundly immoral and unjust," lacking in truth, and "a tragic error that harms the common good." And, in accord with their construal of religious freedom, they asked "all in positions of power and authority to respect the God-given freedom to seek, live by, and bear witness to the truth."[32]

For the bishops, freedom to witness includes the rights of "people in business ... to live out their faith in daily life" and thus to decline products and services to customers such as those seeking photographic or catering services for same-sex weddings.[33] Similarly, the freedom to witness means that employers should not be required to sign a form simply indicating their exemption from paying employees' contraception insurance. The act of signing is for the bishops and other plaintiffs an act complicit in immorality because their action is the mechanism enabling the woman to have (alternate, non-Church-paid) insurance access to contraception. By contrast, the bishops are less insistent about economic policy actions that might be considered immoral or a threat to the common good—despite their arguments to the Supreme Court that Church teachings place a check on businesses against economic exploitation and related ills.[34] In short, the bishops are notably selective in implementing their ethos of religious witness, even as a contrite modernity—and Pope Francis—looks to them to articulate a more economically inclusive sense of the common good.

The postsecular limits in the bishops' position are also conveyed by their lack of acknowledgment that there may be other values at stake in the conflict over religious freedom. They seek to have their understanding of religion and religious freedom affirmed by the courts and the government. But they do not appear to consider how their understanding may impede the moral understanding of others, including the valuing of social inclusivity, which is central to liberal pluralist democracy. The bishops' campaign thus falls short in holding together the postsecular expectation of the reflexive self-critique and mutuality of the religious and the secular. Their religious-based views of moral complicity supersede the secular principles of gender and sexual equality, and the accommodation of related claims (e.g., contraception and same-sex marriage, respectively). And by the same token, as noted, they give greater prioritization to sexual morality than to economic justice.

Limits of the Secular

Just as the bishops' religious freedom campaign unveils the postsecular limits in the Church's reasoning, it also unveils limits in the secular understanding of religion. In liberal democratic societies, religious freedom and the institutional differentiation of church and state tend to compartmentalize religion. In some sense, these arrangements are a concession to the secular idea that if religion does not disappear—as was assumed by Enlightenment thinkers—it will at least be confined to its own separate sphere, and citizens will have the freedom to act on their religious beliefs within that space.

This may seem like a reasonable and practical solution to the persistence of religious belief (uneven secularization). The religious landscape in Western democratic societies has always been more complicated, however, than reflected in any simple view of church–state separation. Sociohistorical differences across countries have given rise to a lot of variation in religious organizational structures, the interplay of religion and political culture, and the particular trajectories of church–state relations.[35] In the United States, the Catholic Church's origins as an outsider, immigrant church in a historically Protestant society propelled it to develop a robust infrastructure of schools, colleges, hospitals, charities, social services, and media organizations. These complemented, reinforced, and extended its faith-based worship structures, primarily defined by the parish.

This infrastructure has been highly adaptive to the changes in American society and in Catholic life over the past several decades. It is also highly responsive to meeting the needs of non-Catholics who are variously underserved by government, private, and for-profit entities. Today, therefore, while there are many Catholic schools and colleges that are Catholic in terms of history, mission, and identity, they enroll and employ large numbers of non-Catholics. Similarly, Catholic hospitals and social service organizations care for and employ many non-Catholics. Indeed, underscoring both the economic ills of modernity and the functional relevance of the Church's institutional presence in secular society, Catholic Charities USA is the country's largest non-governmental provider of social services. Further, all these organizations are participants in professional-organizational fields that require their interaction with several non-Catholic and nonreligious organizations, including other colleges and hospitals, accreditation and professional societies, and federal, state, and local government. In short, in conducting its everyday institutional routines, the Church is simultaneously entangled in the religious and the secular.

A strong secularist might argue that the Church is not required to provide these educational, health, and social services (and indeed, has no business in doing so, despite the evident secular gaps they help fill). Continuing this line of reasoning, the charge is that if it voluntarily chooses to do so—and to accept government financial subsidies toward such activities—then it should also accept the rules that pertain to nonreligious providers in their respective organizational fields. Secular critics argue, in short, that if the Church provides health and social services, it should abide by secular expectations and silence its religious objections to practices it considers immoral.[36] Such secular convictions conflict with the religious convictions of the U.S. bishops and others who object to certain practices. Public-sphere theorists have confidence in the state's ability to mediate conflicts arising from the clash of religious and secular convictions.[37] They assume the state is neutral toward any particular religion and in enforcing the democratic principles of religious freedom and church–state differentiation.

However, what is secular and what is religious are not untainted by history and culture and, as in individual lives, they blur and frequently intersect. Generalized cultural values inform how the state and other institutions frame the questions at issue. Thus, as Robert Bellah notes, "the neutrality of a democratic state is always conditioned by its past, and, in particular, by its religious past."[38] In the United States, that religious past is Protestantism, and the translation of its denominational ethos into cultural principles of pluralism, individual freedom, and church–state differentiation. This is the (religious) culture that underlies the state's assumed religious neutrality, and Western secularism more generally. The practical implementation of religious freedom and church–state differentiation, therefore, is rarely straightforward. It is further confounded when, as for the Catholic Church, its distinctive construal of universal morality grounded in natural law (e.g., its teaching on marriage) transcends church–state differentiation and the assumed autonomy of civil law from any particular religion.

Nevertheless, the blurring of the secular and the religious suits the Church's own understanding of religious freedom. It fits with what it argues is its public institutional mission—a mission far more extensive than worship and parish activities. Just as individual Catholics interweave their religious and secular roles, the Church hierarchy does not dissociate its institutional religious identity from its civil-secular identity. It thus chooses to fully participate in the civil-secular sphere, and does so in multiple ways—in education, health care, social services, publishing, and so on, and as a political citizen or lobbyist (e.g., the USCCB). And it does so without renouncing its (religious) understanding of objective moral truths. Therefore, the services Catholic institutions provide, while fully meeting (secular) professional accreditation norms, can—and must—to some extent be on their own terms. As indicated, for example, by the Catholic Health Association (the largest group of nonprofit health-care providers in the U.S.), Catholic hospitals are explicit about their Catholic identity and its role in discerning the ethical and practical challenges confronting health-care providers today. And they are expected to be transparent about the services they do and don't provide.[39] Thus, like individual Catholics, the Church hierarchy, too, sets the terms of its religious engagement. An important difference is that while individual Catholics bring their secular expectations to their interactions with the Church (see chapter 2), the Catholic bishops—and other Catholic institutions to varying degrees—incorporate their specifically religious expectations into their roles and interactions in secular society.

Does the Bishops' Freedom Campaign Bridge the Religious–Secular Divide?

So far in this chapter I have focused on the bishops' elevation of religious freedom. I have done so to show how the postsecular mutuality of the religious and the secular can be used to resist and reframe the secular. Thus, the bishops are able to use religious freedom—a core principle of liberal secular democracy— and frame it in highly accessible cultural language to oppose secular changes undercutting the public relevance of Catholic morality. In doing so, they simultaneously forge a broader definition of the secular. This redefined claim seeks affirmation of the mutuality of the religious and the secular, not alone in the public sphere (as would accord with postsecularity), but in the Church's own identity and, by definition, its execution across several secular institutional fields. How effective is the Church's campaign? In this section I turn to opinion poll data to assess its reception among Catholics and, more broadly, to probe how Americans view the place of religion in the public sphere.

Although the first half of 2012 was a historic moment of unprecedented public activism on religious freedom by the Catholic bishops, its impact on Catholics is quite limited. A Pew poll coinciding with the 2012 Fortnight for Freedom found that only 22 percent of Catholics had heard "a lot" about the bishops' protests, though many more, 42 percent, said they had heard "a little." Given that social desirability generally prompts interviewees to indicate that they do indeed know something about the topic at hand, it is striking that 36 percent admitted they hadn't heard or didn't know about it. Further, the pattern of Catholic awareness was basically the same as for the public as a whole, though fewer non-Catholics indicated hearing "a lot" about the issue.[40] The fact that non-Catholics were as likely as Catholics to be aware of the bishops' activism lends support to the postsecular expectation that religious-based arguments in the public sphere warrant notice from all citizens, irrespective of religious identity. At the same time, it may be seen as further evidence of the secularization of religious authority among contemporary Catholics, thus accounting for their relative inattentiveness or indifference to the bishops' campaign.

Catholics who attend church weekly were somewhat more likely (78 percent) than other Catholics (69 percent) to report hearing about the issue. However, only a third (32 percent) of Catholics who attend Mass monthly or more often said the priest had spoken about religious freedom at Mass.[41] This is quite remarkable because the bishops' campaign had specifically requested that all parishes dedicate explicit attention to prayer, catechesis, and public action on the issue. The apparent reality that few did illuminates a gap between the bishops' public policy agenda and priests' assessment of what is important in their localized settings. We saw a similar gap in the relative lack of local parish discussion of Francis's encyclical on the environment (see chapter 3). This pattern further conveys the interpretive pluralism within Catholicism: the differences of opinion among Catholic laity; between the laity and the Church hierarchy; between some Catholic institutional employers and the bishops (evident over the ACA mandate); and between the pope and the bishops and priests in their public priorities.

Catholics' Construal of Threats to Religious Freedom

Among Catholics who had heard about the bishops' concerns, a majority (56 percent) said they agreed with them, with weekly Mass-goers (68 percent) more likely than other Catholics (49 percent) to do so.[42] The motif of religious liberty is, as I have argued, a highly accessible cultural idiom. Nonetheless, its meanings and practical translation necessarily vary depending on the context of its discussion and the larger political and cultural questions at issue. Not surprisingly, given the doctrinal and political differences among Catholics (see chapter 2), including on climate change (see chapter 3), they also disagree about religious freedom. In September 2012, a couple of months after the first Fortnight for Freedom campaign, a national survey documented polarization among Catholics. A fourth (24 percent) said they "completely agree" that the right of religious liberty is being threatened in America today" and a fifth (19 percent) said they "completely disagree."[43]

Surveys of liberal (Call to Action, or CTA) and conservative (Catholic League, or CL) Catholics that I conducted in late Spring and early September 2015 echoed this polarization. And the respondents' written comments explaining their views unveiled the emotional intensity underlying the divide. Almost all the conservative (CL) respondents (97 percent) agreed that "the right of religious liberty is being threatened in the U.S. today," but among liberal (CTA) respondents, only 27 percent did.[44] They were far more likely instead to disagree with the statement. One person simply commented: "I don't personally know of anyone [in the U.S.] who feels threatened for practicing their faith." Another said, "We are allowed to worship (or not) when and where we please." A similar view was expressed by the handful of CL respondents who don't think there is a threat to religious liberty. One commented: "We can still pray, we can still go to Mass, and we can still affirm we believe in God. Nothing has been done to oppose religion itself."

These comments convey the typically secular view of religious freedom—one that focuses on an individual's right to worship and churches' entitlement to provide worship and other primarily religious activities. Very few liberal respondents acknowledged the broader political tensions in the United States with respect to religion, including the impact of secularism. One person noted:

> The Affordable Care Act and other laws have religious groups required to pay for health choices of employees that are not sanctioned by the various religious groups who need to apply for waivers. Also, same sex marriages put religious groups in a bind if the state requires all those with license to officiate to offer such services. Secularization in itself infringes upon religious communities.

Other liberal Catholics who agreed that religious liberty is being threatened tended to focus on the situation of religious minorities in the United States (e.g., Jews, Muslims), and potential or actual discrimination against them.

Reflecting CTA Catholics' greater attunement than average Catholics to Church politics, most interpreted the question in the context of the bishops' religious freedom campaign. And inverting the bishops' claims, many argued it is the bishops and their allies who are threatening religious freedom—threatening that of Catholics who reject Church teachings on sexuality and gender, or that of Americans more generally as a result of the push for greater correspondence between Church teachings and American law. Relatedly, some suggested that controversy over religious freedom is politically manufactured, a "straw man" created by the bishops that, while stoking fear, seeks to restore Catholic morality and Biblical teachings.

Conservative Catholics' Changing World

Catholic League (CL) respondents, by contrast, largely echoed the bishops' arguments. They emphasized the threats posed to religious freedom by what they see as anti-family and anti-life policies, including the ACA and the legalization of gay marriage. The following quotes capture the intensity with which some spoke of these perceived infringements:

> I believe there is a war on religion in this country, I see the recent Supreme Court decision on same-sex marriage only the beginning of the threat to our religious freedom.
>
> Laws passed on health care and same sex marriage affect the rights of religious people to engage in commerce. You are forced to either change jobs or compromise your beliefs as a result.
>
> The right to practice my faith is utmost to me. But the change in marriage and the present acceptance of abortion and my belief in traditional marriage and the right to life is constantly at odds with the secular world. I am considered a bigot or less than a woman if I defend my views on gay marriage and abortion.

For conservative Catholics, these social and legal changes are not just undercutting the value of religious freedom in the abstract. They are subjectively experienced as undercutting in a highly personal way their sense of Catholic identity. Thus, some CL respondents talked about secularism and the impact of a changing culture in specifically undermining Catholicism (as opposed to Christianity or religion in general). For such respondents:

> Everywhere you turn, God has been removed. The church, along with the home, is about the only place where someone can "flaunt" their Catholicity without being put down in some form or another.
>
> As a Catholic, I appreciate the fact that Catholics in America were marginalized for a long time. They had to work hard to be accepted by the mainstream, and they have made great contributions to our country. Now, the actions of many groups (including the current [Obama] administration) suggest that they would prefer us to be marginalized again.

Like the bishops, many CL respondents explicitly rejected a narrow view of religious liberty as confined to belief and worship, and thus its exclusion of the relevance of religious conscience vis-à-vis laws and public policy. For these Catholics:

> I should be able to choose when and how I worship, and how and what I am involved in. Congress keeps saying I have the freedom to worship which means stay inside the church but don't bring my religious beliefs and action outside in public.
>
> It seems that the current administration is looking to marginalize religion and to reduce it to private practice. The idea that the government can determine what qualifies as a religious group is somewhat frightening.
>
> Our faith is who we are in society. If we cannot practice our faith, we are not free. No one should be forced by a man made law to disobey the Natural Law of God.

Notwithstanding conservative Catholics' alignment with the bishops, some were also critical of Church leaders (as well as of Catholic institutions and laity), and of what they saw as their role in undermining both Catholicism itself and its public expression. Thus:

> We are being forced to pay for abortions. We are being forced to accept the homosexual agenda. Parents' rights on what they want to teach their children are being denied. In our own Catholic schools the teachers have no morals. Instead of getting good nuns to teach they hire gays and lesbians . . . the teachers' minds are corrupt. How can they teach our children? Priests are giving up celibacy or having homosexual relations. Nuns and sister are lesbians and are not standing up for their spouse Jesus Christ. Nuns on the bus. "Hey, look at me!" Where is the humility? The biggest threat is coming from the inside of the Church. Cardinal Dolan MC of the St. Patrick's Day Parade—let the gays in to parade and not the prolife [supporters]. Get rid of that group of bishops who don't teach the teachings of Christ. If you're not with Him you're against Him.
>
> Our dioceses are filled with weak and/or "cafeteria" Catholics. The pope was right when he condemned careerism, that is a major problem. The pro-life movement's endurance for almost half a century tells me our bishops just don't get it! They need to humble themselves and put on their martyrs' robes and truly act as the apostles of Christ. If Christ showed up he'd bring a truckload of millstones for our worldly bishops.

Beyond religious freedom, these views reflect the frustration some conservative Catholics have with a changing culture—and a changing Church. Liberal and moderate Catholics may be impatient with what they regard as a far too slow pace of change in the Church. While the conservative view conveyed here is reflective of a minority opinion among American Catholics, it highlights the Church's postsecular dilemma. The Church is pushed by moderate Catholics—and postsecularity—to be open to modernity and secular currents. It is simultaneously pushed by conservative Catholics to maintain its moral beliefs in the face of cultural change, an expectation that also has some accord with the postsecular affirmation of the relevance of religion in preserving ethical truths.[45] The bishops appear successful in reinforcing, or even perhaps providing, the rhetorical content of conservative Catholics' critique of secularism and government intrusion on religion. They are far less successful, however, in modulating the views of liberal Catholics. Very few of them acknowledged, for example, the tension posed by secularism to the public relevance of mainstream religious beliefs. Thus, the bishops' campaign contributes to reinforcing rather than bridging, as would be in line with postsecularity, the religious (conservative)—secular (liberal) divide within Catholicism and, by extension, American society.

Americans' Views of Religion in the Public Sphere

A sharpening of the divide between the secular and the religious is seen more generally in public opinion on the friendliness of government to religion. In 2009, 17 percent of Americans said the Obama administration was unfriendly toward religion, but this figure had almost doubled by January 2016, with 30 percent saying so.[46] This was a tumultuous few years. The bishops' religious freedom campaign was not the only politically relevant force. The actual policy and cultural changes in and of themselves (e.g., the ACA, expansion of same-sex marriage), the rise of the Tea Party, and a sharpening of Republican partisanship all undoubtedly contributed to the increase in the perception of a religiously unfriendly, Obama administration.

Yet pointing to the ambiguity in Americans' regard for public religion, there was little overall change in the perception of religion's influence in American life across the interval of Obama's presidency. Less than two years into President Obama's first term, in the summer of 2010, 67 percent of Americans said they thought religion was losing its influence on American life. This dipped slightly to 66 percent in 2012, but had increased to 72 percent in September 2014, when the bishops' campaign was in full swing. By January 2016, however, it had basically reverted, at 68 percent, to its 2010 level.[47] This was so despite the Supreme Court's legalization of gay marriage seven months earlier (June 2015). In sum, despite the politics of religious freedom and the actual secularizing cultural, legal, and policy changes in American society, the public perception of religion's influence has stabilized at the same level evident prior to the height of the various controversies.

In light of the postsecular expectation of mutual public respect for religious and secular arguments, the perception of religion's influence may be less important than how any such perceived increase or decrease is evaluated. Overall, since 2002, there has been a relatively steady increase in the number of Americans saying that religion is losing its influence.[48] Indeed, this trend parallels the steady pattern of increase in religious disaffiliation in America. As previously noted, the proportion of religiously unaffiliated Americans increased in the 1990s and had tripled to 25 percent by 2017. For the most part, a slim majority of those who think religion is losing its influence on American life see it as a bad thing (e.g., 51 percent in 2016).

Context, of course, is important. The terrorist events of 9/11 prompted a sharp increase in the number perceiving an increase in religion's influence. Underscoring the sensitivity of public attitudes to the immediate sociopolitical reality, this perception had already begun to recede by December 2001, and in March 2002 was at the same level as a year earlier. In this context—given the perceived association of religion, specifically Islam, with terrorism—Americans were comparatively less likely to regard religion's losing influence as a bad thing.[49]

In general, however, religion's perceived loss of influence is polarizing, with approximately half of Americans seeing it as a bad thing and the other half a good thing. Catholics (55 percent) and mainline Protestants (57 percent) are internally split, with over half of each group seeing religion's waning influence as a bad thing. Not surprising, given the cultural polarization between evangelicals and the religiously unaffiliated, three times as many evangelical (74 percent) as unaffiliated (26 percent) Americans say religion's losing influence is a bad thing.[50] A basically similar pattern is evident in regard to churches speaking out on social and political issues. Catholics are again split, with 48 percent agreeing that they should speak out and the other half disagreeing. Mainline Protestants are similarly divided, while two-thirds of white evangelicals (66 percent) and one-third of the unaffiliated (32 percent) say that churches should express their sociopolitical views.[51]

The Limits in the Reflexivity of Religion

The postsecular expectation that moderate religious voices should be actively present in the public sphere comes with the equally important expectation that both secular and religious actors should self-critique their own beliefs and their relative place in a pluralistic society where, by definition, there are diverse religious and secular views. This is a challenging task amid the cut and thrust of cultural politics and social change. As noted above, evangelicals are more supportive than other religious and secular citizens of public religion. However, opinion poll data also suggest that they most likely are not aspiring for reflexive religious-secular dialogue, but for more public visibility for their particular religious views. One in two evangelicals (50 percent) say they perceive discrimination against their religious group, a third (34 percent) say "it is becoming more difficult to be religious in the U.S," and a third (30 percent) say they think of themselves as a minority because of their religious beliefs.[52] In this context, when individuals say they want more religion in the public sphere, it more likely means they want more of *their* religion and less of those beliefs with which they disagree.

We see similar limits in the Catholic bishops' activism on religious freedom. The bishops argue that their advocacy is to defend the religious freedom of all religious citizens and the common good of American society. Their 2012 foundational statement on religious freedom states:

> We [Americans] are stewards of this gift [of freedom] not only for ourselves but for all nations and peoples who yearn to be free. Catholics in America have discharged this duty of guarding freedom admirably for many generations. . . . We have been staunch defenders of religious liberty in the past. We have a solemn duty to discharge that duty today. We need, therefore, to speak frankly with each other when our freedoms are threatened. Now is such a time. As Catholic bishops and American citizens, we address an urgent summons to our fellow Catholics and fellow Americans to be on guard, for religious liberty is under attack, both at home and abroad. . . . This is not a Catholic issue. This is not a Jewish issue. This is not an Orthodox, Mormon or Muslim issue. It is an American issue.

Yet, the bishops were relatively silent on the vocal threats by Donald Trump during the 2016 Republican presidential campaign to monitor mosques and to ban Muslims (including American citizens) from entering the United States.[53]

In December 2015, Archbishop Lori, chairman of the bishops' Committee for Religious Liberty, responded to questions from the Catholic News Service specifically about terrorism and Trump's remarks. He stated, "As citizens and as believers, Christians and Catholics in the United States cannot possibly countenance denying people entry into the country due solely to religious affiliation." He also said that proposals to ban Muslims raise "great religious freedom alarms."[54]

The bishops, however, did not issue any subsequent statements on this particular question over the remaining duration of the campaign. Across 2016, it was not listed on the bishops' website as among the current threats to religious freedom in the United States. Nor was it explicitly mentioned, for example, in Archbishop Lori's June 2016 Fortnight for Freedom homily. By January 2017, it seemed that the bishops had decided that this was more of a migration than a religious freedom issue. On the same day President Trump issued an executive order banning the admission of all refugees into the United States, and a temporary ban on the admission of all individuals from seven Muslim-majority countries (January 27), the bishops' Committee on Migration issued a statement denouncing the policy. By contrast, the bishops' Committee for Religious Liberty maintained silence, appearing to suggest, like Trump, that "this is not about religion."

Some individual bishops—including Cardinals Tobin and Cupich, and Bishop McElroy, all of whom were promoted by Francis—separately issued statements denouncing the ban. By the end of the day on January 30, the president and vice president of the USCCB issued a joint statement praising their fellow bishops' responses defending "God's people" and asking all Catholics to stand in "defense of human dignity." The first comment from the bishops' Committee for Religious Liberty appeared on January 31. In a short statement jointly issued with two other committees, the bishops noted the rights of all religious minorities and, addressing "our Muslim brothers and sisters," the bishops stated: "[W]e stand with you and welcome you."[55]

Again, in contrast, the bishops' Committee for Religious Liberty was not slow in responding to President Trump's retention of an executive order prohibiting federal government contractors from discriminating against employees based on sexual orientation and gender identity. Trump's statement was issued on the evening of January 31, and the bishops' response "expressing concern and disappointment" was posted on the USCCB website by February 1, 2017. The religious liberty committee was similarly quick in responding to President Trump's October 2017 decision broadening employers' contraception mandate exemption, praising it in a statement posted on the USCCB website the same day it was announced.[56] These policy issues are complex, and the bishops' organizational structure includes several committees and policy areas. Such factors may impede the coherence and timeliness of some of the bishops' actions. Nonetheless, the relative silence of the bishops' Committee for Religious Liberty on the Muslim ban adds to the evidence suggesting that their religious-freedom activism is focused primarily on pushing back against American secularism.

Conclusion

Secularization is the settled reality of Western society. It is uneven but, as argued throughout this book, secular expectations drive everyday life. This includes the state's and other secular institutions' assumptions and practices. It also includes Catholics' own expectations of the Church. Perhaps because secularization is the de facto reality, postsecular theorizing does not consider the possibility that moderate religious actors might use their postsecular authority to push back against secularism. Yet this precisely is a new and significant dimension of the U.S. bishops' activism. Their specific claim— namely, the mutuality of the religious and the secular across the Church's diverse institutional activities—and their explicit consciousness of language use and messaging strategies place their activism in accord with the postsecular turn (whether intended as such or not).

The bishops' campaign shows that the opening provided by postsecular society cannot be used to confine the Church's public engagement to economic and social justice issues. For the Church, the rescuing of modernity's ills includes the impeding of an accelerated secularism and the reassertion of what it defines as universal moral truths. The assumed neutrality of the state in mediating the conflict between religious and secular convictions is thus being challenged by the Catholic Church, the sort of moderate public religion a contrite modernity looks to for ethical redirection. The Church not only claims a public voice in societal debate, as befits both secular and postsecular expectations; it also claims the freedom to act on its religious beliefs in several secular fields (e.g., health, social services, education). It thus feels entitled to reject secular policies that it views as requiring complicity in (sexually) immoral acts (e.g., contraception insurance).[57] Such claims are the source of its conflict with the state and with secular society more broadly, including many Catholics.

Religious and secular currents intersect in multiple ways and across multiple domains. And their blurred interweaving, especially in the self-understanding of Catholicism, complicates the translation of the secular principle of religious freedom. The complexities are exacerbated today due to increased secularization in society and in the Church. At the same time, the Church's (natural law) understanding of sexual and family morality limits its own reflexivity, and its ability to negotiate the secular claims and expectations of others, including Catholics. The Church's tradition of reflexivity, however, is nonetheless a critical resource for the Church as it seeks renewed relevance in the lives of Catholics and in society at large. Its potential to do so was on full display at the Synod on the Family, the focus of the next chapter.

6

The Synod on the Family

THE CHURCH'S DIALOGUE WITH DIFFERENCE

OPENING THE 2014 Synod on the Family, Pope Francis implored the bishops to use the opportunity to speak openly and honestly. Synod assemblies, he said "are not meant to discuss beautiful and clever ideas, or to see who is more intelligent." Forthright dialogue, rather, is what is required:

> One general and basic condition is this: speaking honestly. Let no one say: "I cannot say this, they will think this or this of me. . . ." It is necessary to say with parrhesia [candidly] all that one feels. After [a previous meeting] . . . in which the family was discussed, a Cardinal wrote to me, saying: "what a shame that several Cardinals did not have the courage to say certain things out of respect for the Pope, perhaps believing that the Pope might think something else." This is not good, this is not synodality, because it is necessary to say all that, in the Lord, one feels the need to say: without polite deference, without hesitation. And, at the same time, one must listen with humility and welcome, with an open heart, to what your brothers say. Synodality is exercised with these two approaches.[1]

To speak candidly about "the realities and the problems" of the Church, as Francis envisioned the Synod,[2] shows a remarkable postsecular sensibility. It demonstrates the openness to particular empirical realities, and to differences in how to interpret those realities, that is a hallmark of postsecular dialogue. Francis's remarks are in accord with postsecular expectations in other ways, too, whether intended as such or not. They convey his interest in transparency and intellectual honesty and in moving beyond the strategic maneuvering that frequently distorts intra-Church (as well as public) debate about important issues. Telling his fellow bishops not to fear offending him or others with their opinions is a startling departure from John Paul II's emphasis on deference to magisterial authority (see chapter 4).

This chapter focuses on the Synod on the Family, and how its convening, its preparations, its organizational structure, its conduct, and its deliberative content and outcomes meet postsecular expectations. The following pages show that there is much evidence to suggest the Synod can be considered a postsecular event owing to its able negotiation of the mutual relevance of doctrinal ideas and Catholic secular realities. Although marked by clericalism and doctrinal politics, it managed to talk openly about diverse realities and how they complicate Church teachings on family life. And through a deliberative process, it managed to forge a way forward in Catholic teaching on divorce and remarriage. Before turning to the Synod itself, I first provide some background on its significance and the unprecedented nature of its preparations.

Convening the Synod

Synods are called "extraordinary"—as this one was—if they are convened to deal with matters requiring "immediate attention" and "a speedy solution." They are "ordinary" if the topic is more general but still important. In either case, they are significant opportunities for the Church to take stock of issues central to its doctrine and institutional life.[3] From the moment it was announced (in October 2013), the Synod on the Family promised to be extraordinary for several reasons. First, it was on the family, a topic of special relevance in the everyday lives of Catholics. Prior to 2014–2015, the most recent synod on the family was in 1980. This was early in John Paul II's papacy, and a time when Western patterns of family life and sexual behavior were less diverse than today.

Second, Catholic doctrine on the family encompasses Church teachings on sexuality, contraception, marriage, divorce, and gay relationships—all controversial issues. Third, the Synod was a two-year process, contrasting with the more typical convening of a synod as occurring within a single two- to three-week period (see Table 6.1). Phase one was the Assembly in Rome in October 2014, and phase two, a year later, in October 2015. This two-stage process was designed to allow for the assessment of family issues and challenges at phase one, and following those deliberations and further reflection, to reconvene in October 2015 to devise proposals for dealing

Table 6.1 Timeline of the Synod of Bishops on the Family

October 8, 2013: Pope Francis announces the convocation of an extraordinary general assembly of the Synod of Bishops on "The Pastoral Challenges of the Family in the Context of Evangelization"

November 2013: The Vatican Secretariat for the Synod releases the preparatory document (*lineamenta*), including survey questions, for dioceses to use and respond to in preparation for the October 2014 Synod

June 2014: The Secretariat for the Synod issues a working document (*instrumentum laboris*) summarizing the responses received to its pre-Synod survey questions

October 5–19, 2014: The Extraordinary Synod on the Family convenes at the Vatican

October 13, 2014: Synod midterm report is issued

October 18, 2014: Synod final report is issued

December 2014: The Secretariat for the Synod issues a new preparatory document (*lineamenta*) including additional questions for dioceses, based on the 2014 Synod deliberations

June 2015: The Secretariat for the Synod issues a new working document (*instrumentum laboris*) in preparation for the October 2015 Synod

October 4–25, 2015: The Ordinary Synod on the Family convenes at the Vatican

October 9, 2015: Synod working group reports are released based on week one discussions

October 14, 2015: Synod working group reports are released based on week two discussions

October 21, 2015: Synod working group reports are released based on week three discussions

October 24, 2015: Synod 2015 final report is issued

April 2016: *Amoris Laetitia* is published; Pope Francis's Post-Synodal Apostolic Exhortation (discussed in chapter 7)

---

with the challenges Catholics encounter in trying to abide by Church teachings on the family. Thus, there was a general expectation that this synod would—or could—be a more momentous event than were previous thematic meetings. And, as I argue, it also held much postsecular promise.

Preparing for the Synod:
Assessing Catholics' Lived Experiences

It was evident as soon as Francis announced his decision to convene a synod that the particular realities and problems of family life, and not simply Church ideals, were to be center stage. Almost a full year prior to the Synod's first meeting, the Vatican issued a preparatory document that included a series of questions for every Catholic diocese to answer based on experiences in its diocese.[4] In this unprecedented move, the Vatican demonstrated that it was seeking to have a prolonged conversation about the family that would be informed by empirical data about how Catholic families are structured and how they live. It also signaled that those data would be used not to condemn the range of contemporary families but, rather, to explore how the Church might proactively respond to the pastoral challenges Catholics encounter in their actual family circumstances. The Vatican's data-gathering request thus focused attention on the relevance of lived experience in Catholic theology, a dimension that tends to be underacknowledged in official Church statements on sexual morality (see chapter 4). It also amplified Francis's emphasis on the need for continuous dialogue between ideas and realities (e.g., *JG* #231–233). Accordingly, the data-gathering initiative suggested that the idea of natural law, for example—notwithstanding its centrality in Catholic teaching (see chapter 4)—may need to be bracketed while the realities of Catholics' relationships and families are reckoned with.

Assessing Diverse Realities

The preparatory questions distributed by the Vatican were wide-ranging and recognized the diversity of contemporary families.[5] The questionnaire asked about the extent to which Catholic married couples know, understand, and practice Church teachings on marriage and on contraception; and the efforts undertaken by the Church in marriage preparation, couple formation, and children's religious socialization. It also asked about couples in "irregular" unions such as cohabiting, same-sex, divorced, and remarried situations. These questions probed the prevalence of, and the pastoral efforts and difficulties encountered in dealing with, such couples and their children, as well as these families' expectations of the Church and the sacraments. Of further note, given the contested nature of interpretive authority in the Church (see chapter 2), the Vatican asked how Catholics understood the separate contributions of scripture, the magisterium, and natural law in the Church's teaching. And it inquired about how natural law is received among nonpracticing Catholics and nonbelievers, as well as in civil society and the culture at large. Additional questions asked about the broader cultural and political context impacting marriage-related issues in a given diocese or country.

There was a great deal of variation in the procedures followed by dioceses and national bishops' conferences in finding answers to these questions, and in summarizing and presenting their findings. And, paralleling the Vatican's data initiative, several Catholic activist groups and organizations in the United States and elsewhere used the Vatican's questions in surveys of their own members and, in turn, submitted data reports and proposals of their own to the Vatican in anticipation of the Synod.[6] The Vatican thus unleashed a great data-gathering frenzy during the winter and spring of 2013–2014. The consultation, in the words of the Synod's General Secretariat, "generated significant reflection among the people of God." By June 2014, "about 90 percent of the world's bishops' conferences and about 800 Catholic organizations or individuals" had submitted responses to the preparatory questionnaire.[7] The range of respondents was outlined in the summary report of the findings released (as an *instrumentum laboris*, or pre-synod working document, hereafter referred to as *Summary*) by the Synod Secretariat:

> A great number of detailed responses to the questions was submitted by the . . . Eastern Catholic churches . . . the episcopal conferences, the departments of the Roman Curia and the Union of Superiors General. In addition, other responses—categorized as observations—were sent directly to the General Secretariat by a significant number of dioceses, parishes, movements, groups, ecclesial associations and families, not to mention academic institutions, specialists both Catholic and non-Catholic, all interested in sharing their reflections.[8]

The large body of data collected did not uncover any major finding that would have surprised sociologists who study Catholicism. In the United States, the bishops' curt summary of the responses underscored the gap between Catholic teaching and Catholics' behavior and attitudes. The findings prompted the U.S. bishops' conference president, Archbishop Kurtz, to comment on the "need for greater, effective teaching on key tenets of the faith, such as the indissolubility of marriage, the importance of sexual difference for marriage, the natural law, and the married couple's call to be open to life."[9] Reports from bishops' conferences in Western European countries similarly reflected the many points of divergence between Catholics and Church teachings.[10] Much of the data pointed, as the bishops of England and Wales elaborated, to Catholics' experiences of the Church as "being out of touch, unbending or unrealistic" regarding sexual ethics, same-sex relationships, and contraception.[11]

Postsecular Import

Although the data gathered were more confirmatory than revelatory, the groundbreaking significance of the exercise cannot be overstated. It is highly significant in terms of both Church practice and postsecular expectations. For the first time in history, Church officials were publicly asking questions about Catholic phenomena they had previously either marginalized or framed as contradictory of Catholicism. Thus, they named the realities of divorced and remarried Catholics, Catholic same-sex relationships, cohabiting Catholics, and contraception-using Catholics. The public character of the Vatican inquiry is important because it literally opened up social and theological conversation about these issues. It did so not alone by acknowledging their empirical reality but also by asking what is being done or could be done to make the Church more responsive to and inclusive of these realities. Further demonstrating empirical openness, the Vatican subsequently distributed a set of follow-up questions to dioceses based on points that emerged in the 2014 Synod discussions. Church officials in the United States and elsewhere have long reiterated that Church teaching is not molded by sociological studies or opinion polls.[12] Yet now, the Vatican itself was publicly spearheading a purposeful, global empirical inquiry on sex and family matters, and in the process showing a postsecular openness to secular reasoning and to diverse secular realities.

A postsecular sensibility is additionally projected in other important ways. First, convening a synod on such a significant Catholic subject demonstrates the willingness of the Church to examine how its teachings and pastoral programs may have gone off-track in meeting contemporary families. As such, holding a synod projects a contriteness that, like modernity, the Church too needs to urgently address some failures. Second, it amplifies the recognition that the secularization of Catholic life—as seen in the prevalence of divorce, cohabitation, same-sex relationships, and contraception use among Catholics—is not necessarily devoid of God's presence. It affirms, rather, that the religious and the secular are interwoven into and embodied by contemporary Catholics (see chapter 2). This is also in tune with the cognitive reset expounded by Francis who, in accord with Catholic theology, stresses that God is in history, not just in the past but also in the present and the future (see chapter 3). And, third, it conveys that Church leaders are open to the reflexive examination of Church teachings and practices—without necessarily leading to, determining, or closing off the possibility of changes in doctrine and practice. This reflexivity is reminiscent of Vatican II, but the Synod went a step further. It explicitly opened the bishops' dialogue to the lived experiences of Catholic laity as collated in response to the Vatican's preparatory survey and its post-2014 Synod follow-up questions. Thus the Synod's commitment to a two-year, two-stage process of discernment and dialogue was not merely an intrahierarchical process but, rather, one that entailed the (mediated) voices and experiences of Catholics at large.[13]

The Quest for New Doctrinal Language

A postsecular openness and reflexivity was further apparent in the explicit consciousness the Synod preparations showed toward doctrinal language. The Jesuit historian John O'Malley called Vatican II a "language event." He emphasized the transformation in the rhetorical style and language used in its deliberations and formal documents—the use, for example, of the inclusive "People of God" phrase to denote the relevance of the laity in Church matters.[14] This change in language is not simply a superficial rewording of an existing principle. More significantly, it reflects and conveys new meanings, such as Vatican II's doctrinal rebalancing in the relation between the hierarchy and the laity (see chapter 2). That the Synod on the Family might, too, be a "language event" was fueled by a remarkable acknowledgment by the Vatican. Its pre-Synod data *Summary* (# 20–27, 30) noted that the language of natural law requires a more meaningful and accessible translation. Given the centrality of natural law in Catholic teaching (see chapter 4), this was a startling recognition. Although Pope Benedict had previously commented on the communicative limits of natural law,[15] the public articulation of this view in the context of the Synod preparations showed a new forthrightness for the Church.

The inaccessibility of natural law, the Vatican suggested, is partly due to the complexity of its reasoning. It also noted its tendency to be misunderstood and, indeed, to be conflated with its inverse (e.g., natural spontaneity), as well its perceived incompatibility with new scientific theories (e.g., evolutionary biology). As elaborated in the pre-2014 Synod *Summary*:

> Very few responses and observations demonstrated an adequate, popular understanding of the natural law. [#21] . . . The responses

and observations also show that the adjective natural often is understood by people as meaning "spontaneous" or "what comes naturally." Today people tend to place a high value on personal feelings and emotions, aspects that appear "genuine" and "fundamental" and therefore to be followed "simply according to one's nature".... Today in not only the West but increasingly every part of the world, scientific research poses a serious challenge to the concept of nature. Evolution, biology and neuroscience, when confronted with the traditional idea of the natural law, conclude that it is not "scientific." (*Summary* #22)

In what can be considered a postsecular response to the Vatican's assessment that "natural law is perceived as an outdated legacy" (*Summary* #22), Church officials called for "a renewal of language" (#30). This strategic move recognizes that in order to persuade people to a particular interpretation of Church teaching, the arguments need to be translated into an everyday idiom that makes sense to ordinary individuals. In the Vatican's view, it is not the particular teaching that lacks authority, but the language in which it is framed. Thus the Vatican argued,

> The language traditionally used in explaining the term natural law should be improved so that the values of the Gospel can be communicated to people today in a more intelligible manner. (*Summary* #30)

It further affirmed that in working toward a "rereading of the concept of the natural law in a more meaningful manner in today's world," the language should be "accessible to all" (#30). In sum, the Church's pre-Synod data-gathering process confirmed its realization that a central element in the language used to outline Catholic teaching falls short of contemporary resonance and thus requires an alternative vocabulary.

Clericalism and Postsecular Expectations

The empirical openness shown in the Synod's preparations did not extend to the composition of its participants. In particular, the Synod's postsecular potential was impeded by its exclusion of women as voting participants, and thus as authoritative voices. Because gender equality is a core principle of modernity and of liberal democratic societies, a secular idiom assumes the inclusion of men and women as full participants in contemporary debates. This expectation would be especially prominent when the subject at hand is not an intra-Church matter alone but, instead, one impacting Catholics' embodied public identities, as family and marital status (and gender) necessarily do.[16] As already discussed, the Catholic Church excludes women from ordination (see chapter 4). Therefore, the ordained hierarchical structure of the Church and its sites of discourse (e.g., at the Vatican and in dioceses and parishes) are heavily masculinized.[17] Because the Synod was a meeting of bishops, most of those who participated were ordained men. Historically, however, as John O'Malley explains, until Vatican I (1869–1870), "the presence of the laity was taken for granted" in Church councils. The 1917 Code of Canon Law formalized Vatican I's "exclusively clerical precedent," though Vatican II allowed a small number of lay men and women auditors.[18]

The Synod on the Family continued Vatican II's concession. A number of lay men and women and nonordained religious sisters (nuns) and brothers participated. None of the women participants, however, had voting rights. A total of 192 of the 253 individuals at the 2014 session were voting participants; and nonvoter experts and auditors included fourteen married couples. In all, twenty-five women participated. At the 2015 session, there were 279 voting participants; and among an additional fifty-one nonvoters (including seventeen married couples), thirty were women.[19] In sum, women made up approx. 10 percent of those participating in the Synod, though none of them was eligible to vote.[20]

The exclusion of women as voting participants is entangled with their exclusion from ordination. It also, however, transcends priestly status. The nuns who participated as representatives of women's religious orders were not allowed to vote. Yet, their counterparts representing male religious orders were, one of whom was not an ordained priest but was a nonordained religious brother. In short, as Church teaching emphasizes, gender differences matter (see chapter 4). And they mattered more than ordination in determining who was allowed to vote at the Synod. A similar pattern of women's exclusion was seen in the Vatican commission established by Francis to study reform of the marriage annulment process; it included nine men, one of whom was not ordained, and no women.[21] There is, however, an even mix of women and men on Francis's commission studying the question of women deacons.[22]

Many Catholics found it especially jarring that a synod on the family would exclude women as authoritative voices. This view was sharply articulated by former Irish president Mary McAleese, a practicing Catholic, and who prior to being president served as an occasional adviser to the Irish Catholic bishops. She stated:

> There is something profoundly wrong and skewed [about] ... male celibates [meeting] to review the Catholic Church's teachings on family life. ... The very idea of ... people who have decided they are not going to have any children, not going to have families, not going to be fathers and not going to be spouses—so they have no adult experience of family life as the rest of us know it—but they are going to advise the pope on family life; it is completely bonkers.[23]

Whether or not readers agree with McAleese, the all-male celibate composition of the Synod visibly underscored the exclusionary clericalism of the Church that is of concern to many. As noted earlier (see chapter 4), the Church's self-enclosed clerical culture is seen by ordinary Catholics—and by Francis—as the root of the hierarchy's disconnect from Catholics' lived realities.

Beyond the issues raised by women's marginal presence, the Synod's post-secular potential was further impeded not only by the small number of lay participants but also by the narrow range of the lay views that were represented. Despite the breadth of views and experiences yielded in response to the Vatican survey, little of this diversity was on show during the Synod meetings. Some lay auditors, for example, were employees of bishops' conferences or conservative religious organizations, and thus perhaps constrained by their job status. Others were advocates of natural family planning, a method that finds favor among a small minority of Catholic laity. The Vatican's *Summary* of its pre-Synod survey results noted that:

> A good number of episcopal conferences mention that when the teaching of the church is clearly communicated in its authentic, human and Christian beauty, it is enthusiastically received for the most part by the faithful. ... On the other hand, many respondents confirmed that even when the church's teaching about marriage and the family is known, many Christians have difficulty accepting it in its entirety. (#13)

Yet, while aware of the difficulties that large numbers of Catholics have in accepting Church teachings, the Synod did not show interest in hearing first-hand from some such individuals and couples, preferring instead to hear from those for whom Church teachings appear to be relatively unproblematic.[24]

Therefore, despite its commitment to engage with "families as they are" (*Summary* #31), the Synod did not fully avail itself of the opportunity to do so. Its clericalism diluted its engagement with the family diversity that is a Catholic and a secular reality. Symbolically, it fell short of conveying a lay-inclusive and gender-inclusive Church, thus losing an opportunity to showcase the Church's contrite commitment to institutional renewal and evangelization. And, further from a postsecular perspective, it was a missed opportunity to concretely demonstrate—with the whole world watching— that, yes, indeed, God is in the secular, "is in the world of today" as Francis states (see chapter 3)—even as Catholics' embodiment of those secular realities complicates Church doctrine and pastoral practices. The Synod's hesitancy to include the spoken voices of diverse Catholics—those whose lives are partially at odds with official Church teaching—reinforced the perception of a (celibate male) hierarchy that is distant from Catholics' everyday realities. It did so, moreover, despite the Vatican's pre-Synod attention to those realities. Nevertheless, as I show in the next section, those realities, despite the marginalization of lay participants, infused the Synod deliberations and pushed forward its dialogue and outcomes.

The Synod: The Dialogue of Catholic Ideas and Catholic Realities

The dialogue produced by the Synod reflected the contested nature of the questions at issue. In particular, it illuminated a deep divide between the bishops over the "irregular" sexual and living situations of gay, and divorced and remarried Catholics. The overarching tension (as on contraception) is between doctrinal traditionalists and moderates. The former argue that Church teaching in these areas cannot change and that neither conscience nor compassion can displace objective moral truth and the truths of the faith concerning marriage. Conversely, doctrinal moderates argue that Church teaching necessarily evolves and, in the context of family life, needs to be responsive to allow Catholics who are in non-Church-approved relationships to fully participate in the Church's sacramental life.

The two reports issued by the 2014 Synod, a midterm and a final report, illuminated both the doctrinal divide and the centrality of language regarding this divide.[25] The midterm report, which summarized the "reflections and . . . dialogues" of the Synod's first week of deliberations, used remarkably conciliatory language in discussing gay, cohabiting, and divorced and remarried Catholics. However, after the Synod's official rapporteur, Cardinal Erdo, presented the report to his fellow participants, several bishops immediately disavowed it in the Synod meeting and subsequently in the press. They argued that it was not an accurate or a balanced summary of the bishops' deliberations. The main objections were "that the text lacked certain necessary references to Catholic moral teaching," scarcely referred to "the concept of sin," and "departed from John Paul II's theology of marriage by seeming to approve of same-sex couples." So contentious was the report that even its principal author blamed another bishop for the moderate language used to discuss same-sex relations.[26] Taking account of these objections and following further discussion within the Synod's ten working groups during the 2014 Synod's second week, the final report was strikingly different in tone and content regarding these specific issues.

Same-Sex Relationships

The 2014 midterm report had a three-paragraph section (#50–52) on "welcoming homosexual persons." It noted that "homosexuals have gifts and qualities to offer to the Christian community." And in a soft questioning tone, it asked whether "we" can offer them "a welcoming home," one which accepts and values their sexual orientation without compromising Church teaching on family and marriage. It acknowledged the mutual sacrifice and support that same-sex partners can provide each other. It also noted that the Church "pays special attention" to the children living with same-sex couples and that priority always should be given to children's needs and rights. Nonetheless, the report affirmed that same-sex unions could never be on a similar footing as heterosexual marriage. It also stated that pressure should not be placed on the Church to align its policies to conform to international bodies and others who subscribe to "gender ideology."

The final 2014 report—issued a week later—had a shorter, two-paragraph section on homosexuality (#55–56).[27] Instead of the welcoming vocabulary in the midterm report, it used the more technical language found in previous Church statements, using phrases such as "persons with homosexual tendencies." Further, the section omitted the Synod's earlier acknowledgment that "homosexuals have gifts." It instead framed the issue as a family problem. It noted that: "Some families have members who have a homosexual tendency," and given this situation, the "synod fathers" wondered what pastoral attention would be appropriate given that homosexual unions—quoting words from a previous Vatican statement—can never be considered even remotely analogous to God's plan for marriage and family. While the bishops reiterated the Church's condemnation of discrimination against "men and women with a homosexual tendency," they also repeated their argument that "exerting pressure" on the Church regarding same-sex marriage is "totally unacceptable."

The shift seen in these reports encapsulated a clear reassertion of both the Church's opposition to same-sex relationships and the authoritative nature of its teaching. The document quoted by the bishops was the 2003 statement from the Congregation for the Doctrine of the Faith (see chapter 4) outlining opposition to the legal recognition of same-sex unions. By quoting this statement, the bishops not only reaffirm the moral unacceptability of gay relationships; importantly, they also remind people of its grounding in Vatican authority. The reassertion of Church teaching is not only conveyed by the deletion of welcoming language, it is further communicated by casting "homosexuality" as a family problem rather than a salient dimension of personal identity. In this framing, gays are not considered mature persons or moral agents in their own right but, rather, as members of families—and thus presenting *problem families* that require some form of special pastoral attention. Further, gays are stripped of their sexual identity; they are no longer "homosexual persons" but, instead, people who have "homosexual tendencies." That such tendencies are considered aberrations has long been articulated in Church teaching (see chapter 4). Indeed, the 2003 statement quoted in the Synod report is the first sentence in a paragraph that continues by stating: "Marriage is holy, while homosexual acts go against the natural moral law" and in scripture are condemned "as a serious depravity."

The substance and tone set by the final 2014 report largely settled the discourse on same-sex relations that would subsequently characterize both the preparations for the 2015 Synod and its actual deliberations. In December 2014, the Vatican issued a new preparatory document (*lineamenta*) to assist the bishops in their reflections in preparation for the Synod's October 2015 meeting.[28] However, though it was issued as part of the Synod's ongoing deliberations, it appeared to short-circuit the reflective–dialogical process by circumscribing its parameters. The *lineamenta* explicitly indicated its intention to assist the bishops:

> to avoid in their responses a formulation of pastoral care based simply
> on an application of doctrine that would not respect the conclusions
> of the extraordinary synodal assembly [of October 2014] and would
> lead their reflection far from the path already indicated.[29]

In other words, it conveyed that the bishops' reflections should be in accord with existing conclusions. In this vein, discussing same-sex relations, the document noted that "The pastoral care of persons with homosexual tendencies poses new challenges today due to the manner in which their rights are proposed in society." Rejecting any such pressure toward change, it repeated the same substantive points and with similar language as articulated in the 2014 final report (discussed earlier).[30]

A subsequent working document (*instrumentum laboris*) issued in June 2015 brought a slightly different emphasis, one that seemed to restore recognition to the pastoral needs of gay individuals in their own right. Somewhat echoing the more inclusive spirit of the 2014 midterm report, it stated:

> It would be desirable that dioceses devote special attention in their pastoral programs to the accompaniment of families where a member has a homosexual tendency and of homosexual persons themselves. [31]

Yet six months later, the report issued at the conclusion of the 2015 Synod basically reiterated the same points and used much the same language as the (more negative) 2014 final report. The tone and vocabulary were slightly more inclusive. The single paragraph on gays (#76) began by noting that "the Church's attitude, like that of her Master," offers boundless love to all people without exception and regardless of sexual orientation. And it did not talk of "homosexual tendencies."[32] However, it maintained a "family members" framing. It stated that "specific attention is given to guiding families with homosexual members," but it was silent about pastoral programs that might minister to "homosexual persons themselves" as identified in the June working document. It also reiterated the Church's opposition to same-sex marriage and again rejected pressure on the Church to change its teaching. This paragraph was approved by 86 percent of the bishops, well over the two-thirds majority required for its adoption by the Synod.[33]

In sum, there has been no shift in the Church's official teaching on gays and, over the course of the Synod, a clear reversal occurred in the attempt to use more "meaningful language" in talking about gays. The Synod's pushback against a more inclusive stance toward gay Catholics can be understood in light of the bishops' perception of the threat same-sex marriage poses to the Church's core teaching on marriage, and to the natural-law assumptions regarding sexual difference and complementarity built into that teaching (see chapters 4 and 5). Moreover, outside of the United States and Western Europe, support for same-sex relationships, and especially for gay marriage, is less prevalent than it is for contraception or for divorce and remarriage.[34] It is also perhaps a less pastorally urgent issue than divorce and remarriage (simply based on comparing the incidence of gay relative to divorced and remarried Catholics). These factors, therefore, may embolden the opposition of some conservative bishops, while tempering the support of some liberal bishops who instead may have opted to push more strongly for change regarding divorced and remarried Catholics.

The Synod, nevertheless, offered evidence of some important linguistic and symbolic gains. It did not explicitly reiterate the Vatican's previous phrasing from the 1970s and 1980s that homosexuality is an "objectively disordered" orientation, or that homosexual acts contravene natural law (see chapter 4). Further, although the Synod gave short shrift to the personal sexual identity and pastoral needs of gay individuals and couples, this might possibly be interpreted as a move away from the Church's earlier focus on "homosexual acts." In this tacit recalibration, the Church is giving lower priority to the relatively private sexual activities of gays. This is displaced by a focus on pushing back against the legalization of same-sex marriage and other secular policies that undermine the Church's moral authority and institutional identity (see chapter 5).

Discerning Change in Church Teaching on Divorced and Remarried Catholics

As on same-sex relations, the Synod's 2014 midterm report provoked controversy over how it summarized the bishops' deliberations on divorced and remarried Catholics. However, unlike the Synod's lack of explicit inclusivity toward gay Catholics, the final 2015 report affirmed a new inclusiveness toward divorce and remarried Catholics. The changes are not without ambiguity. But indicative of the fact that some modulation of the status quo was achieved, each of the three paragraphs on divorce in the final 2015 report failed to win the approval of a fourth or more of the voting bishops.[35] By contrast, only 14 percent voted against the paragraph on gays. Some bishops may have voted against any of these paragraphs because they believed they were not sufficiently inclusive of those in "irregular" situations. In the context of Catholic teaching, however, it is more likely that those who voted no, at least on divorce and remarriage, did so because they felt the wording leaned toward doctrinal moderation. Their concern reflects an anxiety— reminiscent of Paul VI's hesitancy on contraception—that doctrinal change undermines the Church's authority and the constancy of what they consider to be a necessarily unchanging Church doctrine. Additionally, for some such bishops, voting no likely signaled that "We are not giving into the secular agenda," a view confidently declared by Cardinal Pell at the end of the 2014 Synod.[36]

On initial reading, it is not self-evident where the change or even equivocation occurs in the evolution of the Synod's thinking. The language and tone across each of the reports are inclusive and noncondemnatory. The 2014 mid-term report spoke of "appreciating the positive values" rather than the "limitations and shortcomings" contained by those who participate in the Church's life "in an incomplete and imperfect way" (#20). Subsequent reports did not mention "positive values," but the 2014 final report reiterated that "the grace of God works also in [such persons'] lives, giving them the courage to do good, to care for one another in love and to be of service to the community in which they live and work" (#25). Continuing this positive tone, the 2014 final report also stated that those:

> who are divorced and remarried require careful discernment and an accompaniment of great respect. Language or behavior that might make them feel an object of discrimination should be avoided, all the while encouraging them to participate in the life of the community. The Christian community's care of such persons is not to be considered a weakening of its faith and testimony to the indissolubility of marriage, but precisely in this way the community is seen to express its charity. (#51)

Reflecting the dialogical openness encouraged by Francis, subsequent documents (e.g., the December 2014 *lineamenta* and the June 2015 *instrumentum*) outlined the core tension between the bishops regarding the participation of remarried Catholics in the Church. The division was essentially between "spiritual communion" conveyed through participation in Mass but not the Eucharist, and "sacramental communion"—the freedom to receive the Eucharist. These documents also explicitly noted the bishops' various points of disagreement as to which participatory and penitentiary (confessional) paths are pastorally appropriate and in accord with canon law.

The Integration of Difference

Careful review of the documents reveals a critical linguistic shift in the pre-Synod 2015 working document (*instrumentum laboris*) issued in June that year. That document introduces the vocabulary of "integration" and explicitly signals the importance of the integration of divorced and remarried Catholics into the Church. This is the first time in the synod process that this word is employed in this particular context. And it is used both in the report text and in two separate headings, such as in denoting "The Integration of Divorced and Civilly Remarried Persons in the Christian Community" (#121). Sociologically, integration entails the crafting of community amid differences,[37] and this is the moral task that emerges in the document. With a strategic linguistic move, the *instrumentum* translates the theme of "careful discernment," emphasized in each preceding report, into a proactive goal. It notes:

> Many parties request that the attention to and the accompaniment of persons who are divorced and civilly remarried take into account the diversity of situations and be geared towards a greater integration of them into the life of the Christian community. (#121)

The paragraph continues by articulating what this might entail. It makes a tactical nod to John Paul II's apostolic exhortation, *Familiaris Consortio* (*FC*), a theology of marriage that doctrinal conservatives argued was missing in the 2014 midterm report. It states:

> Without prejudice to the recommendations made in *Familiaris Consortio* (#84), some suggest that the forms of exclusion currently followed in liturgical and pastoral practice be re-examined as well as those in education and charitable activity. Since these persons are still part of the Church, the aim is to reflect on the opportunity to eliminate these forms of exclusion. (#121)[38]

The elimination of forms of exclusion thus became the task to be tackled by the 2015 Synod. And this is what the Synod largely accomplished. In the 2015 final report, the language of "careful discernment" permeating each of the preceding reports becomes explicitly proscriptive, though not a command. It states:

> Hopefully, dioceses will promote various means of discernment for these [cohabiting and divorced and remarried] people and to involve them in the community to help and encourage them to grow and eventually make a conscious, coherent choice. (#53)

And it continues:

> The baptized who are divorced and civilly remarried need to be more integrated into Christian communities in a variety of possible ways,

while avoiding any chance of scandal. The logic of integration is the key to their pastoral care, a care which might allow them not only to realize that they belong to the Church as the Body of Christ, but also to know that they can have a joyful and fruitful experience in it. . . . Their participation can be expressed in different ecclesial services which necessarily requires discerning which of the various forms of exclusion, currently practiced in the liturgical, pastoral, educational and institutional framework, can be surpassed. Such persons need to feel not as excommunicated members of the Church, but instead as living members, able to live and grow in the Church and experience her as a mother, who welcomes them always, who takes care of them with affection and encourages them along the path of life and the Gospel. (#84)

The language here—of integration while avoiding scandal—encapsulates a persistent tension in the maintenance of Catholicism as a living (secularized) tradition. "Avoiding scandal" concedes acceptance of individuals' particular (irregular) circumstances while simultaneously constraining their freedom to publicly contravene official Church teaching. This is a complicating tension. I leave it aside for the moment in order to focus on the dynamic change accomplished by the Synod, but return to it in the next chapter.

The paragraph's unequivocal insistence on the imperative of integration leaves no doubt as to the Church's definition of the task at hand. Further, the language indicating that divorced and remarried Catholics should not feel excommunicated is a major symbolic milestone. The sense of being excommunicated (while not officially the case) is precisely the feeling experienced by many Catholics who are divorced or in other "irregular" situations (as noted in chapter 2). The document does not indicate that they are welcome to receive sacramental communion. Yet, it pushes open the door to that eventual outcome. If, as the *Catechism* states, the Eucharist is "the source and summit" of Catholic life, it would seem that for imperfect Catholics "to live and grow in the Church" (as the quoted paragraph states), they would—and should— need the Eucharist.[39]

As outlined by the Synod, conscientious discernment is critical to assessing whether it might be valid for divorced and remarried Catholics to possibly receive communion. That process returns to the words of John Paul II (*FC* #84). In particular, it includes his important acknowledgment that each "irregular" situation presents its own circumstances and context, and by extension, the probability of varying degrees of moral responsibility. The 2015 Synod final report states:

> Pope Saint John Paul II offered a comprehensive policy, which remains the basis for the evaluation of these situations: "Pastors must know that, for the sake of truth, they are obliged to exercise careful discernment of situations. There is in fact a difference between those who have sincerely tried to save their first marriage and have been unjustly abandoned, and those who through their own grave fault have destroyed a canonically valid marriage" (*FC* #84). It is therefore the duty of priests to accompany such people in helping them understand their situation according to the teaching of the Church and the guidelines of the Bishop. . . . Under certain circumstances people find it very difficult to act differently. Therefore, while supporting a general rule, it is necessary to recognize that responsibility with respect to certain actions or decisions is not the same in all cases. Pastoral discernment, while taking into account a person's properly formed conscience, must take responsibility for these situations. Even the consequences of actions taken are not necessarily the same in all cases. (#85)

This quote is excerpted from the paragraph (#85) that received the most no votes; it met the consensus threshold but was rejected by close to one-third (31 percent) of the bishops. Given the elevated moral and magisterial authority of John Paul among theologically conservative Catholics, it is ironic that his language and reasoning become pivotal to forging a new consensus on doctrinal change. The Synod draws on his theology of marriage to legitimate the possibility that a conscientious judgment process might allow for communion for divorced and remarried Catholics on a case-by-case basis. The Synod does so even though John Paul, in the same section invoked (*FC* #84), also unequivocally reaffirmed the Church's practice of excluding divorced and remarried Catholics from communion.

Doctrinal Politics

This doctrinal development is a remarkable communicative achievement. It is not untainted by doctrinal politics, however. The bare consensus (especially on #85) crystallized a tense and polemical public debate between high-profile cardinals. It is important to note this doctrinal division because it is another angle on the interpretive diversity within Catholicism. Of further postsecular import, the foregrounding of doctrinal conflict did not sabotage the Synod's focus on the realities of family life nor on finding an inclusive way forward.

The public contentiousness began as early as the fall of 2013, when the Vatican issued the preparatory document for the Synod. From the outset, some bishops were suspicious that the Synod was a vehicle for a predetermined change in Church teaching on marriage. In public interviews and in books and magazine articles, the question debated was whether divorced and remarried Catholics could legitimately have a penitentiary path to Communion. This view was elaborated in diverse forums by German Cardinal Walter Kasper, including in his influential book *The Gospel of the Family*. The idea was forcefully rejected by his fellow German, Cardinal Muller (head of the Vatican's Congregation for the Doctrine of the Faith) and by other high-profile cardinals and theologians.[40]

Opponents of any possible doctrinal or pastoral change argued that "the indissolubility of sacramental marriage," a doctrine confirmed by the Council of Trent and reaffirmed in recent decades by papal and magisterial teaching, "means that there is no possibility of admitting remarried divorcees to the sacraments."[41] In this perspective, "in a sex-saturated culture ... the divorced and civilly remarried can receive the Eucharist (and the other sacraments) even if they share the same home—namely, once they renounce sharing the same bed."[42] This argument accords with John Paul's teaching on sexual continence in his *Familiaris Consortio* (#84), the same document (and indeed from the same paragraph) that ironically, as noted just prior, was used by the Synod to articulate a more inclusive and differentiated understanding of the situations of divorced and remarried Catholics.

Irony aside, the doctrinal division evident between Church officials engages larger overarching questions of whether, when, how, and on what authority can or does Catholic doctrine change. More immediately, it prompted the formation of a relatively dichotomous alignment of bishops that played out during the Synod. In light of postsecular—and Francis's—expectations of sincere dialogical openness to differences, this pre-Synod alignment is important. It would seem to militate against the bishops coming to the Synod with the attitude of communicative openness required of reflexive deliberation. Openness assumes that the bishops participating in the Synod's ongoing candid deliberations might cultivate a more nuanced understanding of the issues relative to their initial position. Yet, as highlighted by the controversy in response to the 2014 midterm report (noted earlier), there was essentially a continuation and a reassertion of the bishops' pre-Synod doctrinal polarization rather than its nuancing or modulation.

Hermeneutic of Suspicion

The apparent doctrinal polarization also exposed a hermeneutic of suspicion among some bishops regarding the integrity of the Synod's communicative procedures. Cardinal Burke, for example, a moderator of one of its discussion groups, publicly criticized the Synod leadership following the 2014 midterm summary. He argued:

> All of the information regarding the synod is controlled by the General Secretariat of the synod, which clearly has favored from the beginning the positions expressed [in the midterm report]. . . . You don't have to be a rocket scientist to see the approach at work, which is certainly not of the church.[43]

He and others also objected to Francis's imposition of moderators and rapporteurs to complement the (mostly conservative) bishops elected as moderators by the bishops themselves. One nonparticipating theologian argued that the Synod's communicative process and procedures stifled "openness and transparency." He further maintained that they exposed its "not-so-hidden agenda [that] feeds into a bigger agenda, which is that of a secular society that threatens the traditional family to its very foundations."[44]

The Synod secretariat had initially intended not to publish its individual working groups' summary reports, but to provide them only to the drafters of the final 2014 report. However, in response to the bishops' insistence that they should be published, they were released on October 16, prior to the conclusion of the Synod (on October 19) and the drafting of the final (2014) report. Consequently, one could compare the final report with the thematic content of the group discussions and identify any distortions. As Cardinal Pell explained: "We wanted the Catholic people around the world to know actually what was going on in talking about marriage and the family."[45]

Nevertheless, a hermeneutic of suspicion—regarding both doctrinal content and communicative procedures—continued into and during 2015. Such criticism flourished in June following the Vatican's release of the pre-Synod (2015) working document (even though that document, as noted earlier, built on the 2014 final report and the *lineamenta* statement of follow-up questions). And it intensified as the bishops assembled that October for the three-week meeting at which they were expected to finalize the Synod's views on the family. On the day the Synod began (October 5, 2015), thirteen high-profile cardinals submitted a letter to Francis criticizing the Synod procedures. They argued that they seemed "designed to facilitate predetermined results on important disputed questions."[46] Although forthright in their criticisms, the letter-signers were less forthright about whose actual views they were expressing. They asked Francis to consider concerns "we have heard from other synod fathers"; and they stated that the "new synodal procedures will be seen in some quarters as lacking openness and genuine collegiality." And in two other instances in the letter, they noted that they were expressing concerns heard from "various fathers" and "a number of fathers." That same day during the Synod discussion at which Francis was present, Cardinal Pell, a signatory to the letter, and other participants articulated similar concerns as outlined in the letter—a letter which was then not yet public.

The following day, Francis strategically intervened and, in unscheduled remarks, rejected the concerns expressed. He forcefully stated that the 2015 Synod was in continuity with the 2014 Synod; that the (heavily criticized) June 2015 working document was approved by the postsynodal council in his presence; that the 2014 documents—the midterm and final reports, as well as the December follow-up statement and questions—were also part of the official discourse; and that the 2015 working document was the basis for the continuing dialogue at the Synod. He also pointed out that "Catholic doctrine on marriage has not been touched," and cautioned against reducing the Synod to discussion of the question of communion for divorced and remarried Catholics. In summarizing Francis's remarks, the official Vatican spokesman further noted that decisions about the procedures were formally approved by Francis and thus not open to revision. In sum, as Vatican observers pointed out, the Vatican rejected the "requests of the letter en bloc," other than a marginal acknowledgment that the Synod was about more than remarried Catholics. Adding to the political and rhetorical intensity, the influential Jesuit editor and Francis ally Antonio Spadaro tweeted from the Synod hall that Francis also exhorted the bishops "not to give in to the conspiracy hermeneutic." That hermeneutic, Francis argued, is "sociologically weak and spiritually unhelpful."[47]

Doctrinal, ideological, and personality conflicts among Church officials, while intriguing, are not new in the Church—Vatican II had plenty of them.[48] The Synod's report writing and procedural controversies highlight that the Synod was far from being an impartial gathering committed to the sincere probing of reasonable claims and counterclaims. It was, rather, a high-stakes doctrinal and political event with strategically aligned partisans, positions, and desired outcomes. From a postsecular perspective, what is interesting is that amid such conflicts, the discourse moves forward: doctrine as a living thing changes, however slightly—but always significantly. Dialogue is far messier than public-sphere theorists convey.[49] It does not occur in a sterile environment but, rather, amid particular realities in which crosscutting experiences, interests, and expectations impinge. This is the case even among what appears as a highly select and relatively homogeneous group (Catholic bishops), and even as they share core values. All the bishops, for example, believe in the sanctity of the Eucharist and in the sanctity of marriage. Consensus, however, does not occur immaculately; it needs a structure and a process. Of particular postsecular relevance, the Synod's dialogue structure required conversation with difference. The next section discusses how this worked, and with what effect.

Communicative Structure: Conversation with Difference

The communicative structure of the 2015 Synod assigned the bishops to thirteen shared-language working groups: four English-language, three French-language, three Italian-language, two Spanish-language, and one German-language group. Though characterized by shared language, the participants in some groups brought wide-ranging geographical and cultural experiences of family life.[50] In any case, irrespective of cultural diversity, the group structure meant that when the bishops were not assembled as one in a plenary session, they had to engage in intragroup, face-to-face dialogue with each other in discussing and reworking the Synod's working document. This method forced the bishops to reciprocally converse with one another, rather than simply indicate their individual approval or disapproval of discrete paragraphs. In retrospect, whether or not it was experienced as such by the participants at the time, the groups "worked" in that they contributed to producing a final document that, though contested, won consensual approval.

The final 2015 report was a major accomplishment because, as noted earlier, it formulated guidelines toward the possibility that divorced and remarried Catholics might be admitted to the sacraments on a case-by-case basis following careful pastoral discernment (#85). The Synod thus marked a way forward for the Church and for Catholics. Further, the report did not repeat John Paul's specific sentence that remarried Catholics are excluded from Communion (*FC* #84). This is symbolically significant, and further projects the report's inclusive intent. In Catholicism, what is said and what is left unsaid can be equally important (see chapter 4). A lesson here is that one never starts from scratch. Quite the contrary. The cumulative stock of lived knowledge available to those engaged in making sense of a particular issue provides a resource for refining or changing the practice in question. Church officials—and the laity—are always immersed in a specific contextual tradition, and they take cues from that tradition, including its disposal of fragments, nuances, and ambiguities. The Synod's new pathway for divorced and remarried Catholics is thus in continuity with the Catholic doctrinal tradition even as it changes it. Such outcomes challenge the assumption that tradition invariably stands in the way of progressive change.[51]

Reciprocal Dialogue

Was this doctrinal change facilitated by a bias toward secularism in the Synod's communicative procedures, as some conservatives allege? Or was it achieved by reciprocal conversation? There is sufficient evidence from the working-group process to suggest that the bishops' personal engagement with each other's different arguments and perspectives played a decisive role.

The Synod's language-based working group methodology ensured that conservative and moderate bishops were mixed rather than based on self-selected doctrinal alignments. This process required conversation with difference and the working out of such differences. The ensuing conversations were not necessarily easy, but they were productive. It is especially noteworthy that it was the German-language group who first outlined the case-by-case framework as a pathway to communion. The group came to this agreement even though its participants were a mix of doctrinal conservatives and progressives, including Cardinal Kaspar, the hierarchy's strongest advocate of communion for remarried Catholics, and Cardinal Muller, one of its strongest opponents (as noted earlier). As recounted by German participant Cardinal Reinhard Marx, the group "extensively debated concepts that are, again and again, considered to be opposites" (e.g., mercy and truth) and other core concepts relevant to the development of the Church's teaching on marriage.[52] Despite clear public evidence of doctrinal disagreement (if not polarization) between Kaspar and Muller prior to the Synod, the group managed to find a resolution and to articulate a way forward on which the group unanimously agreed.[53]

The achievement of this particular group-level consensus is interesting in itself. And from a postsecular perspective, it shows that through the process of reciprocal dialogue consensus can be found amid different convictions. Thus, conversation with difference is not only possible but can also be productive in forging a remedial path in the face of a particular problem. And the consensus achieved—as both Francis and postsecularity would expect—is not one that dilutes or negates the differences at issue. Rather, it engages with the differences precisely to work through them to achieve a new understanding of the problem at hand. Further, the breakthrough achieved seems to have been a critical step in shaping the language of the Synod's final report and carving a Church that seeks to be more integrative of different experiences.

Importantly, too, the wording emerged organically from the group-level discussions themselves rather than having been imposed by the final report writers, a committee of ten clerics composed of Synod-elected and Francis-appointed members. And the change emerged notwithstanding strategic interventions that attempted to circumscribe the inclusive direction of the Synod's conversations. For example, on the first day of the 2015 Synod, Cardinal Erdo made an unscheduled speech to the full assembly in which he invoked John Paul's *Familiaris Consortio* #84 to reaffirm the Church's exclusion of divorced and remarried Catholics from communion. He wanted, he explained at a press conference, to give recognition "to the voice of the Church."[54] It was, however, the *voices* of the Church in conversation that forged the consensus of the Synod's final report. This was possible, in part, because the dialogical process in the language groups ensured attentiveness to diverse experiences and perspectives.

The Execution of Dialogue with Difference

Several of the language-group summaries commented on the intragroup process.[55] Summarizing its first week's discussion, English-C, for example, spoke of the patience required by the working-group format and the challenges they experienced in minimizing "discussions that were more semantic than substantial." It was clear, nonetheless, that despite an "imperfect process," the group managed to have an engaged discussion. According to its summary account:

> The going was very slow indeed at times and we are left wondering how on earth we will manage to make our way paragraph by paragraph through the entire document before the end of the Synod. If the task itself has been unclear in this new Synod format, so too have been our method of working. We have had to shape the method as we have moved through the week, and this has challenged the resourcefulness

and tactical sense of the Moderator, to say nothing of the patience of group members. . . . We have spent considerable time discussing language in a way that looks beyond semantic quibbling. For instance, we had a lengthy discussion about what we meant by "the family."

Like English-C, Italian-A reported that while they had "some difficulty with the synod's reformed process and with the methodology used," they "soon adjusted." Indeed, "after much discussion" they unanimously approved all their amendments. Similarly, French-B commented that they had learned to work better together after each session, and French-C expressed their appreciation for the time given to the groups. Spanish-B "looked very positively" on the methodology being used and "the great freedom and fraternity with which participants can discuss the themes"; for this group, "the agreements outweighed the differences" and they found it possible to reach either consensus or unanimity on the various amendments.

Despite initial difficulties, English-C commented in the second week's reports that their process "has matured after past travails." English-D—composed of twenty-nine people including twenty-one bishops from twenty different countries—noted that "working together and offering commentary and amendments" had become "simpler," and there was unanimity in accepting their second report.

The third series of reports, summarizing the groups' discussions of the contentious issues of divorce and remarriage and gays, acknowledged the intensity of the exchanges. One commented that "the issues surfaced strong feelings and sentiments" (English-A), and English-D noted that participants had a "long exchange" and "much discussion." Given the high stakes, it is not surprising that discussions did not necessarily lead to unanimity for each group—as it did for the German speakers, and for some others (e.g., English-B, Italian-C). English-A reported a majority, but not full agreement on certain marriage-related practices and proposals. English-C participants, though using "good tactics and tenacity," were "evenly divided" or "divided" in their conclusions, and other groups reported similar intragroup divisions (e.g., English-D, French-C).

Though the group experiences varied somewhat, these excerpts convey that the working-group format forced an ongoing conversation among participants during the Synod. Reports from the 2014 Synod similarly spoke of the value of joint discussions and praised the process of "reciprocal listening." Additionally, individual bishops praised the Synod as marked by "genuine dialogue" and "fraternal collegiality," despite disagreements.[56] The Synod dialogical process required the bishops to hear the reasoning of diverse others and to articulate their own claims and counterclaims on various points of disagreement. This was so regardless of whether any of the participants came to a new understanding of some elements of the questions at issue, or whether they changed their mind or reached agreement on any specific proposals.

Independent of persisting disagreements and the outcomes achieved, engagement in sustained dialogue can offer clarity and insight, and a certain solidarity or unity of purpose. As reported in the group summaries and as evident in the vote tally on the final report, many disagreed with the final wording on the more contentious issues (with between a fourth and a third voting against the three paragraphs on divorce and remarriage). Yet the dialogical process itself helps crystalize what, despite differences, is at stake. As English-C phrased it in their first week's summary, "We have spoken in different ways of our different experiences of marriage and the family; yet a profound sense of why they matter has emerged."

Paradoxically, if there was a bias in the Synod's procedures, it was a bias that required dialogue rather than suppressed it (as some Synod critics claimed).[57] This may be understood not as a secular bias (which would favor a dilution of the understanding of marriage as a Church-approved sacrament) but, rather, as a postsecular process. It is postsecular because it required reflexive, reciprocal listening across the twin demands of the Catholic doctrinal-sacramental tradition and the relevance of the secularized experience of marriage, divorce, and remarriage. Further, it did not privilege either conservative or liberal voices. Instead, it required conversations that tackled differences of opinion. That task could not be circumvented, even if some conversations may have been motivated by strategic interests rather than consideration of a larger good (e.g., integration).

Language Consciousness

The group-level discussions also reflected the consciousness of language use that is a marker of postsecular translation. As noted earlier, the 2014 pre-Synod *Summary* indicated that the Church should employ more meaningful and accessible language in communicating its teaching on marriage and family. And almost all of the 2015 Synod working groups similarly emphasized the relevance of this. Groups variously called for more attentiveness to the vocabulary in which the Church presents its doctrine. Many argued that "more attractive," less negative, "less legalistic," and more "optimistic" and "joyful" language should be used in framing the Church's teaching on marriage. Some specifically proposed that alongside "indissolubility," the Church should speak of "marriage as a grace, a blessing, and a lifelong covenant of love."[58] On access to the sacraments, a bishop in English-D (#3) argued that it would not only be more "accurate" and "appropriate" but also less negative to say that people in difficult situations "abstain" rather than are "excluded" from communion. Pondering possible reforms, Spanish-B (#3) suggested that instead of talking of a "penitential way," it may be better and more precise in meaning to call it a "path of reconciliation."

While many groups argued that the Church's language should be "more simple" and "accessible to families," there was simultaneous concern that Church teaching should be clearly, coherently, and unequivocally stated. As English-A (#2) noted, "Though every effort should be made to provide for streamlined attractive language, a primary concern was the clarity of well-grounded explanations of Church teaching on marriage and the family." Some bishops, especially English-B, commented that such clarity was especially necessary amid the cultural confusion regarding marriage. In short, as one cardinal remarked at the 2014 Synod, the bishops want to change the "very harsh language that alienates people," but not the teachings themselves.[59]

The bishops' attentiveness to language conveys a postsecular sensibility. It recognizes that faith-based teachings require translation into a vocabulary that is meaningful to people who, regardless of their level of commitment to the Church, may have difficulty grasping its reasoning on specific issues. Changing the language but not the doctrine is complicated. Yet, the Synod made some progress as measured by its own criterion. Acting on the Vatican's pre-Synod concern over the inaccessibility of natural law, the term is not mentioned in any of the official Synod reports. This shift is a departure from previous iterations of Catholic teaching on sexuality, marriage, and family. Some of the Church's other self-criticized language remains. The reports talk of the "domestic Church," for example, and of the "gospel of the family," despite some bishops (like English-C, #1) having explicitly noted the contemporary obscurity of these "Church-speak" terms. A critical step in the Church's efforts to develop a new language is the significance of its language of omission. As I have highlighted, on the two most contentious issues—same-sex relationships, and divorce and remarriage—the Synod omitted phrases that had been central to its teaching. Such omissions constitute more than a silencing of language; they may be interpreted as nuancing the Church's doctrine on both issues. As such, especially in the Catholic hermeneutic, by not reiterating certain well-worn points, the Church tacitly conveys a shift in its understanding even as it simultaneously reaffirms its teaching. This teaching is clear that: "The Sacrament of Matrimony as a faithful and indissoluble union between a man and a woman, called to accept one another and to welcome life, is a great grace for the human family."[60]

In sum, despite its attention to the importance of finding more accessible language, it is not clear that the Synod should be considered a "language event," as warranted by Vatican II. No new doctrinal phrasing as such emerged. The symbolically important language of discernment and accompanying infused the Synod deliberations and documents. Yet, this phrasing had already become prominent with Francis's statements more broadly (e.g., *Joy of the Gospel*). We can, however, consider the Synod a postsecular event for the various reasons I have articulated here, including its language consciousness.

Conclusion: *The Synod's Postsecular Import*

The Synod's willingness to reflexively examine its teachings on marriage and family life, its openness to Catholics' secular experiences, and its deliberate dialogical engagement with the mutual relevance of doctrinal ideas and Catholic realities support its characterization as a postsecular event. The Synod's achieved consensus on divorce and remarriage—encapsulated in its final report—tilted more toward change than confirmed the status quo (though in continuity with Church doctrine). As such, it pushes Church doctrine and practices toward greater attunement with Catholic and secular realities. This outcome was not *pre*determined by the Synod methodology or by the personalities involved. It was, however, impacted by its methodology and, we can infer, by the reasonableness and diversity of the arguments exchanged in group discussions. It was also influenced by Francis's naming of the problem—the very act of convening an extraordinary Synod that would focus candidly on the diverse realities of Catholic family life—and by the doctrinal and linguistic interventions of specific bishops over the course of the Synod. The Synod's two-year process, and the extensive intrahierarchical and public discussions it stimulated, opened up debate about complicated doctrinal and pastoral questions on issues central to Catholic teaching and to secular society. In doing so, it foregrounded the negotiation of crosscutting religious and secular currents, the Church's own tradition of doctrinal reflexivity, and the diversity of Catholic realities and interpretive activity.

As I have argued, the convening of the Synod and its extensive preparations—in particular its openness to the empirical diversity of Catholics' lived experiences, its expectation of honest and open discussion, and its consciousness of the importance of culturally accessible language in conveying Church teaching—demonstrated postsecular attunement. The Church showed an eagerness to bridge the secular expectations and experiences that challenge its teachings on marriage and sexual relationships, while simultaneously affirming their authoritative nature. The Synod did not formally change Church teaching on marriage, but it refined and moved forward Church doctrine on divorced and remarried Catholics. More generally, its emphasis on the communal integration of couples in "irregular" situations, its reframing of some well-settled previous readings of Church teachings, and its language of omission mark significant symbolic shifts in doctrine and are ones that are more closely aligned with both secular realities and Catholics' experiences and aspirations (including the aspiration to fully participate in the Church despite an "irregularity").

Amid tensions in Catholicism between tradition and change—the religious and the secular—the Synod highlighted the relevance of tradition as a resource for doctrinal change. As I discussed, John Paul II's *Familiaris Consortio*, an authoritative source of theology on marriage, was an important reference point during the Synod deliberations. It could have being instrumental in reinforcing Church teaching on the exclusion of divorced and remarried Catholics from communion. Instead, it was incorporated in ways that helped to facilitate consensus approval of a nuanced but consequential shift in the Church's position. Thus, a resource in the doctrinal tradition becomes a resource for achieving change in the face of secular realities, and does so while simultaneously maintaining continuity with the tradition. Similarly, the Synod implicitly conveyed a symbolically significant deemphasis in the Church's previous focus on gay sexual acts. In contemporary Catholicism, therefore, the living tradition of Catholic doctrine both absorbs and is integrated into the secularization of the Church and of everyday Catholic life.

The Synod also drew attention to the Church's postsecular limits. It highlighted the Church's clerical culture evident in the Assembly's exclusion of women as voting participants, and its more general marginalization of lay Catholics and the diversity of their experiences. The Synod also revealed the intensity of intrahierarchical doctrinal politics, and pointed to the challenge entailed in the postsecular expectation of reciprocal engagement with contrasting convictions. Some bishops' relatively cemented doctrinal alignments, however, provide a reminder that the Church is a human, social institution whose leaders have varied interests and aspirations and who differ in their sensitivity and responsiveness to diverse lived realities.

The public disagreements among the bishops further underscore that no one voice speaks for the Church, including for the Church hierarchy. The exposure of such differentiation reinforces the facticity (and legitimacy) of interpretive diversity within Catholicism, and thus has a secularizing impact. It reminds Catholics (and others) that the teaching authority of the Church embodied by the pope and his fellow bishops is not a monolithic entity characterized by a mystically endowed, doctrinal unanimity. It also points to the fact that doctrine is not calcified and that the process of doctrine formation is messy and contested—and an ongoing interpretive activity. Further, such disagreements expose to Catholic public scrutiny the array of arguments used to favor or oppose a certain doctrinal position. Therefore, even though lay Catholics did not formally participate as voters in the Synod deliberations, in their own conversational circles they can evaluate and reflect on the various arguments aired by the bishops. Attentive followers of the Synod will know, for example, that the bishops initially commented very positively on gay relationships (see the 2014 midterm report), even though that language was subsequently discarded. Intrahierarchical disagreements can thus contribute to Catholics' conscience formation and their discernment of the morality of their past, present, or intended-future sexual and/or marital behavior.

Finally, the Synod validated postsecular expectations of the necessity and fruitfulness of dialogue with difference. The Synod addressed complicated issues that brought forth key tensions in Catholicism. Yet, its communicative structure—in particular its language groups—fostered dialogue among participants with different doctrinal positions, opinions, and perspectives. The intragroup dialogical process yielded some unanimity, but also some disagreements. The disagreements, however, were not sufficient to prevent the achievement of a consensus—a minimum two-thirds' approval—regarding each of the final report's paragraphs, including on its most contested questions. Such consensus can well be considered a positive outcome of the Synod. It is also one that contributes to the Church's postsecular relevance, as it holds together the twin pulls of the religious and the secular within the Church and in society at large.

Postsecular Catholicism

A CONTINUOUS DIALOGUE OF DOCTRINAL IDEAS AND SECULAR REALITIES

MEETING CATHOLICS WHERE they are is what postsecular relevance requires. Francis shows himself to be remarkably open to this encounter. He recognizes that Catholics' lived realities are secular realities and *simultaneously* are infused with God's presence and the meanings and beliefs endowed by Catholicism. The task of encounter requires ongoing conversation between religious ideas and secular realities. This is easier said than done, of course.

Its tensions are well exemplified by *Amoris Laetitia* (*AL*), Francis's response to the Synod on the Family, to which I now turn. I focus in this final chapter on *AL* because its content and contested reception allow me to summarize how Francis amplifies the Church's postsecular relevance while also holding together the dynamic interplay in Catholicism between ideas and realities, tradition and change, and hierarchical authority and interpretive autonomy.

Amoris Laetitia (The Joy of Love)

Published in April 2016, *Amoris Laetitia* (*AL*), underscores the secular accessibility of Francis's discourse.[1] It deploys a mostly straightforward and culturally resonant vocabulary, with several evocative passages on the joys of love building on St. Paul's well-known epistle ("Love is patient and kind . . . "). It elaborates on how "the gaze of love" and the growth of love must be nourished by a couple's ability to listen to one another, to dialogue with an open mind, and to nourish their dialogue through shared experiences (*AL* #128, 137, 139, 141, 145). Invoking the scene of a grateful hug in the film *Babette's Feast*, Francis argues that "since we were made for love, we know that there is no greater joy than that of sharing good things." In his framing, bringing joy to others is at the core of the human vocation; it is a selfless joy of "lovers who delight in the good of those whom they love, who give freely to them and thus bear good fruit" (*AL* #129).

AL extensively emphasizes the importance of discernment, a theme prominent in Francis's remarks from the outset of his papacy and one given much attention at the Synod. Showing an attentive ear to the expectations of American Catholics, *AL* also has a strong emphasis on conscience and lived experience. In what might be considered a rebuke to bishops' and priests' intrusiveness into sexual behavior, Francis asserts that "We have been called to form consciences, not to replace them" (*AL* #37). He insists, nonetheless, that the Church cannot depart from its commitment to the religious-based values of marriage. Yet, he simultaneously demonstrates the self-critique of a contrite Church by explicitly acknowledging deficiencies in the Church's teaching competence. He states:

> At times we have also proposed a far too abstract and almost artificial theological ideal of marriage, far removed from the concrete situations and practical possibilities of real families. This excessive idealization, especially when we have failed to inspire trust in God's grace, has not helped to make marriage more desirable and attractive, but quite the opposite [#36]. We have long thought that simply by stressing doctrinal, bioethical and moral issues, without encouraging openness to grace, we were providing sufficient support to families, strengthening the marriage bond and giving meaning to marital life. We find it difficult to present marriage more as a dynamic path to personal development and fulfillment than as a lifelong burden. We also find it hard to make room for the consciences of the faithful, who very often respond as best they can to the Gospel amid their limitations, and are capable of carrying out their own discernment in complex situations. We have been called to form consciences, not to replace them. (#37)

Further in tune with postsecular expectations, he notes that persuasion, not Church authority, is the approach required to bring people to an appreciation of what the Church teaches; "it is [not] helpful" he states, "to try to impose rules by sheer authority" (*AL* #35). *AL* also reflects the postsecular expectation of attentiveness to empirical realities and Francis's own recurring emphasis that ideas should be in continuous dialogue with realities (*JG* #231). These family realities, in keeping with his concerns about economic inequality (see chapter 3), necessarily include an array of economic problems. *AL* thus elaborates (as did the Synod documents) on how marriage and family life are undermined by poverty, migration, unemployment, and a lack of affordable housing, as well as by domestic violence, pornography, alcohol and drug abuse, consumerism, and narcissism.

But again, Francis notes that the Church must proactively engage with these realities, not simply denounce them. Thus, he states, "there is no sense in simply decrying present-day evils, as if this could change things" (*AL* #35). Conveying that contemporary realities are not a threat to Catholicism, *AL* affirms the diversity of Catholic families, including the "stability" offered by same sex-unions (*AL* #52; see chapter 4). It specifically states that divorced and remarried or cohabiting Catholics are not excommunicated, and should be encouraged to "participate in the life of the [Christian] community" (*AL* #243). However, it does not indicate that they might benefit from the nourishment of the Eucharist, though it explicitly advises this for individuals who have not remarried (*AL* #242). Nonetheless, it acknowledges that the diverse circumstances and extenuating conditions of divorced and remarried Catholics mean that they cannot be rigidly categorized or pigeon-holed (*AL* #298), and it affirms the Synod's recommendation that "irregular" Catholic couples should engage in conscientious discernment of their circumstances in conversation with a priest (*AL* #300), the "internal forum."

AL's stress on discernment, conscience, and particular circumstances bolsters the inference that "irregular" Catholics can—and should—be more fully integrated into the Church and able to avail themselves of an individualized pathway to Communion (as the Synod suggested). Indeed, as Francis unequivocally states, "no one can be condemned forever," as that would be contrary to the logic of the gospel (*AL* #297).[2] He elaborates, moreover, on the relevance in Catholic theology of mitigating factors that reduce moral fault. Of particular significance, he clarifies that "it can no longer simply be said that all those in any 'irregular' situation are living in a state of mortal sin and are deprived of sanctifying grace" (*AL* #301). He also notes that even in situations of objective sin—in which individuals may or may not be subjectively culpable—the person can benefit from the Church's help. Importantly, "in certain cases this can include the help of the sacraments" (*AL* #305; fn. 351). *AL* does not specify which sacraments might be appropriate. But given the context of Synod debate about participation in Communion, it is significant that Francis states here that "the Eucharist is not a prize for the perfect."

The Intricate Dance of Integration in Catholicism

Taken as a whole, *AL* offers a welcoming message to "irregular" Catholics. It extends the possibility of their full integration into the Catholic community, even as Francis acknowledges, quoting Benedict, that no "easy recipes" exist (*AL* #298). In many respects, *AL* represents a delicate postsecular negotiation of faith and reason, of doctrinal ideas and secular realities. The "internal forum" of an individualized pastoral discernment process is spiritually promising. Yet sociologically, it is limiting even as it is also empowering. This is because the internal forum does not confer public legitimacy. Thus, *AL* does not disturb Catholicism's holding together of tradition and change, and simultaneously, the dance of hierarchical authority and individual interpretive autonomy. This is a maneuver that allows the accommodation of both doctrinal truths and changing realities.

It is accomplished through *AL*'s reiteration of the Church's long standing preoccupation with the "avoidance of scandal," a concern that underlies its distinction between private sexual behavior and public behavior or Catholic identity. In this framing, while individual Catholics in "irregular" situations might conscientiously discern (with pastoral advice) the moral appropriateness of their particular relationship, the Church requires that this subjective resolution not be publicized. As Francis states, one "can't flaunt objective sin" (*AL* #297). Church officials say that they don't want the outcome of sincere discernment to stoke misunderstanding of the Church's teaching on marriage, or to stoke perception of a double standard in the Church (*AL* #300). Discernment requires that "love for the Church and her teaching" (*AL* #300) should always come before the individual's own desires. Thus, the integration of divorced and remarried Catholics must be done in ways that avoid "any occasion of scandal" (*AL* #299).

This principle extends to any Catholics in "irregular" situations, including LGBT and cohabiting heterosexual couples. It helps explain, for example, the firing of openly gay and lesbian teachers in Catholic schools. This trend has, in fact, accelerated with Francis's papacy—likely driven both by the increased visibility of married same-sex Catholics and localized episcopal pushback against Francis's articulation of a more inclusive message on sexuality.[3] In the Church's scandal-avoidance frame, one might be subjectively inculpable (absolved from sin), but if one's public identity is objectively contrary to Church teaching, the Church requires suppression of that part of identity that contradicts its teaching. In practical terms, this means that individuals must silence either the public expression of their Catholicism or the public recognition of their divorced and remarried, gay, or cohabiting status.

Bifurcated Identity

This forced choice is highly consequential in the everyday lives of many Catholics. Being gay, or divorced and remarried (without an annulment), are (still) objectively stigmatized identities in official Church teaching. This is so, notwithstanding the impressive symbolic gains in the Church's acceptance of gay Catholics (see chapter 4), its concrete steps toward integrating divorced and remarried Catholics (see chapter 6; and *AL* discussed earlier), and the sociological normalization of gay, divorced, and cohabiting Catholics (see chapter 2). The public visibility of being openly gay or divorced and remarried, in contrast to the privacy of contraception use, for example, means that in practice contraception-using Catholics partake of Communion (with or without absolution despite their objective contravening of Church teaching) and can be visibly engaged in the Church, while divorced and remarried or gay Catholics have that freedom curbed.

For Catholics in "irregular" situations, the hierarchy's scandal-avoidance dictum requires a bifurcated understanding of identity.[4] It conveys that one can be either Catholic or divorced and remarried, but not Catholic *and* divorced and remarried; that one can be either Catholic or gay, but not Catholic *and* gay, and so on. Official Church discourse requires Catholics to choose one over the other; they cannot embody both simultaneously. This bifurcation is in tension with the postsecular recognition that religion matters alongside and in mutual conversation with the secular. It is also contrary to the embodied intersectionality in how Catholics experience identity and engage everyday life (see chapter 2). It is further in tension with the Church's own institutional affirmation of the continuity across religious and secular, private and public activities.

Hierarchical Authority and Interpretive Autonomy

The interpretive autonomy within Catholicism means that, as on other issues, many "irregular" Catholics will actively negotiate the challenges presented to their everyday reality, notwithstanding the Church's scandal-avoidance concerns. Lay Catholics, as I've shown throughout the book, drive the reality-maintenance work of Catholicism. Their practical negotiation of religious and secular expectations contributes to the defining—and the modifying—of the institutional and social reality of Catholicism. Their everyday experiences of sexuality and family life push the hierarchy to revisit doctrines and pastoral practices, and thus accelerate the normalization processes that create and reinforce new realities.[5]

Nonetheless, their everyday reality must still contend with the Church's hierarchical authority. Its reach is exemplified by the pastoral guidelines elaborated by Archbishop Chaput of Philadelphia for the implementation of *AL*. Church teaching, he clarifies, requires divorced and civilly remarried Catholics to abstain from sexual intimacy. Further,

> Even where . . . they live under one roof in chaste continence and have received absolution (so that they are free from personal sin), the unhappy fact remains that, objectively speaking, their public state and condition of life in the new relationship are contrary to Christ's teaching against divorce . . . . where pastors give Communion to divorced and remarried persons trying to live chastely, they should do so in a manner that will avoid giving scandal or implying that Christ's teaching can be set aside. In other contexts also, care must be taken to avoid the unintended appearance of an endorsement of divorce and civil remarriage; thus divorced and civilly remarried persons should not hold positions of responsibility in a parish (e.g., on a parish council), nor should they carry out liturgical ministries or functions (e.g., lector, extraordinary minister of Holy Communion). . . . [T]wo persons in an active, public same-sex relationship, no matter how sincere, offer a serious counter-witness to Catholic belief, which can only produce moral confusion in the community. Such a relationship cannot be accepted into the life of the parish without undermining the faith of the community, most notably the children. Finally, those living openly same-sex lifestyles should not hold positions of responsibility in a parish, nor should they carry out any liturgical ministry or function.[6]

In short, actively engaged Catholics cannot present in public a personal identity that, in Church terms, is contradictory to Catholic teaching. This constriction is not confined to the specific public context of the parish or church ministry but applies as well to any visible Catholic. The threat posed to Church authority by such deviations also accounts for why Church officials criticize Catholic politicians whose actions convey messages contrary to Church teachings on abortion and same-sex relations.[7]

Like Chaput, some other bishops have pushed back against *AL*'s themes of conscience and discernment. A pastoral letter issued by Archbishop Sample of Portland, Oregon, similarly emphasizes that objective moral truth has primacy over conscience, and that fundamental moral truths (e.g., the indissolubility of marriage) do not change regardless of context.[8] And, most notably,

Cardinal Burke (who was also highly critical of the Synod; see chapter 6) has stated that *AL* is not formal teaching but, rather, "a mixture of doctrine and opinion," a highly controversial claim given the authoritative status in Catholicism of an apostolic exhortation (as *AL* is called). He and some other conservative Catholics are thus challenging both the substance and the authority of the theology of marriage articulated by Francis.[9]

Other high-profile cardinals and bishops, however, emphasize that *AL* is consistent with and faithful to Church doctrine. They interpret it as a pastoral document requiring the accompaniment of divorced and remarried Catholics in "a process of discernment and of conscience."[10] Moreover, the Vatican's official newspaper, *L'Osservatore Romano*, published an article by an ecclesiologist explaining that *AL* is indeed authoritative "papal teaching, to which Catholics are obliged to give 'religious submission of will and intellect.'"[11] This is what Francis Sullivan calls "sincere assent" (see chapter 2). As on other issues (e.g., contraception), some will be able to give sincere assent while others will not. Ironically, the nonassenters on *AL*, in contrast to *Humanae Vitae* and other teachings on sexual morality, are doctrinal conservatives.

The views of Cardinal Burke and Archbishop Chaput—clerics well known for the sharp edge of their conservatism—undoubtedly reflect a strand of political backlash against Francis's openness to secular realities. In contradistinction to his emphasis that ideas should not become detached from realities or used to obscure them (*JG* #231), they convey that doctrinal ideas are more important than secular realities. In their view, doctrine should be detached from secular influences rather than complicated by them, a position contrary to the postsecular expectation of religious–secular dialogue.

Nevertheless, these public doctrinal disagreements enrich the diversity of Catholic interpretive activity. Further, they reinforce Catholics' everyday lived knowledge that there may not be one universal teaching applicable to all Catholics in all circumstances. It is from within such everyday experiences that doctrinal ideas get refined, and push the Church to encompass new directions while maintaining continuity with the Catholic (pluralistic) tradition.[12] *AL* accomplishes this even as its meanings, distinctions, and ambiguities are variously contested.

The Process of Change

In any case, no one exhortation alone, or any one event no matter how momentous—such as Vatican II—or as significant as the Synod on the Family, is unequivocally decisive. Rather, the integration of realities and ideas is processual and not achieved by fiat or decree. It is—as Francis notes and as postsecularity expects—a continuing dialogue. Thus, any lost opportunity, such as the silencing of women's ordination, is not lost forever; it can be recovered. New arrangements can emerge from the multiple doctrinal strands already in place. And as we saw with the Synod on the Family, all its various reports—including its midterm and working documents—are, as emphasized by Francis, part of official Church discourse. Any of their slender strands, therefore, including the 2014 midterm report's affirmation of gay Catholics, are grist for ongoing conversations with new and changing realities. This is perhaps the current achievement: the clear acknowledgment of the diversity of Catholic couples and families, including as noted, same-sex unions, the strong affirmation of discernment and conscience, that Church officials are called to form but not to replace conscience, the acknowledgment that sheer authority is not only ineffective but also an inappropriate intrusion on human reason, and the clarification that "irregular" Catholics—those not living in accord with official Church teaching on sexual morality and marriage—are not excommunicated, but are considered integral to the Catholic community (despite limits on the flaunting of objective sin).

Consequently, the cat is out of the bag. There is no going back. Theoretically, the postsecular turn means that the public relevance of religion cannot be denied and contemporary society must adjust to it. By the same token, postsecular Catholicism cannot deny the press of secular experiences and expectations on the articulation of doctrine, and must adjust to the fact that the Church's relevance among Catholics and society at large lies in dialogue *with* secular realities. In short, postsecularity means that neither religious nor secular realities can be denied.

Amoris Laetitia, the Synod on the Family (see chapter 6), and the Church's public engagement on economic inequality and climate change (see chapter 3) stand out as evidence that Catholicism doesn't have to be weighed down by defeatism. It has the resources to recraft—and is recrafting—a realistic narrative in which the Church has renewed relevance for a contrite modernity, as well as for increasingly secularized Catholics. Francis's engagement across these and other issues (including abortion and same-sex relationships; see chapter 4) illuminates the effort to build a more inclusive Catholicism as well as a more inclusive society. The projects are interrelated—necessarily so, given the crosscutting religious and secular influences in the Church, as in society. There are limits to this narrative, of course. In particular, the Church's silencing of debate on women's ordination (see chapter 4) contravenes the postsecular and Francis's emphasis on the need for dialogue between ideas and realities, and also impedes the Church's project of institutional renewal. Similarly, the U.S. bishops' religious freedom campaign, despite its cultural resonance, appears primarily driven by the bishops' interests in impeding the secularization of sexual morality (see chapter 5).

The ongoing dialogue between doctrinal ideas and secular realities in the enactment of Catholicism will again be showcased at the Synod on Youth, taking place in October 2018. It will see further examination of the realities of Catholicism and reflexive engagement with those realities. Young people's life contexts are different to those of their parents and grandparents, underscored by the fact that young American Catholics are part of the most religiously unaffiliated generation. They are strongly committed to the remediation of climate change, and their ethnic–economic divide calls attention to the problems of economic and social exclusion. They are also more likely to identify as LGBT. Further, a large majority of their generation consider gay marriage and heterosexual marriage as equally normal and, for many, cohabiting and other nonmarital relationships are preferred options.[13]

Meeting young Catholics as they are, therefore—listening to their reality, as Francis has indicated, to their "voice, [their] sensitivities . . . [their] faith . . . [and their] criticism"—accentuates the relevance of postsecular expectations.[14] It requires the Church to be publicly engaged on pressing societal issues and simultaneously responsive to Catholics' changing, increasingly secularized definitions of sexual morality and family life. The findings presented in this book suggest that Catholicism is up to that task. It has the doctrinal and institutional resources to do so, and importantly, it has a recent exemplary case—the Synod on the Family—of how it can move forward. Further, notwithstanding the impediments presented by a deep-seated clerical culture, the Church has expressed its resolve to continue its project of renewal.[15] The current focus on youth—the intergenerational linchpin of intra-Catholic and Church-society relations—reinforces this commitment.

The Catholic Church has many resources that well match the postsecular turn. The extent to which it continues to proactively maintain conversation between Church doctrines and secular realities will likely determine both the trajectory of its institutional renewal and its societal relevance. The dialogue between religious and secular expectations—and thus the steering of a contrite modernity and the maintenance of a relevant Catholicism—is both energized and complicated by the fact that the interpretive work of Catholicism is not confined to any single site, voice, or issue. This is so, notwithstanding the structural significance of the Church hierarchy. As shown across this book, such interpretive activity unveils many points of disagreement (including *within* the hierarchy, as well as between laity and Church officials). Different religious traditions deal with doctrinal disagreements in different ways. But in Catholicism, the simultaneous hold of faith and reason and of hierarchical authority and interpretive autonomy guides the development and refinement of doctrine. This means that doctrinal disagreements are part and parcel of its lived reality and thus also of its negotiation of tradition and change. Such disagreements, despite the claims of some commentators, do not portend a schism.[16] Catholicism is a reflexive encounter with diverse, increasingly secularized realities and about finding a good-enough communal unity in and amid such diversity.

Notes

CHAPTER 1

1. The divide was 51 percent (tradition) to 49 percent (change); Pew Research Center, *U.S. Catholics Divided on Church's Direction under New Pope* (Washington, DC: Pew Research Center, February 21, 2013): 1.

2. The Second Vatican Council (Vatican II) affirmed the separation of church and state; see its "Pastoral Constitution on the Church in the Modern World," #73–76, in Walter Abbott, ed., *The Documents of Vatican II* (New York: Herder and Herder, 1966). On the Church's historical expectations that public policy would encode Catholic teachings, see, for example, John H. Whyte, *Church and State in Modern Ireland* (Dublin: Gill and Macmillan, 1980).

3. *Catechism of the Catholic Church* (Dublin: Veritas, 1994), #2180 n1118.

4. See Andrew Greeley, *Religion in Europe at the End of the Second Millennium* (New Brunswick, NJ: Transaction, 2003); Pew Research Center, *Religion in Latin America: Widespread Change in a Historically Catholic Region* (Washington, DC: Pew Research Center, November 13, 2014); Bendixen and Amandi International/Univision, *Global Survey of Roman Catholics* (January 2014); and Angela Coco, *Catholics, Conflicts and Choices* (Durham, UK: Acumen, 2013).

5. Max Weber, quoting Leo Tolstoy. See Max Weber, "Science as a Vocation," in H. H. Gerth and C. W. Mills, eds., *From Max Weber: Essays in Sociology* (New York: Oxford University Press, 1919/1943), 143.

6. Arlie Hochschild, *Strangers in Their Own Land* (New York: New Press, 2016), probes the marginalization felt by white, conservative, middle- and working-class Americans.

7. On the relation between science and values, see Weber, "Science as a Vocation"; and on trust in science, see Gordon Gauchat, "Politicization of Science in the Public Sphere: A Study of Public Trust in the United States, 1974–2010," *American Sociological Review* 77 (2012): 167–187.

8. Jurgen Habermas, in Virgil Nemoianu, "The Church and the Secular Establishment: A Philosophical Dialog between Joseph Ratzinger and Jurgen Habermas," *Logos* 9 (2006): 17–42, 26.

9. John XXIII, December 1961, announcing his decision to convoke Vatican II for some time in 1962; see Abbott, *Documents of Vatican II*, 704. For secular scholarly critique of the role of scientific and technical rationality in perpetuating inequality and human destruction, see Max Horkheimer and Theodor Adorno, *The Dialectic of Enlightenment* (Stanford, CA: Stanford University Press, 1972/2002).

10. John XXIII's opening speech at Vatican II, October 11, 1962, in Abbott, *Documents of Vatican II*, 712.

11. Ibid.

12. The everyday changes included a new understanding of the central role of the laity in the life of the Church and in society; the language used in the Mass, from Latin to English or other native languages; and the affirmation of conscience and religious freedom.

13. "Pastoral Constitution," #2; and Abbott, *Documents of Vatican II*, 3 n2. For an introduction to Vatican II, see Abbott, *Documents of Vatican II* for its texts and for commentaries on them. See also John O'Malley, *What Happened at Vatican II* (Cambridge, MA: Harvard University Press, 2008), and Melissa Wilde, *Vatican II* (Princeton, NJ: Princeton University Press, 2007).

14. Jurgen Habermas, "Notes on Post-Secular Society," *New Perspectives Quarterly* 25 (2008): 17–29, 11; Jurgen Habermas, *An Awareness of What Is Missing: Faith and Reason in a Post-Secular Age* (San Francisco: Ignatius Press, 2010), 73, 75; and Habermas in Nemoianu, "Church and Secular Establishment," 26. This acknowledgment of the public value of religion marked a major shift in Habermas's thinking. His earlier writings on the public sphere and his theory of communicative action rejected even moderate religion as a resource in public discourse, owing to its limited rationality. For a critique, see Michele Dillon, "The Authority of the Holy Revisited: Habermas, Religion, and Emancipatory Possibilities," *Sociological Theory* 17 (1999): 290–306.

15. See, for example, Robert Bellah, Richard Madsen, William Sullivan, Ann Swidler, and Steven Tipton, *Habits of the Heart: Individualism and Commitment in American Life* (Berkeley: University of California Press, 1985); and Mary Ann Glendon, *Abortion and Divorce in Western Law* (Cambridge, MA: Harvard University Press, 1987).

16. See, for example, David J. O'Brien, *Public Catholicism* (New York: Orbis Books, 1989); and Jose Casanova, *Public Religions in the Modern World* (Chicago: University of Chicago Press, 1994).

17. See Nathan Hatch, *The Democratization of American Christianity* (New Haven, CT: Yale University Press, 1989).

18. On the secularization of education and public culture in the United States that intensified in the late nineteenth century, see Christian Smith, "Introduction: Rethinking

the Secularization of American Public Life," in Christian Smith, ed., *The Secular Revolution* (Berkeley: University of California Press, 2003), 1–96.

19. Max Weber, *The Protestant Ethic and the Spirit of Capitalism* (New York: Scribner's, 1904–1905) traces the secularization of wealth from its early Calvinist origins.

20. Robert Jones, Daniel Cox, Betsy Cooper, and Rachel Lienesch, *Exodus: Why Americans Are Leaving Religion—And Why They're Unlikely to Come Back* (Washington, DC: Public Religion Research Institute, September 2016).

21. Mark Chaves, "Secularization as Declining Religious Authority," *Social Forces* 72 (1994): 749–774.

22. On the democratization of Christianity, see Hatch, *Democratization*. On the cultural significance of denominationalism, see R. Stephen Warner, "Work in Progress toward a New Paradigm for the Sociological Study of Religion in the United States," *American Journal of Sociology* 98 (1993): 1044–1093. On religious freedom and church shopping in American lives in the 1940s and '50s, see Michele Dillon and Paul Wink, *In the Course of a Lifetime: Tracing Religious Belief, Practice, and Change* (Berkeley: University of California Press, 2007), 60–79.

23. My discussion of Catholic interpretive autonomy builds on my earlier research in Michele Dillon, *Catholic Identity: Balancing Reason, Faith, and Power* (New York: Cambridge University Press, 1999).

24. Habermas, "Notes," 3–4. On the tensions and complexities in Habermas's use of postsecularity, see Michele Dillon, "Jurgen Habermas and the Post-Secular Appropriation of Religion: A Sociological Critique," in Philip Gorski, David Kim, John Torpey, and Jonathan Van Antwerpen, eds., *Probing the Post-Secular* (New York: New York University Press/Social Science Research Council, 2012), 249–278; and other essays in that volume. See also William Barbieri, ed., *At the Limits of the Secular* (Grand Rapids, MI: Eerdmans, 2014).

25. Habermas, "Notes," 7; Habermas, *Awareness*, 16.

26. Habermas, "Notes," 11; Habermas, *Awareness*, 16, 22.

27. Habermas, *Awareness*, 16, 23. See also Robert Wuthnow, *The God Problem. Expressing Faith and Being Reasonable* (Berkeley: University of California Press, 2012), 39–40.

28. Throughout this book, when I reference "the U.S. bishops," I am referring to the collective voice of the U.S. bishops articulated through its collaborative organization, the U.S. Conference of Catholic Bishops (USCCB), and its various committees (see www.usccb.org). Individual bishops may disagree with statements issued by the USCCB. On the cultural frames used by the U.S. bishops on abortion, see Michele Dillon, "Cultural Differences in the Abortion Discourse of the Catholic Church: Evidence from Four Countries," *Sociology of Religion* 57 (1996): 25–36.

29. Wuthnow, *God Problem*, 39–40.

30. Habermas, in Nemoianu, "Church and Secular Establishment," 27.

31. Habermas, *Awareness*, 76.

32. Habermas, *Awareness*, 18, states: "My motive for addressing the issue of faith and knowledge is to mobilize modern reason against the defeatism lurking within it. Postmetaphysical thinking cannot cope on its own with the defeatism concerning reason which we encounter today both in the postmodern radicalization of the 'dialectic of the Enlightenment' and in the naturalism founded on a naïve faith in science."

33. See, for example, the crisis observations of John McGreevey, *Catholicism and American Freedom* (New York: Norton, 2003), 289–293; Peter Steinfels, *A People Adrift: The Crisis of the Roman Catholic Church in America* (New York: Simon and Schuster, 2003); and Hans Kung, "Church in Worst Credibility Crisis since Reformation," *Irish Times*, April 16, 2010, www.irishtimes.com.

34. In the U.S., fifteen dioceses have declared bankruptcy as a result of financial costs incurred from lawsuits related to sex abuse; see, for example, Dan Morris-Young, "Great Falls-Billings Diocese Becomes Fifteenth to File for Bankruptcy," *National Catholic Reporter*, April 3, 2017, www.ncronline.org. On the range of issues raised by the sex-abuse crisis, see, for example, Jean Bartunek, Mary Ann Hinsdale, and James Keenan, eds., *Church Ethics and Its Organizational Context: Learning from the Sex Abuse Scandal in the Catholic Church* (Lanham, MD: Rowman & Littlefield, 2006). On its impact on the credibility and pastoral leadership of Church leaders, see William D'Antonio, Michele Dillon, and Mary Gautier, *American Catholics in Transition* (Lanham, MD: Rowman & Littlefield, 2013), 83–86.

35. On lay-hierarchy divisions in American Catholicism, see D'Antonio et al., *Catholics in Transition*; Jerome Baggett, *Sense of the Faithful* (New York: Oxford University Press, 2009); and Mary Ellen Konieczny, *The Spirit's Tether: Family, Work and Religion among American Catholics* (New York: Oxford University Press, 2013).

36. Michael Hout and Claude Fischer, "Explaining Why More Americans Have No Religious Affiliation: Political Backlash and Generational Succession, 1972–2012," *Sociological Science* 1 (2014): 423–447; Jones et al., *Exodus*; and Pew Research Center, *America's Changing Religious Landscape* (Washington, DC: Pew Research Center, May 2015).

37. Jones et al., *Exodus*, 4, and Pew, *America's Changing Landscape*, 9, estimate that 13 percent of Americans are former Catholics.

38. See Jones et al., *Exodus*, 3, on generational disaffiliation. On young Catholics, see Christian Smith, Kyle Longest, Jonathan Hill, and Kari Christoffersen, *Young Catholic America* (New York: Oxford University Press, 2014). See also D'Antonio et al., *Catholics in Transition*, 139–150.

39. Benedict outlined his apology in a "Pastoral Letter to the Catholics of Ireland," March 19, 2010. He issued the letter not long after the Irish bishops had gone to Rome at his invitation to give an accounting of Ireland's sex-abuse cases. In pointing to secularization, he cited the loosening of Catholic faith and of adherence to Church teachings. The letter—and all papal encyclicals, exhortations and formal addresses, statements, and letters that I reference in this book are easily accessed

from the Vatican's website: http://w2.vatican.va/content/vatican/en.html (filtered by "Supreme Pontiffs").

40. In June 2002, a few months after the *Boston Globe's* exposure of the sex-abuse scandals in the United States, the U.S. bishops' then president, Bishop Wilton Gregory, apologized for the bishops' derelict leadership regarding abuse; see Teresa Watanabe, "US Bishops Apologize for Scandal," *Los Angeles Times*, June 14, 2002. Most recently, Australian archbishops have apologized for their leadership failures; see "Australian Archbishops: Leadership on Abuse was 'Catastrophic Failure,'" *Catholic News Service*, February 24, 2017, www.catholicnews.com.

41. Benedict, "Letter to the Catholics of Ireland."

42. See, for example, Cardinal Ratzinger's pre-Conclave address (April 18, 2005) to his fellow Cardinals convened at the Vatican for the conclave that would elect him pope.

43. Ratzinger, in Virgil Nemoianu, "The Church and the Secular Establishment: A Philosophical Dialog between Joseph Ratzinger and Jurgen Habermas," *Logos* 9 (2006): 17–42, 27–30,

44. Benedict, in his 2007 encyclical *Spe Salvi* #22.

45. See *New York Times*, April 2, 2014, A17.

46. The Eucharist, the *Catechism* (#1324) states, is "the source and summit" of Catholic faith.

47. See, for example, Laurie Goodstein, "New Fight on a Speaker at a Catholic University," *New York Times*, May 17, 2012, A20. More generally, some bishops such as Archbishop Chaput denounce Catholic colleges that give awards to Catholic and non-Catholic political leaders (e.g., President Obama) whose public positions deviate from the Church's teachings on sexual morality. See, for example, Chaput's Tocqueville Lecture on Religious Freedom, delivered at the University of Notre Dame, September 15, 2016, www.archphila.org.

48. On religion as discursive community, see, for example, Habermas, *Awareness*, 76, and Wuthnow, *God Problem*, 38–39. On Vatican II's construal of interpretive community, see Dillon, *Catholic Identity*, 45–53; and chapter 2 in this book.

49. Peter Berger and Thomas Luckmann, *The Social Construction of Reality* (New York: Anchor Books), 19–20, state: "Everyday life presents itself as a reality interpreted by [ordinary individuals] and subjectively meaningful to them as a coherent world. . . . [It] is not only taken for granted as reality by [them] . . . in the subjectively meaningful conduct of their lives. It is a world that originates in their thoughts and actions, and is maintained as real by these."

CHAPTER 2

1. Michael Hout and Claude Fischer, "Why More Americans Have No Religious Preference: Politics and Generations," *American Sociological Review* 67 (2002): 165–190; Hout and Fischer, "Explaining Why More Americans"; Jones et al., *Exodus*; and Pew, *America's Changing Landscape*, 9.

2. On the changing demographic composition of U.S. Catholicism, see D'Antonio et al., *Catholics in Transition*, 29–36. Approximately 2 percent of Americans convert to Catholicism; see Pew, *America's Changing Landscape*, 9.

3. Seventy percent of white but 80 percent of Hispanic Catholics say that Jesus's Resurrection is personally very important to them. For a comparison of Hispanic and white Catholics' faith beliefs and attitudes toward official church teachings, see D'Antonio et al., *Catholics in Transition*, 54–56, 75–77.

4. Gene Burns, *The Frontiers of Catholicism: The Politics of Ideology in a Liberal World* (Berkeley: University of California Press, 1992), 50.

5. The data reported here on Catholics' beliefs and practices are from D'Antonio et al., *Catholics in Transition*, 48–60.

6. The proportion of Catholics who get married in a Catholic church has declined; see http://cara.georgetown.edu/frequently-requested-church-statistics/. Catholics are as likely as other Americans to get married, but fewer of them are marrying in church. See Mark Gray, *NineteenSixtyFour Blog*, CARA (Center for Applied Research in the Apostolate), Georgetown University, September 26, 2013, nineteensixty-four.blogspot.com/.

7. See Pope John XXIII's December 1961 statement convoking Vatican II, in Abbott, *Documents of Vatican II*, 704–705.

8. The quote is from paragraph #60 in *Rerum Novarum*. Additionally, in pointing to the continuity between Catholics' religious and secular duties, *Rerum Novarum* praised Catholic individuals and associations who work to improve social conditions. It stated: "Those Catholics are worthy of all praise—and they are not a few—who, understanding what the times require, have striven, by various undertakings and endeavors, to better the condition of the working class by rightful means. They have taken up the cause of the working man, and have spared no efforts to better the condition both of families and individuals; to infuse a spirit of equity into the mutual relations of employers and employed; to keep before the eyes of both classes the precepts of duty and the laws of the Gospel" (#55). Subsequent pre-Vatican II encyclicals extending the themes in *Rerum Novarum* include Pius XI's *Quadragesimo Anno* (1931) and John XXIII's *Pacem in Terris* (1963). The encyclicals and exhortations of specific popes can be accessed at the Vatican's website: http://w2.vatican.va/content/vatican/en.html (filtered by "Supreme Pontiffs").

9. John XXIII's statement (issued on December 25, 1961) convoking Vatican II, in Abbott, *Documents of Vatican II*, 704–705.

10. This quote is from paragraph #43, and the two prior quotes from paragraph #55 and 56, respectively, in "Pastoral Constitution."

11. "Pastoral Constitution," #56.

12. This quote is from paragraph #36 in "Dogmatic Constitution on the Church," in Abbott, *Documents of Vatican II*.

13. This quoted passage is from "Pastoral Constitution," #43 and 62. On hierarchical authority, see "Dogmatic Constitution," #18–21, 25.

14. Dillon, *Catholic Identity*, 48, argues that the new framework adopted at Vatican II "sought to balance the supreme authority of the Church hierarchy with an emphasis on respect for lay competence and reasoned dialogue among all Church members. . . . Vatican II thereby shifted, whether intentionally or not, the system of power relations in the Church. The redrawing of interpretive authority validated an understanding of religious identity derived from a more egalitarian, communal sense of Church ownership rather than from the Church hierarchy's universal definitions alone."

15. Pope Benedict, "What Has Been the Result of the Council?" in James Carroll, ed., *Vatican II: The Essential Texts* (New York: Image Books, 2005/2012), 3–13. On how a hermeneutic of reform is in continuity rather than in discontinuity with the larger Catholic tradition, see David Tracy, *Plurality and Ambiguity* (San Francisco: Harper & Row, 1987); and Joseph Komonchak, "Interpreting the Council and its Consequences," in James Heft with John O'Malley eds., *After Vatican II: Trajectories and Hermeneutics* (Grand Rapids, MI: Eerdmans, 2012), 164–172.

16. "Pastoral Constitution," #59.

17. Burns, *Frontiers*, 50.

18. See, for example, Dillon and Wink, *In the Course of a Lifetime*, 80–99, a longitudinal study of Catholics and Protestants; and the Pew Research Center's cross-sectional survey data in *Faith in Flux: Changes in Religious Affiliation in the U.S.* (Washington, DC: Pew Research Center, April 2009), 23–24.

19. Pew, *Faith in Flux*, 24.

20. Dillon, *Catholic Identity*.

21. Eighty-six percent, in D'Antonio et al., *Catholics in Transition*, 52–54.

22. On conscience, see "Pastoral Constitution," #16 and 41; more specifically on religious freedom, see *Declaration on Religious Freedom (RF)*, #9–10, in Abbott, *Documents of Vatican II*.

23. See John Mahoney, *The Making of Moral Theology: A Study of the Roman Catholic Tradition* (Oxford: Oxford University Press, 1987), 259–274; and James Keenan, *A History of Catholic Moral Theology in the Twentieth Century* (New York: Continuum, 2010), 122–123.

24. I discuss the issue of Church authority in *Catholic Identity*. On contraception, see Leslie Tentler, *Catholics and Contraception: An American History* (Ithaca, NY: Cornell University Press, 2004), 230.

25. John Seidler and Katherine Meyer, *Conflict and Change in the Catholic Church* (New Brunswick, NJ: Rutgers University Press, 1989), 104–106.

26. For analysis of the response of American Catholics to *Humanae Vitae*, see Michael Hout and Andrew Greeley, "The Center Doesn't Hold: Church Attendance in the United States, 1940–1984," *American Sociological Review* 52 (1987): 325–345. D'Antonio et al., *Catholics in Transition*, 110, finds that 31 percent of self-identified Catholics attend Mass once a week. Pew finds that 39 percent report

weekly participation; Pew Research Center, *U.S. Catholics Open to Non-Traditional Families* (Washington, DC: Pew Research Center, September 2015), 40. Though both surveys use representative samples, the difference may be due to the lessened impact of social desirability in the impersonal, online format used by *Catholics in Transition* compared to Pew's phone interviews.

27. See Ann Patrick, *Liberating Conscience: Feminist Exploration in Catholic Moral Theology* (New York: Continuum, 1997). Keenan, *History of Catholic Moral Theology*, 145–146, points out: "The development of moral theology from the late 1960s to 1980 was largely guided by . . . dedicated priests whose work in moral theology prompted others to participate in the reconstruction of the field. . . . Ministering pastorally to the laity especially in the face of classical church teachings on birth control, masturbation, divorce, remarriage, and homosexuality, these priests first offered pastoral adaptations to resolve the gulf between the Church's norms and the experience that the laity lived. In time, they realized that their task was not to offer pastoral adaptations, which after all often upheld the norms. Rather, they needed to determine what indeed made a moral decision an objectively right one." More generally, on the nuances and complexities in Catholic sexual ethics see, Lisa Sowle Cahill, *Sex, Gender, and Christian Ethics* (New York: Cambridge University Press, 1996).

28. D'Antonio et al., *Catholics in Transition*, 50.

29. On Catholics' attitudes toward same-sex marriage, see Pew Research Center, *Support for Same-Sex Marriage Grows, Even Among Groups That Had Been Skeptical* (Washington, DC: Pew Research Center, 2017), 6. On sexual morality more generally, see D'Antonio et al., *Catholics in Transition*, 72–83; Pew Research Center, *U.S. Catholics View Pope Francis as a Change for the Better* (Washington, DC: Pew Research Center, March 6, 2014), 4; Pew Research Center, *Support for Same-Sex Marriage at Record High* (Washington, DC: Pew Research Center, June 8, 2015); and Pew, *U.S. Catholics Open to Non-Traditional Families*. On LGBT Catholic self-identification, see Pew Research Center, *A Survey of LGBT Americans* (Washington, DC: Pew Research Center, June 2013), 92. Close to half of American Catholics (47 percent) say they have a close friend or family member who is LGBT; Pew, *Support for Same-Sex Marriage at Record High*, 15. On Catholics' divorce and cohabitation rates, see Pew, *U.S. Catholics Open to Non-Traditional Families*, 10, 55; see also D'Antonio et al., *Catholics in Transition*, 177; Gray, *NineteenSixtyFour Blog*, September 26, 2013; and Michael Hout, "Angry and Alienated: Divorced and remarried Catholics in the United States," *America*, December 16, 2000.

30. In October 2015, after Francis's U.S. visit, 81 percent of Catholics had a favorable view of him, down from 86 percent in June 2015 and 90 percent in February 2015; see Pew Research Center, *Positive Impact of Pope Francis on Views of the Church, Especially Among Democrats and Liberals* (Washington, DC: Pew Research Center, October 7, 2015), 2. The data supporting change in Church teachings on birth control, celibacy, and women priests, and recognizing same-sex marriages are

from Pew, *U.S. Catholics View Pope Francis as a Change for the Better*, 11. These figures are consistent with trend data since the late 1980s; see William D'Antonio, James Davidson, Dean Hoge, and Katherine Meyer, *American Catholics: Gender, Generation, and Commitment* (Walnut Creek, CA: AltaMira Press, 2001); and D'Antonio et al., *Catholics in Transition.*

31. The survey data on sexual attitudes come from D'Antonio et al., *American Catholics: Gender, Generation and Commitment*, 43, 49. On John Paul's leadership, see David Moore. "Pope John Paull II Controversial Figure Among U.S. Catholics," Gallup News Service, October 16, 2003.

32. On Catholic interpretive pluralism, see Tracy, *Plurality and Ambiguity*. My argument here and elsewhere (e.g., *Catholic Identity*; D'Antonio et al., *Catholics in Transition*) contrasts with the interpretation offered by Christian Smith (e.g., in Smith et al., *Young Catholic America*), who defines Catholic commitment in narrow terms, primarily constituted by weekly Mass attendance, belief in transubstantiation, and agreement with official Church teaching on contraception and sexual morality.

33. The Council acknowledged "how great a distance lies between the message she offers and the human failings of those to whom the gospel is entrusted" ("Pastoral Constitution," #43). It further argued that the laity should be given "every opportunity . . . so that, according to their abilities and the needs of the times, they may zealously participate in the saving work of the Church" ("Dogmatic Constitution," #33); and it not only permitted—but obliged—them to express informed opinions on Church issues. As elaborated in "Dogmatic Constitution," #37: "An individual layman, by reasons of the knowledge, competence, or outstanding ability which he may enjoy, is permitted and sometimes even obliged to express his opinion on things which concern the good of the Church." See also Dillon, *Catholic Identity*, 48–52.

34. Tricia Bruce, *Faithful Revolution: How Voice of the Faithful Is Changing the Church* (New York: Oxford University Press, 2011); William D'Antonio and Tony Pogorelc, *Voices of the Faithful* (New York: Herder & Herder, 2007).

35. Konieczny, *Spirit's Tether*; James Davidson Hunter, *Culture Wars: The Struggle to Define America* (New York: Basic Books, 1991).

36. See Dillon, *Catholic Identity*, 164–193; and Baggett, *Sense of the Faithful.*

37. Thirty-two percent of ever married white Catholics compared to 45 percent of ever married white mainline Protestants have ever been divorced; see Pew, *Catholics Open*, 55. See also Gray, *NineteenSixtyFour Blog*, September 26, 2013.

38. For example, very few Catholics in Chile (10 percent), Argentina (16 percent), and Brazil (17 percent) say divorce is morally wrong; Pew, *Religion in Latin America*, 80.

39. Seventy-two percent of self-identified U.S. Catholics say that one can be a good Catholic without having one's marriage approved by the Church, and 69 percent say one can be a good Catholic without obeying Church teachings on divorce and remarriage; D'Antonio et al., *Catholics in Transition*, 50. White Catholics are more

likely than Hispanic Catholics to express these views, even though cohabitation is more common among Hispanic than among white Catholics; D'Antonio et al., *Catholics in Transition*, 55; and Pew, *Catholics Open*, 60.

40. Personal interviews with a small number of divorced Catholics at an early stage of this project brought my attention to variation in how divorced Catholics construe their relationship to the Church. It is estimated that around 25 percent of cohabiting or divorced and remarried Catholics attend Mass at least weekly, and most who attend receive Communion; Pew, *Catholics Open*, 41.

41. Because the obligation of the sacrament of marriage ends with death ("till death do us part"), widows and widowers can freely contract a second marriage.

42. See Mark Gray, Paul Perl, and Tricia Bruce, *Marriage in the Catholic Church: A Survey of U.S. Catholics*, CARA report 2007, Center for Applied Research in the Apostolate, Georgetown University, 2007, 92, 168. The Pew Research Center, using a more generalized question asking divorced Catholics whether they or their former spouse have, or have sought, an annulment, reports that 26 percent have; Pew, *Catholics Open*, 56. On comparative and historical trends in Catholic annulments, see Melissa Wilde, "From Excommunication to Nullification," *Journal for the Scientific Study of Religion*, 40 (2001): 235–249.

43. Pew, *Catholics Open*, 10; and Hout, "Angry and Alienated."

44. Most Catholics who attend Mass (including those in an "irregular" marital or cohabiting situation) tend to partake of communion; Pew estimates that 15 percent of current self-identified Catholics are ineligible to receive communion owing to cohabitation or divorce and remarriage without an annulment. See Pew, *Catholics Open*, 42–43, 60.

45. Catholics' confusion about and disregard of Church teachings on divorce and remarriage are illuminated across the large number of comments posted online by readers of the *New York Times* in response to two, same-day front-page articles on divorced Catholics. See Michael Paulson, "As Vatican Revisits Divorce, Many Catholics Long for Acceptance," and Diantha Parker, "Stories of Catholic Marriage and Divorce," both *New York Times*, January 24, 2015.

46. In online surveys I conducted in 2015 of chapter leaders and associates of the liberal Catholic organization Call to Action (CTA), and of members of the conservative Catholic organization the Catholic League for Religious and Civil Rights (CL), relatively similar proportions of liberal (CTA, 21 percent) and conservative (CL, 18 percent) respondents reported being personally impacted by the Church's teachings on divorce and remarriage. In an open question asking how the teachings personally impacted them, almost half (47 percent) of CTA respondents spontaneously commented on the negative aspects of annulment. By contrast, only a fifth of CL respondents mentioned annulment, and were as likely to comment on its positive as its negative aspects. I am very grateful to Dr. William Donohue, President of the Catholic League for Religious and Civil Rights, who facilitated my survey of Catholic League respondents, and to Bob Heinemann at Call to

Action (CTA) for facilitating my survey of CTA chapter leaders and allies. The CTA ($N = 185$) survey was completed in April 2015, and the CL ($N = 937$) survey in September 2015. On the range of reasons American Catholics in general offer for not seeking an annulment, see Pew, *Catholics Open*, 57.

47. Similar themes of frustration are apparent in comments about annulments posted online to the *New York Times* in response to a front-page article on Francis's stream-lining of the annulment process. See Jim Yardley and Elisabetta Povoledo, "Pope Francis Announces Changes for Easier Marriage Annulments," *New York Times*, September 8, 2015.

48. Save Our Sacrament Inc. states that it is "an organization comprised of both current and former Respondents in marriage annulment cases. We represent over one thousand individuals who have contacted us in need of help. Most of these respondents have experienced what could be termed 'abuse' on psychological, emotional and moral levels, by priests working in diocesan marriage tribunals"; see www. SaveOurSacrament.org. I am grateful to Jan Leary for helpful background information on SOS. For a personal account of her negative experience of the annulment process, see Sheila Rauch Kennedy, *Shattered Faith* (New York: Henry Holt, 1997). For a more positive view of annulment's therapeutic value, see Kathleen Jenkins, *Sacred Divorce: Religion, Therapeutic Culture, and Ending Life Partnerships* (New Brunswick, NJ: Rutgers University Press, 2014).

49. Bellah et al., *Habits of the Heart*, discuss what they see as the pervasiveness of a narcissism in everyday American culture, religion, and spirituality. For a more nuanced empirical analysis, see Paul Wink, Michele Dillon, and Kristen Fay, "Spirituality, Narcissism and Psychotherapy: How Are They Related?," *Journal for the Scientific Study of Religion* 44 (2005): 143–158. On the therapeutic nature of the religiosity of young Catholics and Protestants, see Christian Smith and Melinda Lundquist Denton, *Soul Searching: The Religious and Spiritual Lives of American Teenagers* (New York: Oxford University Press, 2005).

50. Francis A. Sullivan, *Magisterium: Teaching Authority in the Catholic Church* (New York: Paulist Press, 1983).

51. Ibid., 162.

52. Ibid., 163–166; see also Mahoney, *Roman Catholic Tradition*, 271–274, 289–301. I similarly discuss this issue in *Catholic Identity*, 14–15.

53. On cognitive complexity and political ideology, see Philip Tetlock, "Cognitive Structural Analysis of Political Rhetoric: Methodological and Theoretical Issues," in S. Iyengar and W. McGuire, eds., *Explorations in Political Psychology* (Durham, NC: Duke University Press, 1993), 380–405.

54. For example, 43 percent of college graduates compared to 38 percent of those with a high school or less education attend Mass weekly. And while 65 percent of college graduates report that they receive communion every time they go to Mass, this is true of only 35 percent of those with some college or less education; Pew, *Catholics Open*, 41–43. On the influence of Catholic education on Church commitment

and attitudes to the Church's teaching authority among Catholics in general, see D'Antonio et al., *Catholics in Transition*, 58–60. Similarly, a majority of the leaders (52 percent) and members (58 percent) of Voice of the Faithful (VOTF), an organization that sprung up in response to the exposure of the Church's sex-abuse scandals to advocate for various institutional reforms, were educated in Catholic colleges; see D'Antonio and Pogorelc, *Voices*, 39, 53.

55. On the centrality of social justice in Catholicism, see David Hollenbach, *The Common Good and Christian Ethics* (Cambridge: Cambridge University Press, 2002); and Joseph Palacios, *The Catholic Social Imagination: Activism and the Just Society in Mexico and the United States* (Chicago: University of Chicago Press, 2007).

56. Two-thirds (67 percent) of U.S. Catholics say that helping the poor is an element of Catholicism that is personally very important to them; D'Antonio et al., *Catholics in Transition*, 50–51.

57. Robert Jones, Daniel Cox, and Juhem Navarro-Rivera, *The 2012 American Values Survey* (Washington, DC: Brookings Institution and Public Religion Research Institute, 2012), 59–62.

58. Fifty-two percent of white Catholics voted for George Bush in 2000, 56 percent in 2004 (even though the Democratic nominee, John Kerry, was a practicing Catholic), and 52 percent voted for John McCain in 2008. See Pew Research Center, *How the Faithful Voted: A Preliminary 2016 Analysis* (Washington, DC: Pew Research Center, November 9, 2016).

59. Clem Brooks and Jeff Manza, "A Broken Public? Americans' Responses to the Great Recession," *American Sociological Review* 78 (2013): 727–748.

60. Among white Catholics, 31 percent of Republicans and 28 percent of Democrats report weekly Mass attendance; 68 percent of Republicans and 70 percent of Democrats support immigration reform. By contrast, 73 percent of Republicans compared to 45 percent of Democrats favor reduced government spending; see D'Antonio et al., *Catholics in Transition*, 130–133.

61. Because the U.S. Census does not include questions about religious affiliation, this figure is based on survey estimates; see the CARA report, *The Emerging Church in the United States*, Center for Applied Research in the Apostolate, Georgetown University, November 2016.

62. Twenty-seven percent of Hispanic Catholic millennials compared to 12 percent of white Catholic millennials report currently living with a partner; D'Antonio et al., *Catholics in Transition*, 142. On some of the pastoral challenges Hispanics' socioeconomic disadvantage present for the Catholic Church, see Hosffman Ospino and Patricia Weitzel-O'Neill, *Catholic Schools in an Increasingly Hispanic Church* (Chestnut Hill, MA: Boston College, School of Theology and Ministry and School of Education, 2016).

63. Thirty percent of Hispanic, 36 percent of Black, and 12 percent of white children are poor; Jessica Carson, Marybeth Mattingly, and Andrew Schaefer, *Gains in*

Reducing Child Poverty, But Racial-Ethnic Disparities Persist (University of New
Hampshire, Durham, NH: Carsey School of Public Policy, 2017), National Issue
Brief #118.

64. Andrew Greeley, *The American Catholic: A Social Portrait* (New York: Basic
Books, 1977).

65. D'Antonio et al., *Catholics in Transition*, 144, 146.

66. Catholics deal with polarizing divisions, in part, by seeking out parishes whose doc-
trinal and cultural emphases fit with their own leanings. See Konieczny, *Spirit's
Tether*; Baggett, *Sense of the Faithful*; and Tricia Bruce, *Parish and Place: Making
Room for Diversity in the American Catholic Church* (New York: Oxford University
Press, 2017).

CHAPTER 3

1. Pope Leo XIII's *Rerum Novarum* (Of New Things), issued in 1891, marks the
beginning of the Church's framing of the ethical challenges presented by a
changing industrial and urban economy. In 1931, Pope Pius XI revisited these
same issues in *Quadragesimo Anno*. John Paul's *Centesimus Annus* (1991) was
written to mark the one hundredth anniversary of *Rerum Novarum*. His two
other most relevant socioeconomic encyclicals are *Laborem Exercens* (1981),
and *Sollicitudo Rei Socialis* (1987), which marked twenty years since Paul VI's
Populorum Progressio (which focused on world economic development). In pre-
paring to write *Centesimus Annus*, John Paul invited leading economists from
across the globe to discuss the changes in the world economy following the col-
lapse of the Soviet Union and the new political independence of Poland and
the other former Soviet bloc countries; see Institute for Advanced Catholic
Studies, *The Capstone*, Spring/Summer 2016, 1. On the U.S. bishops' articulation
of Catholic social teaching in the American policy context, see Burns, *Frontiers
of Catholicism*, 97–129. All papal encyclicals and other formal statements can be
accessed at the Vatican website: http://w2.vatican.va/content/vatican/en.html
(filtered by "Supreme Pontiffs").

2. See, for example, John XXIII's 1963 encyclical, *Pacem in Terris*; and Vatican II's
"Pastoral Constitution."

3. The interview was conducted by the influential Jesuit Antonio Spadaro, editor
of the Rome-based Jesuit journal *Civilta Cattolica*, and was published in *America*
magazine and online (September 30, 2013). In Poland for World Youth Day activities, he told the gathered crowd at an outdoor Mass in Czestochowa (close to the
shrine of the Black Madonna) that God does not dwell in history books but, rather,
in "everyday affairs" and "concrete activities." See Joshua McElwee, "Francis Tells
Poles: God Not in a History Book, But People's Real Lives," *National Catholic
Reporter*, July 28, 2016, www.ncronline.org.

4. Andrew Greeley, *The Catholic Imagination* (Berkeley: University of California Press, 2000), 77.

5. "Pastoral Constitution," #44.

6. Paul VI, December 7, 1965.

7. Ibid.

8. John Paul, *The Gospel of Life* (Evangelium Vitae) (New York: Random House, 1995), #11 and 12.

9. Ratzinger, pre-Conclave speech, 2005. Available on http://w2.vatican.va/content/vatican/en.html

10. Although Francis issued the encyclical *Lumen Fidei* in July 2013, it was primarily written by Benedict prior to his resignation. On this point, and on the writing of *JG*, see the remarks introducing *JG* in *Origins* 43, no. 28 (December 5, 2013), www.originsonline.com.

11. For example, John Paul's (1990) statement on Catholic universities, *Ex Corde Ecclesiae*, specifically states that Catholic theologians "are to be faithful to the Magisterium of the Church as the authentic interpreter of Sacred Scripture and Sacred Tradition" (Article 4). On theologians' views of John Paul's overreach of magisterial authority, see Dillon, *Catholic Identity*, 221–241; and Keenan, *History of Catholic Moral Theology*, 130–134.

12. Benedict, interview August 5, 2006, prior to his first visit as pope to Germany. Available on http://w2.vatican.va/content/vatican/en.html.

13. Hollenbach, *Common Good*, 226.

14. See "Francis, Capitalism, and War: The Pope's Divisions," *The Economist* online blog, June 24, 2014, www.economist.com/.

15. Burns, *Frontiers of Catholicism*, 108.

16. Conservative political commentators in the United States, including Rush Limbaugh and Glenn Beck, criticized Francis as Marxist. See, for example, Michael Sean Winters, "The Right Blasts Francis (Again)!," *National Catholic Reporter*, March 12, 2014, www.ncronline.org. A Lexis-Nexis search of English-language newspapers showed that the theme of Francis and Marxism circulated in the United States, Ireland, the United Kingdom, Canada, Australia, New Zealand, India, Egypt, and South Africa.

17. See Philip Bump, "Who Is More Fallible on Economics: Paul Ryan or Pope Francis?," *The Atlantic*, December 26, 2013, www.theatlantic.com.

18. For an introduction to liberation theology, see John Berryman, *Liberation Theology* (Philadelphia: Temple University Press, 1987). On Benedict, see, for example, Ian Fisher and Larry Rohter, "The Pope, Addressing Latin America's Bishops, Denounces Capitalism and Marxism," *New York Times*, May 14, 2007, A10.

19. During John Paul's papacy, other prominent liberation theologians, including Leonardo Boff, were silenced by the Congregation for the Doctrine of the Faith, under then Cardinal Ratzinger. On the increasing rapprochement between the Vatican today and liberation theology, see Joshua McElwee, "Pope Meets with

Liberation Theology Pioneer," *National Catholic Reporter*, September 25, 2013, www.ncronline.org.

20. See, for example, "Pope's Apostolic Doctrine Under Cloud of Marxism," *New India Express*, December 17, 2013; "Pope Francis shrugs off allegations of Marxism," *Irish Independent*, December 16, 2013, accessed at: www.lexisnexis.com/hottopics/lnacademic.

21. See, for example, "A Hard Pope for Capitalists to Love," *The Globe and Mail* (Canada), January 13, 2014, accessed at www.lexisnexis.com/hottopics/lnacademic; and Jim Yardley, "A Humble Pope, Challenging the World," *New York Times*, September 19, 2015, A6.

22. Benedict, Address to Workers and Leaders of Catholic Charities and Members of the Pontifical Council *Cor Unum*, the Vatican office in charge of coordinating and promoting the Church's charitable activity, January 19, 2013. Available on http://w2.vatican.va/content/vatican/en.html; and *Caritas in Veritate*, his 2009 encyclical (#34).

23. Benedict, Address to the Members of the Diplomatic Corps Accredited to the Holy See, January 2007.

24. Benedict, Address to the Members of the Diplomatic Corps Accredited to the Holy See, January 2013.

25. On the relationship between politics and markets, see Charles Lindblom, *Politics and Markets* (New York: Basic Books, 1977). Precisely because of the structural interrelation between economic and political elites, the charge of Marxism leveled at Francis's discourse by both political and economic leaders would not surprise Marxists.

26. Such well-positioned critics underscore the continuity between religious and secular roles. The interwoven continuity embodied across secular and religious identities was on full public display during Francis's address to Congress in September 2015: all three of the most senior leaders hosting him were Catholic: then Speaker John Boehner, Minority Leader (and past Speaker) Nancy Pelosi, and Vice President (and Senate President) Joe Biden.

27. USCCB, "Federal Budget Choices Must Protect Poor, Vulnerable People, Says U.S. Bishops' Conference," April 17, 2012, accessed at www.usccb.org. See also Laurie Goodstein, "A Jesuit Rebuke for Ryan," *New York Times*, April 25, 2012, A16; "Paul Ryan's Social Extremism," editorial, *New York Times*, August 27, 2012, A18. More generally, on bishops' advocacy for minimum wage increases, see, for example, Thomas Kaplan, "Cardinal and Bishops Urging Albany to Raise the Minimum Wage," *New York Times*, May 2, 2012, A27.

28. "Pope Should Stick with Religion and Avoid Economics." *National Post* (*The Financial Post*) (Canada), November 28, 2013, accessed at www.lexisnexis.com/hottopics/lnacademic.

29. On the threat posed by environmental degradation, see, for example, Jurgen Habermas, *Legitimation Crisis* (Boston: Beacon Press, 1975), 35, 41–43.

30. Paul VI, 1971, *Octogesima Adveniens*, Apostolic letter on the 80th anniversary of *Rerum Novarum*. "Man is suddenly becoming aware that by an ill-considered exploitation of nature he risks destroying it and becoming in his turn the victim of this degradation" (#21).

31. In *Redemptor Hominis* (1979), #15, John Paul wrote:

    We seem to be increasingly aware of the fact that the exploitation of the earth, the planet on which we are living, demands rational and honest planning. At the same time, exploitation of the earth not only for industrial but also for military purposes and the uncontrolled development of technology outside the framework of a long-range authentically humanistic plan often bring with them a threat to man's natural environment, alienate him in his relations with nature and remove him from nature. Man often seems to see no other meaning in his natural environment than what serves for immediate use and consumption. Yet it was the Creator's will that man should communicate with nature as an intelligent and noble "master" and "guardian," and not as a heedless "exploiter" and "destroyer."

    On ecology as a moral issue, see John Paul, *Centesimus Annus* (1991), #37, 38.

32. See, for example, Benedict, January 2007, Address to the Diplomatic Corps; Ker Than, "Pope Preaches Green at UN," *National Geographic News*, April 18, 2008, accessed at www.news.nationalgeographic.com; and *Caritas in Veritate*, #32, 48, 49, 51.

33. See, for example, Cary Funk and Brian Kennedy, *The Politics of Climate* (Washington, DC: Pew Research Center, 2016); Lawrence Hamilton, "Where Is the North Pole? An Election Year Survey on Climate Change," National Issue Brief 107 (2016), Carsey School of Public Policy, University of New Hampshire; Coral Davenport, "Conservative to Fund Republicans Who Back Climate Change Action," *New York Times*, June 30, 2016, A19; and Philip Schwadel and Erik Johnson, "The Religious and Political Origins of Evangelical Protestants' Opposition to Environmental Spending," *Journal for the Scientific Study of Religion* 56 (2017): 179–198.

34. In the postsecular frame, the empirical reality of religion's persistence is more important than the theoretical assumption (secularization thesis) or the ideological presumption (Enlightenment fundamentalism) of secularity and the disappearance of religion; see chapter 1, this volume.

35. Francis's quotes of Benedict are from *Caritas in Veritate* and his World Day of Peace Address, 2010.

36. Francis's critique of the techno-economic paradigm echoes a pessimistic analysis of post–World War II consumer society outlined by theorists associated with the Frankfurt School, most notably Max Horkheimer and Theodor Adorno, *The Dialectic of Enlightenment* (Stanford, CA: Stanford University Press, 1972/2000). Habermas is a second-generation Frankfurt School theorist, but as I emphasize in chapter 1, he is confident that a contrite modernity's failings (e.g., economic inequality, climate change) can be remedied.

37. See Catholic News Service, "Margin Notes," on the news conference for the publication of *Laudato Si,'* in *Origins* 45, no. 8 (June 26, 2015), www.originsonline.com.

38. "The Pope and the Environment. What Would Jesus Do About Global Warming?" *The Economist*, June 20, 2015, 35–36.

39. Rosie Scammell, "Cardinal Pell: Church Has No Particular Expertise in Science," *Religion News Service*, July 17, 2015, www.religionnewsservice.org.

40. On conservatives' response, see, for example, Christopher Hale, "Rick Santorum Wants Pope Francis to Leave Science to the Scientists Only When It's Convenient for Him," *Washington Post*, June 4, 2015, www.washingtonpost.com. Prior to the encyclical's release, several conservative political individuals and groups rejected Francis's foray into climate change discussion; see, for example, Coral Davenport and Laurie Goodstein, "Pope's Climate Plan Vexes Right," *New York Times,* April 28, 2015, A1. On the response to *LS* more generally, see Catholic News Service, "Religious and Civil Leaders Weigh in on Pope's New Encyclical," *The Pilot*, June 26, 2015, 1, 8; Carol Glatz, "Encyclical Comes at Crucial Time with Message for All, Speakers Say," *The Pilot*, June 26, 2015, 8–9; and Mary Wisniewski, "Scientists Welcome Pope's Encyclical on Climate Change," *Irish Independent*, June 18, 2015, 37. Although a degree in science is not a prerequisite for having an informed opinion about climate change issues, Francis does in fact have scientific expertise—he has a degree in chemistry.

41. On Catholic bishops' use of social scientific arguments in the Irish divorce debate, see Michele Dillon, *Debating Divorce: Moral Conflict in Ireland* (University Press of Kentucky, 1993), and of scientific arguments in abortion debates in the United States and elsewhere, see Dillon, "Cultural Differences."

42. On post-*Laudato Si'* activities, see, for example, Brian Roewe, "Catholic Coalition Files Amicus Brief Backing Clean Power Plan," *National Catholic Reporter*, April 5, 2016; Marie Venner, "Monterey, Calif., Diocese Enters 'New Era' with Sustainable Energy Program," *National Catholic Reporter*, October 3, 2016; Marie Venner, "Chicago Parishes Look to Do More with Less Through Energy Efficiency," *National Catholic Reporter*, June 28, 2016, www.ncronline.org. See *National Catholic Reporter*'s "Eco Catholic" reporting for many examples of Catholic engagement in climate change initiatives.

43. For information on Catholic Covenant activities, see www.catholicclimatecovenant.org.

44. See Gerard O'Connell, "Vatican Backs Pan-Amazonian Church Network to Protect 30 Million People and the Environment," *America*, March 6, 2015, www.americamagazine.org. The network's acronym is REPAM and includes the Catholic Church and other institutions in Brazil, Colombia, Ecuador, Guyana, Peru, Surinam, French Guyana, Peru, and Venezuela.

45. The percentages reported in this paragraph are from Pew Research Center, *Catholics Divided over Global Warming* (Washington, DC: Pew Research Center, June 16, 2015), 5, 2, 1.

46. Italics in original. The report is from Yale University's Program on Climate Change Communication and George Mason University's Center for Climate Change Communication. The data the authors report are from a nationally representative panel survey of self-identified Catholics, evangelicals, and non-evangelical Protestants conducted in March 2015 and October 2015; see E. Maibach, A. Leiserowitz, C. Roser-Renouf, T. Myers, S. Rosenthal, and G. Feinberg, *The Francis Effect: How Pope Francis Changed the Conversation about Global Warming*, Report by George Mason University and Yale University (Fairfax, VA: George Mason University Center for Climate Change Communication, 2015).

47. The data I cite in this section are findings from Maibach et al., *The Francis Effect*.

48. Ibid., 48. Contemporary Catholics also show limited awareness of the U.S. bishops' religious freedom campaign (see chapter 5, this volume); as was also the case in the 1980s in regard to the U.S. bishops' pastoral letters on economic justice and nuclear disarmament; see William D'Antonio, James Davidson, Dean Hoge, and Ruth Wallace, *American Catholic Laity in a Changing Church* (Kansas City, MO: Sheed and Ward, 1989), 166–170.

49. Maibach et al., 11–12. In a poll conducted by CARA (Center for Applied Research in the Apostolate) in May 2016 on "Attitudes about Climate Change" (cara. georgetown.edu/climate), almost one year after *LS* was released, 32 percent of Catholics, 24 percent of non-evangelical Christians, and 29 percent of religiously unaffiliated Americans reported they had heard or read about *LS*. The low levels of reported awareness (24 percent in the Yale–George Mason survey in Fall 2015; and 32 percent in the CARA May 2016 survey) are striking given that the surveys primed respondents by specifically mentioning Francis and his encyclical's topic in the question asked. Parishes that did not literally discuss the encyclical may have nonetheless alerted their parishioners to its release. For example, the weekly bulletin at St. Paul's Parish in Wellesley, Massachusetts, for July 5, 2015, included an excerpt from a statement from the U.S. Catholic bishops encouraging "efforts to bring about discussion on issues affecting the environment (climate change, consumption, pollution, stewardship of the land) that is civil and constructive." It also provided the link to the website of the USCCB, which in turn had a link to *Laudato Si'* and to several other documents and resources on the environment in Catholic teaching. The church's bulletin also featured "The Saint Francis Pledge" about protecting God's creation and working toward the remedying of climate change.

50. Maibach et al., 12.

51. A Public Religion Research Institute (PRRI) fall 2014 survey conducted in partnership with the American Academy of Religion found that 5 percent of white and 22 percent of Hispanic Catholics say that their clergy leaders discuss climate change often. Five percent of evangelicals and 10 percent of white mainline Protestants say that their clergy leaders discuss climate change often. See Robert Jones, Daniel Cox,

and Juhem Navarro-Rivera, *Believers, Sympathizers, and Skeptics* (Washington, DC: PRRI, 2014), 31.

52. John Gehring, *The Francis Effect: A Radical Pope's Challenge to the American Catholic Church* (Lanham, MD: Rowman & Littlefield, 2015), 176–177.

53. Maibach et al., *The Francis Effect*, 8.

54. Hamilton, *North Pole*, 3; and Funk and Kennedy, *The Politics of Climate*, 4–6. See also Gauchat, "Politicization of Science in the Public Sphere," 167–187.

55. In Chapter 4 I discuss the relation between Catholics' changing attitudes toward same-sex marriage and their understanding of the Church's official position. More generally on opinion formation biases, see Dan Kahan, Hank Jenkins-Smith, and Donald Braman, "Cultural Cognition of Scientific Consensus," *Journal of Risk Research* 14 (2011): 147–174.

56. On opinion change, the Pope' influence, and concern, see Maibach et al., *The Francis Effect*, 14–16, and on human actions, 18–19. In fact, the survey finds an increase Spring to Fall (from 22 percent to 29 percent) in the proportion of Catholics who agree with the statement that they "have personally experienced the effects of global warming." (Most say they "somewhat"—from 20 to 25 percent, rather than "strongly" agree—from 2 to 4 percent.) The authors suggest that the "pope's discussion may have amplified people's perceptions that summer's extreme weather is linked to changes in the climate"; Maibach et al., *The Francis Effect*, 27. The summer of 2015 did have some extreme weather, as the authors note. But given that people's perceptions of objectively severe weather seem to be mediated by their existing political partisanship, it would be hard for Francis to have an impact in shifting perceptions, net of the subjective experience of severe weather and individuals' already existing political stance on the issue. On partisanship and climate change attitudes, see Lawrence Hamilton and Mary Lemcke-Stampone, "Was December Warm? Family, Politics and Recollections of Weather," National Issue Brief #100 (2016), Carsey School of Public Policy, University of New Hampshire.

57. Maibach et al., *The Francis Effect*, 35. In fact, Catholics are more likely to show either no change or a small decline (2 to 3 percentage points) in the proportions supporting the regulation of carbon dioxide, funded research on renewable energy sources, and tax rebates for energy-efficient purchases (e.g., cars, solar panels); see Maibach et al., *The Francis Effect*, 89–91.

58. John Schwartz and Tatiana Schlossberg, "Little Debating a Climate Divide," *New York Times*, October 18, 2016, D5. On election priorities, see Lydia Saad, "Global Warming Concern at Three-Decade High," Gallup poll, March 14, 2017, accessed at www.gallup.org. On voting preferences, see Pew, *How the Faithful Voted: A Preliminary 2016 Analysis*. On Trump's views, see Davenport, "Conservative to Fund Republicans."

59. Maibach et al., *The Francis Effect*, 23.

60. This opinion was expressed by 45 percent of white and 57 percent of Hispanic Catholics; see Jones at al., *Believers, Sympathizers, and Skeptics*, 12–14.

61. The findings discussed here are from Maibach et al., *The Francis Effect*, 75–81. Large proportions of Catholics also agree that climate change is an agricultural (60 percent), economic (51 percent), and health (54 percent) issue; and the pre- and post *Laudato Si'* surveys found large increases in the proportions seeing them as such.

62. C. Roser-Renouf, E. Maibach, A. Leiserowitz, G. Feinberg, and S. Rosenthal, *Faith, Morality and the Environment: Portraits of Global Warming's Six Americas,* Report of Yale University and George Mason University (New Haven, CT: Yale Program on Climate Change Communication, 2016), 1.

63. Fifty-six percent of the unaffiliated (and 48 percent of Catholics) say global warming is a "very serious problem" and 57 percent say it is caused by human activity (compared to 47 percent of Catholics). Among mainline Protestants, the respective percentages are 41 percent and 42 percent; Pew, *Catholics Divided over Global Warming*, 5, 6, 8.

64. Pew Research Center, *In U.S., Pope's Popularity Continues to Grow* (Washington, DC: Pew Research Center, March 5, 2015).

65. In 2015, 21 percent of Americans self-identified as Catholic and 23 percent as unaffiliated; Pew, *America's Changing Religious Landscape*, 9. Maibach et al., *The Francis Effect*, 3, state that they did not include "non-religious" Americans due to their relatively small numbers and sample size limitations.

66. Center for Applied Research in the Apostolate (CARA), *Attitudes about Climate Change,* Catholic Poll, May 2016 (Washington, DC: Georgetown University, 2016), 5. (cara.georgetown.edu/climate)

67. On cognitive bias, see Kahan et al. "Cultural Cognition."

68. On civil religious themes in American public discourse, see Robert Bellah, "Civil Religion in America," *Daedalus* 96 (1967): 1–21; Bellah et al., *Habits of the Heart*; and Philip Gorski, *American Covenant: A History of Civil Religion from the Puritans to the Present* (Princeton: Princeton University Press, 2017).

69. Strong nationalist themes surged in the 2016 U.S. presidential campaign and are salient in several European countries, telegraphed by the majority vote in June 2016 in favor of Great Britain's withdrawal from the European Union, and by the significant parliamentary gains of the Alternative for Germany party in Germany's September 2017 national election. On the ethical challenges of a global cosmopolitanism, see Ulrich Beck and Edgar Grande, "Varieties of Second Modernity: The Cosmopolitan Turn in Social and Political Theory Research," *British Journal of Sociology* 61 (2010): 409–443; and Lisa Sowle Cahill, *Global Justice, Christology, and Christian Ethics* (New York: Cambridge University Press, 2013).

70. On the Church as a transnational actor, see Ivan Vallier, *Catholicism, Social Control, and Modernization in Latin America* (Englewood Cliffs, NJ: Prentice Hall, 1970); Eric O. Hanson, *The Catholic Church in World Politics* (Princeton, NJ: Princeton University Press, 1987); and Mehran Tamadonfar and Ted Jelen, eds., *Religion and Regimes: Support, Separation, and Opposition* (New York: Lexington Books, 2014).

71. See Thomas Banchoff and Jose Casanova, eds., *The Jesuits and Globalization* (Washington, DC: Georgetown University Press, 2016).

CHAPTER 4

1. Rogers Brubaker, *Grounds for Difference* (Cambridge, MA: Harvard University Press, 2015), 26, notes that sex and gender categories are both externally defined and "deeply inhabited categor[ies] of difference at the core of most people's understanding of who they are."

2. John Gallagher, *Time Past, Time Future: An Historical Study of Catholic Moral Theology* (New York: Paulist Press, 1990), 29–47, 115–119.

3. Keenan, *History of Catholic Moral Theology*, 2–3.

4. James Joyce, *A Portrait of the Artist as a Young Man* (London: Penguin, 1916), 126, 144–145.

5. Keenan, *History of Catholic Moral Theology*, 120–126.

6. Burns, *Frontiers*, 22–46, 49–50, argues that the Church's prioritization of "faith and morals" over sociopolitical issues dates to the "papal struggle with liberalism" in the late nineteenth and early twentieth centuries. The Vatican's loss of its political battle with liberalism gave it "a newfound autonomy from liberal society," and even an "autonomy to develop new ideological forms and even expand its authority over what had been politically defined as religious issues" (25).

7. Natural law, Benedict explains, is "a common law that precedes dogma . . . [its principles are derived] from nature, from man's reason." See Benedict, "Prepolitical Moral Foundations of a Free Republic," in Hent DeVries and Lawrence Sullivan, eds., *Political Theologies: Public Religions in a Post-Secular World* (New York: Fordham University Press, 2006), 261–268, 265.

8. See, for example, Andrew Greeley, *American Catholics Since the Council* (Chicago: Thomas More Press, 1985); Dillon, *Catholic Identity;* and Keenan, *History of Catholic Moral Theology.*

9. Keenan, *History of Catholic Moral Theology*, 123, 119, argues that *Humanae Vitae* was "the first significant papal endorsement of neo-manualism after Vatican II." He states, "In the twentieth century, with this emerging moral magisterium, moral truth became identified with papal and episcopal utterances."

10. See Kristin Luker, *Abortion and the Politics of Motherhood* (Berkeley: University of California Press, 1984), on the moral complexities in pro-choice and pro-life activists' worldviews on abortion.

11. Benedict's annual address to members of the diplomatic corps, January 7, 2013.

12. Cathleen Kaveny, "The Spirit of Vatican II and Moral Theology: *Evangelium Vitae* as a Case Study," in James Heft with John O'Malley eds., *After Vatican II: Trajectories and Hermeneutics* (Grand Rapids, MI: Eerdmans, 2012), 43–67.

13. Since 1973, when the U.S. Supreme Court legalized abortion (with its *Roe v. Wade* decision), public opinion on abortion has been relatively stable, with about

one-fifth of Americans opposed to abortion in all circumstances, one-fifth in favor of abortion in any circumstance, and 60 percent in favor of legal abortion but with certain restrictions. Fifty-six percent of white Catholics and 43 percent of Hispanic Catholics support legal abortion in all or most circumstances, as do 68 percent of white mainline Protestants and 79 percent of religiously unaffiliated Americans; fewer in all groups say that abortion is morally acceptable; see Michele Dillon, "Asynchrony in Attitudes toward Abortion and Gay Rights: The Challenge to Values Alignment," SSSR 2013 Presidential Address, *Journal for the Scientific Study of Religion* 53 (2014): 1–16.

14. Paul VI's Commission on birth control distinguished between contraception and abortion (though Paul VI subsequently denounced both in *Humanae Vitae*). For a historical perspective on the conflation and dissociation of abortion and contraception, see Tentler, *Catholics and Contraception*, 38, 91–92, 170–171.

15. See, for example, D'Antonio et al., *Catholics in Transition*, 59.

16. John Paul, *Veritatis Splendor*, 321.

17. Heather Boonstra, "Abortion in the Lives of Women Struggling Financially," *Guttmacher Policy Review* 19 (2016): 46–52.

18. Congregation for the Doctrine of the Faith, "Considerations Regarding Proposals to Give Legal Recognition to Unions Between Homosexual Persons," *Origins* 33, no. 11 (August 14, 2003), www.originsonline.com. LGBT Catholics push back against such categorizations and dynamically construe everyday identities that show the normalcy of being LGBT *and* Catholic; see, for example, Dillon, *Catholic Identity*, 115–163; Todd Fuist, "'It Just Always Seemed Like It Wasn't a Big Deal, Yet, I Know for Some People they Really Struggle With It': LGBT Religious Identities in Context," *Journal for the Scientific Study of Religion* 55 (2016): 770–786; and Donileen Loseke and James Cavendish, "Producing Institutional Selves: Rhetorically Constructing the Dignity of Sexually Marginalized Catholics," *Social Psychology Quarterly* 64 (2001): 347–362.

19. U.S. Bishops, "Ministry to Persons with a Homosexual Orientation," *Origins* 36, no. 24 (November 23, 2006), www.originsonline.com.

20. Wuthnow, *God Problem*, 36–37.

21. By extension, the Vatican also rejects the "gender ideology" of gender and sexual fluidity; see, for example, Pope Benedict XVI, "Christmas Greetings to Members of the Roman Curia," December 21, 2012. Francis reaffirms complementarity in *LS* #155, and calls its rejection, "ideological colonization."

22. Bishop Richard Malone, Chairman of the USCCB Committee on Laity, Marriage, Family Life and Youth, commenting on National Marriage Week USA (February 7–14, 2016) and World Marriage Day (February 14, 2016); see www.usccb.org.

23. Benedict, 2012 annual diplomatic address.

24. Congregation for the Doctrine of the Faith, "Considerations," 2003.

25. Michael Lawler and Todd Salzman, "Human Experience and Catholic Moral Theology," *Irish Theological Quarterly* 76 (2011): 35–56.

26. Pew Research Center, *In Gay Marriage Debate, Both Supporters and Opponents see Legal Recognition as "Inevitable"* (Washington, DC: Pew Research Center, June 6, 2013), 21; and Pew, *U.S. Catholics Open to Non-Traditional Families*, 3.

27. A slight majority of white Catholics (52 percent), white mainline Protestants (52 percent), and the religiously unaffiliated (53 percent) say that people are born gay or lesbian; 7 percent in each group say it is a result of a person's upbringing; 28 percent of white Catholics and one-third of mainline and unaffiliated say it is a choice; Pew, *Gay Marriage Debate*, 12.

28. Bellah et al., *Habits of the Heart*.

29. Nineteen percent of same-sex couple households include children under age 18; and among LGBT individuals under age 50, either living alone or with a spouse or partner, 48 percent of women and 20 percent of men, are raising a child; see Gary Gates, "LGBT Parenting in the U.S.," February 2013, Williams Institute, UCLA.

30. Seventy-nine percent of LGBT Americans say the Catholic Church is "unfriendly" toward LGBT people; Pew Research Center, *A Survey of LGBT Americans* (Washington, DC: Pew Research Center, June 13, 2013), 12.

31. Vatican II stated: "In pastoral care, appropriate use must be made not only of theological principles, but also of the findings of the secular sciences, especially of psychology and sociology. Thus the faithful can be brought to live the faith in a more thorough and mature way" ("Pastoral Constitution," #62).

32. See Dillon, *Debating Divorce*; and Dillon, "Cultural Differences."

33. See Spadaro interview. Francis repeats this theme in *JG* #35.

34. Benedict, 2012 annual diplomatic address.

35. He also criticizes "the politics of reproductive health" (*AL* #42).

36. On the importance of language in meaning creation in everyday life, see Berger and Luckmann, *Social Construction*, 34–46; and Wuthnow, *God Problem*, 4, who states: "language is behavior" and thus confers meaning. On abortion and excommunication, John Paul stated:

    The Church's canonical discipline, from the earliest centuries, has inflicted penal sanctions on those guilty of abortion. This practice, with more or less severe penalties, has been confirmed in various periods of history. The 1917 Code of Canon Law punished abortion with excommunication. The revised canonical legislation continues this tradition when it decrees that "a person who actually procures an abortion incurs automatic excommunication" . . . . In the Church, the purpose of the penalty of excommunication is to make an individual fully aware of the gravity of a certain sin and then to foster genuine conversion and repentance. (*Gospel of Life* #62)

37. In canon law, because abortion is a "grave sin" incurring excommunication, it can only be absolved by the Pope, the bishop, or by priests authorized by them (*Catechism* #1463).

38. John Paul II, Holy Thursday Address, 1983.

39. See Spadaro interview.

40. The quote on marriage is from Francis; see Joshua McElwee, "Francis Marks Anniversary with Interview on Sex Abuse, Women, Contraception," *National Catholic Reporter*, March 5, 2014, www.ncronline.org. See also Paddy Agnew, "Pope Francis Enters Debate over Italy's Same-Sex Unions Bill," *Irish Times*, January 24, 2016, www.irishtimes.com. See Sarah MacDonald, "Cardinal Marx: Society Must Create Structures to Respect Gay Rights," *National Catholic Reporter*, June 28, 2016, www.ncronline.org; Patsy McGarry, "Church Must Apologise to Gay People, Pope's Adviser Declares," *Irish Times*, June 23, 2016, www.irishtimes.com; Reuters, "Pope Francis Says Church Should Apologize to Gays," *New York Times*, June 27, 2016, A8.

41. Recent guidelines from the Vatican's Congregation for the Clergy (issued on December 8, 2016) specifically repeat earlier Church language that men who "practice homosexuality, present deep-seated homosexual tendencies or support the so-called 'gay culture'" should not be considered eligible for the priesthood. All priests, gay or straight, are obliged to observe a vow of celibacy. The specific mention here of homosexual tendencies and the absence of any mention of heterosexual tendencies suggest that the Vatican still sees something troubling (if not disordered) about homosexual tendencies; see http://en.radiovaticana.va/news/2016/12/08/vatican_issues_new_guidelines_for_priestly_formation/1277681.

42. See, Pew, *Support for Same-Sex Marriage Grows*; and Robert P. Jones, Betsy Cooper, Daniel Cox, and Rachel Lienesch, *Majority of Americans Oppose Laws Requiring Transgender Individuals to Use Bathrooms Corresponding to Sex at Birth Rather than Gender Identity* (Washington, DC: Public Religion Research Institute, 2016). A third (36 percent) of Catholics who support same-sex marriage say (correctly) Francis is opposed, and 15 percent say they don't know his position. Among Catholics who oppose same-sex marriage, close to two-thirds say (correctly) that the pope opposes it, 15 percent say he supports it, and 22 percent say they don't know his position. See Robert Jones and Daniel Cox, *The Francis Effect?: U.S. Catholic Attitudes on Pope Francis, the Catholic Church, and American Politics* (Washington, DC: Public Religion Research Institute/Religion News Service, 2015), 9.

43. On everyday situational definitions, habits, and normalization processes, see William I. Thomas, *The Unadjusted Girl* (Boston: Little, Brown, 1923), 43–44; and Berger and Luckmann, *Social Construction*, 53. On cultural bias, see Kahan et al., "Cultural Cognition."

44. Congregation for the Doctrine of the Faith, "Inadmissibility of Women to Ministerial Priesthood," *Origins* 25 (November 30, 1995): 401, 403–405.

45. See, for example, D'Antonio et al., *Catholics in Transition*, 100–102; Bendixen and Amandi International, *Global Survey*, 21; and Pew, *Religion in Latin America*, 107.

46. Congregation for the Doctrine of the Faith, "Vatican Declaration: Women in the Ministerial Priesthood," *Origins* 6 (February 3, 1977): 517, 519–531; and Dillon, *Catholic Identity*, 60–64, 168–173.

47. John Paul II, "Letter to Women," *Origins* 25 (July 27, 1995): 137, 139–143.

48. See, for example, Brubaker, *Grounds for Difference*, 24–26.
49. Greeley, *Catholic Imagination*, 108, accounting for Catholic women's and men's support for women's ordination.
50. See, for example, Tracy, *Plurality and Ambiguity*; and Mahoney, *The Making of Moral Theology*.
51. *Catechism*, #1324, 1325, 1327.
52. John Paul II, "Ordinatio Sacerdotalis," *Origins* 24 (June 9, 1994): 49–52.
53. Congregation for the Doctrine of the Faith, "Inadmissibility of Women," 405.
54. In *Joy of the Gospel* (#104), Francis states:

    Demands that the legitimate rights of women be respected, based on the firm conviction that men and women are equal in dignity, present the Church with profound and challenging questions that cannot be lightly evaded. The reservation of the priesthood to males, as a sign of Christ the Spouse who gives himself in the Eucharist, is not a question open to discussion, but it can prove especially divisive if sacramental power is too closely identified with power in general.
55. "Pastoral Constitution," #43; as I note in chapter 2.
56. "Pastoral Constitution," #62, states: "the deposit of faith or revealed truths are one thing; the manner in which they are formulated without violence to their meaning and significance is another."
57. Several Catholic organizations advocate for women priests, including Women's Ordination Conference, Women's Ordination Worldwide, CORPUS, and Roman Catholic Womenpriests-USA. Based on a 2011 nationally representative sample of American self-identified Catholics, 62 percent of women and 61 percent of men expressed support for women's ordination; D'Antonio et al., *Catholics in Transition*, 100–101. Sixty-eight percent of Catholics say the Church should allow women to become priests; see Pew, *U.S. Catholics View Pope Francis as a Change for the Better* (Washington, DC: Pew Research Center, March 6, 2014), 4.
58. In 2011, 31 percent of women reported weekly Mass attendance, down from 43 percent in 1993 and from 52 percent in 1987; and whereas 58 percent of women in 1987 said that the Church was among the most important parts of their lives, this declined to 49 percent in 1993, and to 38 percent in 2011 (and with just 22 percent of young white women saying so); see D'Antonio et al., *Catholics in Transition*, 90–92, 148. On the Vatican's investigation of American nuns, see, for example, Laurie Goodstein, "Vatican Reprimands a Group of U.S. Nuns and Plans Changes," *New York Times*, April 19, 2012, A16; Laurie Goodstein, "American Nuns Vow to Fight Vatican Criticism," *New York Times*, June 2, 2012, A11; and Laurie Goodstein, "Friendly Move From Vatican Clears Nuns," *New York Times*, April 17, 2015, A1, 14. On criticism of feminist theologians, see, for example, Laurie Goodstein, "Nun's Book is Criticized by Bishops," *New York Times*, April 1, 2011, A22; Paul Vitello, "After Bishops Attack Scholar's Book, Trying to Grasp New Bounds of Debate," *New York Times*, April 12, 2011, A19; and Laurie Goodstein and Rachel Donadio, "Vatican Scolds Nun for Book on Sexuality," *New York Times*, June 5, 2012, A13.

59. The Church's condemnation of sexism was first expressed in a draft pastoral letter on women that the U.S. bishops were writing in 1988, but which after successive drafts failed to win the support of two-thirds of the bishops, a threshold required for it to qualify as the "teaching authority" of a pastoral letter; see Dillon, *Catholic Identity*, 64–65.

60. In *Amoris Laetitia* (*AL* #54), Francis states, "If certain forms of feminism have arisen which we must consider inadequate, we must nonetheless see in the women's movement the working of the Spirit for a clearer recognition of the dignity and rights of women."

61. Francis, Weekly Wednesday General Audience, April 29, 2015. Reported by Joshua McElwee, "Francis Firmly Backs Equal Pay for Women, Citing Christian 'Radical Equality,'" *National Catholic Reporter*, April 29, 2015, www.ncronline.org.

62. Congregation for the Doctrine of the Faith, "Women in the Ministerial Priesthood," 523.

63. For Francis, motherhood, in particular, is essential to societal well-being, because "mothers are the strongest antidote to the spread of self-centered individualism" (*AL* #174).

64. See Spadaro interview.

65. See Dillon, *Catholic Identity*, 164–193.

66. Francis, "Christmas [2014] Greeting to Curia Officials," in *Origins* 44 (January 8, 2015), www.originsonline.com. Francis's appointment and promotion of bishops committed to social justice, such as Archbishop Cupich in Chicago, his first U.S. appointment (and whom he subsequently made a Cardinal), can be seen as an attempt to disincentivize clericalism.

67. This quote is from a letter released by the Vatican, from Francis to Cardinal Marc Ouellet in his role as the head of the Pontifical Commission for Latin America; Joshua McElwee, "Francis: Spirit Works in Laypeople, Is Not Property of the Hierarchy," *National Catholic Reporter*, April 26, 2016, www.ncronline.org.

68. On standpoint analysis, see Dorothy Smith, *The Conceptual Practices of Power* (Boston: Northeastern University Press, 1990). On the arbitrariness of institutional classifications and practices, collective misrecognition, and how religious language (e.g., of sacrifice) euphemizes power relations, see Pierre Bourdieu, *Practical Reason: On the Theory of Action* (Stanford, CA: Stanford University Press, 1991), 92–126. On the arbitrariness of categories, see also Michel Foucault, *The Order of Things* (London: Tavistock, 1974), xv.

69. In my 2015 survey of Call to Action (CTA) chapter leaders and associates, over two-thirds of respondents rank as top priorities: placing women in Vatican leadership positions (71 percent), ordaining women (69 percent), removing the ban on artificial contraception (69 percent), reducing clericalism (69 percent), and increasing the role of the laity (69 percent).

70. See Spadaro interview.

71. See Smith, *Conceptual Practices of Power* on women's standpoint and its exclusion from "ruling texts."
72. In the Spadaro interview, Francis notes that women are essential to the Church. In August 2016, he appointed a twelve-member commission (including six women), to study the possibility of allowing women to serve as deacons; see Joshua McElwee, "Francis Institutes Commission to Study Female Deacons, Appointing Gender-Balanced Membership," *National Catholic Reporter*, August 2, 2016, www.ncronline.org. The CDF symposium on the role of women in the Church took place in September 2016, with mostly women theologians and biblical scholars discussing the roles women have historically had in the Church and might possibly play in the future; see Cindy Wooden, "Doctrinal Congregation Convokes Meeting on Role of Women in the Church," *National Catholic Reporter*, September 29, 2016, www.ncronline.org.
73. Benedict, "Prepolitical Moral Foundations," 265. I discuss this further in chapter 6.
74. Vatican II affirmed the principle of episcopal collegiality in the sense that it is not the pope alone who is a teaching authority but, rather, the pope in agreement with his fellow bishops, as stated in "Dogmatic Constitution," #8. Yves Congar, *Tradition and Traditions: An Historical and Theological Essay* (New York: Macmillan, 1967), 336–337, sees the assertion of magisterial authority as a move to make the papacy a source rather than a mediator or interpreter of divine revelation. Despite appeals to hierarchical authority, it is important to keep in mind that there is not necessarily a "universal consensus" among bishops on doctrinal issues (see chapter 6). See also the remarks of retired San Francisco Bishop Francis A. Quinn, "How the Pope Might Renew the Church," opinion editorial, *New York Times*, September 18, 2015, www.nytimes.com.
75. Habermas, in Neomianu, "Church and Secular Establishment," 26; and as noted in chapter 1.
76. On relativism and moral truth, see, for example, Ratzinger, pre-Conclave speech, 2005; and Francis *JG* #61, 64, 80.
77. Benedict, "Prepolitical Moral Foundations," 265.
78. Ibid., 266.

CHAPTER 5

1. U.S. bishops (USCCB), *Amicus Curiae* (friend of the court) brief submitted in the *Hobby Lobby* case to the U.S. Supreme Court (January 28, 2014), 12–13. This brief, and all other documents and statements discussed or referenced in this chapter pertinent to the U.S. bishops' religious freedom activism are (unless indicated otherwise) available to read/download from the website of the U.S. Conference of Catholic Bishops, www.usccb.org/issues-and-action/religious-liberty/index.cfm.
2. On the institutionalization of religious freedom in the U.S., see Bellah, "Civil Religion in America." On global religious discrimination, see, for example,

Pew Research Center, *Global Restrictions on Religion Rise Modestly in 2015, Reversing Downward Trend* (Washington, DC: Pew Research Center, April 11, 2017), which among global incidents against both Christians and Muslims, reports an increase in government force against Muslims in Western Europe.

3. The U.S. Conference of Catholic Bishops sponsored a full one-page advertisement in the *New York Times* on December 21, 2011, arguing against the mandate and its refusal to protect conscience rights. The signatories included Cardinal Dolan, then Archbishop and president of the USCCB, and several university presidents, as well as health-care, social service, and other administrators and executives.

4. Catholic organizations that accepted the government compromise include the Catholic Health Association of the United States (CHA), which comprises approximately 2,000 Catholic hospitals and health-care facilities, making it the largest group of nonprofit health care providers in the United States (see www.chausa.org); Catholic Charities USA, a network of Catholic nonprofit agencies providing a range of social services to poor and other underserved groups across the United States (www.catholiccharitiesusa.org); the Association of Jesuit Colleges and Universities, which represents 28 Jesuit colleges and universities in the United States (www.ajcunet.org); and the Leadership Conference of Women Religious (LCWR), which represents the leaders of congregations of women religious (nuns) in the United States accounting for approximately 80 percent of all religious sisters (www.lcwr.org). See Laurie Goodstein, "Obama Shift on Providing Contraception Splits Critics," *New York Times*, February 4, 2012, www.nytimes.com. One of the original signers, the Little Sisters of the Poor subsequently filed a lawsuit claiming that the administrative burden of having to sign the opt-out exemption form imposed an undue burden on their conscience. During his U.S. visit, Pope Francis privately visited the Little Sisters of the Poor in Washington, D.C.

5. On May 21, 2012, 43 Catholic dioceses/bishops (including New York, Washington, St. Louis, and Dallas), and several schools and social service agencies filed lawsuits in 12 federal courts; Laurie Goodstein, "Bishops Sue over Mandate to Provide Birth Control," *New York Times*, May 22, 2012, A13. By December 2013, approximately 90 lawsuits representing 300 individual and institutional plaintiffs had been submitted to the federal courts challenging the mandate; USCCB President Archbishop Kurtz's letter to President Obama, December 2013.

6. U.S. bishops (USCCB), *Amicus Curiae* (Friend of the court) brief submitted to the U.S. Court of Appeals for the Tenth Circuit, in support of the Little Sisters of the Poor and other plaintiffs (March 3, 2014), 11, www.usccb.org/issues-and-action/religious-liberty/index.cfm.

7. In 2001, for example, 35 percent of Americans expressed support for same-sex marriage, and by 2012, 48 percent did; currently 67 percent do. See Pew, *Support for Same-Sex Marriage at Record High*, 28–29, and Pew, *Support for Same-Sex Marriage Grows*, 6.

8. Despite an early public apology in 2002 from the U.S. bishops by their then president, Bishop Wilton Gregory, for derelict leadership regarding priest sex abuse

(Watanabe, "U.S. Bishops Apologize for Scandal"), individual bishops have varied in the public contrition shown; see, for example, Joshua McElwee, Brian Roewe, and Dennis Coday, "U.S. Bishop Finn, Symbol of Church's Failure on Sex Abuse, Resigns," *National Catholic Reporter*, April 21, 2015, www.ncronline.org. In June 2011, the U.S. bishops issued their revised *Charter for the Protection of Children and Young People*, which included new norms adopted in response to the ongoing legal and pastoral issues presented by the problem of priest sex abuse (since 2002 when it was first published); see www.usccb.org/issues-and-action/child-and-youth-protection/upload.

9. Lori's lecture, "Religious freedom in the Year of Mercy," was delivered to the Institute for the Psychological Sciences on May 19, 2016, at Divine Mercy University.

10. In their 2009 pastoral letter on marriage, the bishops also noted that "The vision of married life and love that we have presented in this pastoral letter is meant to be a foundation and reference point for the many works of evangelization, catechesis, pastoral care, education and advocacy carried on in our dioceses, parishes, schools, agencies, movements and programs"; www.usccb.org/issues-and-action/marriage-and-family.

11. Social movement scholar James Jasper, *The Art of Moral Protest* (Chicago: University of Chicago Press, 1997), 140, uses "moral shock." He argues that social movements are contingent both on political opportunity structures and on the cultural resources deriving from a group's shared beliefs and moral visions. Gene Burns, *The Moral Veto: Framing Contraception, Abortion and Cultural Pluralism in the United States* (New York: Cambridge University Press, 2005) uses "moral frame."

12. These data are from Pew Research Center, *2015 Global Attitudes Survey* (Washington, DC: Pew Research Center, November 2015). Not all Western citizens are as affirming as Americans of the principle of religious freedom: the United States, 84 percent; Germany, 71 percent; U.K., 68 percent; France, 52 percent; Italy, 75 percent; Poland, 55 percent; Spain, 58 percent; Canada, 62 percent; Australia, 54 percent.

13. See, for example, Dillon, "Cultural Differences."

14. Only one bishop, Archbishop John Myers of New Jersey, mentioned religious freedom, and he confined it to just one brief paragraph in his response to New Jersey's court ruling in 2006 on the equal rights of gay couples.

15. Cordileone, 2011 statement. The other messaging themes in the bishops' initiative were sexual difference, the good of children, and the common good.

16. The Ad Hoc Committee for Religious Liberty; see *Origins* 41, no. 19 (October 13, 2011). www.originsonline.com.

17. Statement of the Administrative Committee of the USCCB, March 14, 2012.

18. The bishops submitted a broad range of testimony and letters on religious freedom/conscience; see www.usccb.org for an updated, detailed list.

19. The statement, "Our First, Most Cherished Liberty," issued in April 2012, was unanimously endorsed by the 40 bishops of the conference's Administrative Committee. Its unanimity, and that of another one issued by that committee on

the HHS contraceptive mandate, was emphasized by the chairman of the Ad Hoc Committee for Religious Liberty, Archbishop Lori.

20. The committee also urged that the liturgical feast of Christ the King, which typically occurs in November, "a feast born out of resistance to totalitarian incursions against religious liberty—be a day specifically employed by bishops and priests to preach about religious liberty, both here and abroad" (Archbishop Lori, April 2012). On the cultural and "civil religious" significance of Independence Day, see Bellah, "Civil Religion in America."

21. U.S. Bishops, Strategic Plan, 2017–2020, www.usccb.org.

22. Archbishop Lori, Fortnight for Freedom 2016, opening homily.

23. See, for example, Dillon, "Cultural differences"; and David Yamane, *The Catholic Church in State Politics: Negotiating Prophetic Demands and Political Realities* (Lanham, MD: Rowman and Littlefield, 2005).

24. Lori's homily opening the 2016 Fortnight for Freedom is available on www.usccb.org.

25. U.S. Bishops, April 2012 statement, "Our First, Most Cherished Liberty."

26. See, for example, Jeffrey Alexander, *The Civil Sphere* (New York: Oxford University Press, 2006).

27. "Radical" and "reductive" are the words used by Benedict (during the *ad limina* visit of a group of U.S. bishops to the Vatican in January 2012); Lori uses "aggressive" in a December 2013 homily on religious liberty and the poor.

28. "Homily at Mass Opening the first Fortnight for Freedom" (in 2012). Available on www.usccb.org.

29. Cardinal Wuerl's homily, closing Fortnight Mass, July 4, 2013. Available on www.usccb.org.

30. U.S. Bishops, "Our First, Most Cherished Liberty," April 2012.

31. USCCB, *Amicus Curiae, Hobby Lobby* brief, 7.

32. Archbishop Kurtz, June 26, 2015.

33. These words drawing on the USCCB, *Amicus Curiae, Hobby Lobby* brief are restated in fact sheets distributed by the USCCB (such as the fact sheet "The Right to Practice Faith in Business"). The specific examples are used in the USCCB fact sheet "Marriage and Religious Freedom," one of several fact sheets on religious freedom available on the USCCB website, www.usccb.org.

34. USCCB, *Amicus Curiae, Hobby Lobby* brief, 13–14.

35. See, for example, Casanova, *Public Religions*; Tamadonfar and Jelen, *Religion and Regimes*; and Paul Manuel, Lawrence Reardon, and Clyde Wilcox, eds., *The Catholic Church and the Nation-State: Comparative Perspectives* (Washington, DC: Georgetown University Press, 2006).

36. See, for example, the claims articulated in Erica Hellerstein and Josh Israel, "A Bishop in the Exam Room: When Faith Dictates Health Care Instead of Science," in Center for American Progress (CAP) Action Fund, *Think Progress* (Washington, DC: CAP, June 22, 2016).

37. Habermas, *Awareness*, 20–21; and John Rawls, *Political Liberalism* (New York: Columbia University Press, 2005).

38. Robert Bellah, "Response to 'Religion in the Public Sphere' by Jürgen Habermas," Kyoto Laureate Symposium, University of San Diego, March 4, 2005, unpublished manuscript, University of California-Berkeley, Department of Sociology, 3. See also, Bellah, "Civil Religion in America." I discuss this same point in Dillon, "Jurgen Habermas."

39. See the resources on the website of the Catholic Health Association of the United States, www.chausa.org.

40. Among non-Catholics, 14 percent said they heard a lot about the bishops' religious freedom concerns, 40 percent a little, and 41 percent didn't know about the issue. See Pew Research Center, *Catholics Share Bishops' Concerns about Religious Liberty* (Washington, DC: Pew Research Center, August 2012), 1.

41. Ibid. The proportions are for white Catholics.

42. Ibid.

43. Public Religion Research Institute (PRRI)/Brookings Institution, *2012 American Values Survey* (Washington, DC: PRRI and Brookings Institution, 2012), 43 (raw data tables).

44. In the targeted Catholic surveys I conducted in 2015, 92 percent of Catholic League (CL) respondents indicated that they "completely agree" that "the right of religious liberty is being threatened in the U.S. today," and an additional 5 percent said they "mostly agree." Among Call to Action (CTA) respondents, 9 percent "completely" and 18 percent "mostly" agreed, whereas 45 percent "mostly" and 28 percent "completely" disagreed with the statement.

45. See chapter 1; and Habermas, "Notes" and Habermas, in Neoimanu, "Church and Secular Establishment."

46. Pew Research Center, *Faith and the 2016 Campaign* (Washington, DC: Pew Research Center, January 2016), 57.

47. Pew Research Center, *Public Sees Religion's Influence Waning* (Washington, DC: September 22, 2014), 44; and Pew, *Faith and the 2016 Campaign*, 41, 55.

48. Pew, *Influence Waning*, 44; and Pew, *2016 Campaign*, 41, 55.

49. In March 2002, 44 percent of individuals told pollsters that religion's loss of influence on American life was a bad thing. The proportions were higher subsequently: 50 percent in 2006, 53 percent in 2010, 49 percent in 2012, 56 percent in 2014, and 51 percent in 2016; Pew, *2016 Campaign*, 56.

50. Ibid., 42. On the continuing significance of religious identity as a cultural boundary in the U.S., see Penny Edgell, Douglas Hartmann, Evan Stewart, and Joseph Gerteis, "Atheists and Other Cultural Outsiders: Moral Boundaries and the Non-Religious in the United States," *Social Forces* 95 (2016): 607–638.

51. Pew, *Influence Waning*, 8.

52. Evangelicals are twice as likely as Catholics to say it has become more difficult to be religious. In September 2014, 18 percent of Catholics said that in recent years

it has become more difficult to be Catholic in the United States, 8 percent said it has become easier, and 73 percent said there has been no change; Pew, *Influence Waning*, 18.

53. See, for example, "This Land Is Our Land," *The Economist*, November 28, 2015, 24–25.

54. Junno Arocho Esteves, "Archbishop Lori Says Proposals to Restrict Religion Raise 'Alarms,'" *Catholic News Service*, December 11, 2015, www.catholicnews.com.

55. Between January 25 and January 27, 2017, the bishops' Committee on Migration issued three statements on this and related refugee/immigration issues; for all statements referenced here, see www.usccb.org. On Trump's remarks, see Peter Baker, "'This Is Not About Religion,' President Says of Order," *New York Times*, January 30, 2017, A1.

56. The sexual/gender identity discrimination statement was jointly issued by Archbishop Lori, chairman of the Committee for Religious Liberty, and Archbishop Chaput, chairman of the Committee on Laity, Marriage, Family Life and Youth; www.usccb.org.

57. See, for example, USCCB, *Amicus Curiae*, Little Sisters of the Poor Brief, 24.

CHAPTER 6

1. These quotes are from Francis, respectively, at the Synod's opening Mass homily, October 5, 2014; and his Synod Greetings (opening message), October 6, 2014. Francis's speeches (and exhortations and encyclicals) are available at: http:// w2.vatican.va/content/vatican/en.html.

2. Francis, Synod Greetings, October 6, 2014.

3. Synods are collegial assemblies of the Church's bishops. They were common in early Church history, and in the spirit of Vatican II were reinstituted by Pope Paul VI in 1965 to foster greater consultation between the pope and the bishops. Since then (and prior to 2014), there had only been two extraordinary synods: one in 1969 to discuss ways to enhance cooperation between the Vatican and national conferences of bishops and one in 1985 to mark the 20th anniversary of the closing of Vatican II; see Holy See Press Office, "Synod of Bishops," www.vatican.va/news_services/press/ documentazione/documents/sinodo/sinodo_documentazione-generale_en.html#.

   The Synod on the Family was referred to as an Extraordinary General Assembly of the Synod of Bishops; but technically, the October 2014 assembly was an Extraordinary General Assembly, and the October 2015 meeting an Ordinary General Assembly. The deliberations of a synod's participating bishops typically result in a formal, post-synodal document subsequently issued by the pope with a view to articulating a way forward on the subject addressed by the synod. In April 2016, Francis issued *Amoris Laetitia* in response to the Synod on the Family; I discuss it in chapter 7.

4. See "Preparatory Document for 2014 Synod on the Family," *Origins* 43, no. 25 (November 21, 2013), www.originsonline.com.

5. For the list of questions, see ibid.

6. See Peter Fagan, "Voices of the People: Responses to the Vatican survey in preparation for the Extraordinary Synod on the Family," Johns Hopkins School of Medicine, Baltimore, MD. The survey was commissioned by member groups of Catholic Organizations for Renewal, including Call to Action, Dignity USA, New Ways Ministry, Voice of the Faithful, CORPUS, and Women's Ordination Conference, among others.

7. The quote is from the introduction to the summary of responses to the Vatican's pre-Synod preparatory questions, in the working document (*instrumentum*) of the Synod of Bishops General Secretariat, "Pastoral Challenges of the Family in the Context of Evangelization," *Origins* 44, no. 10 (July 17, 2014), www.originsonline. com; hereafter referred to as *Summary*.

8. *Summary*, "Introduction."

9. Christine Schenk, "Underreported Survey Responses for Synod on the Family, a Valuable Tool for the Vatican," *National Catholic Reporter*, June 19, 2014, www.ncronline.org. See also Patricia Zapor, "Synod Reports Point to Poor Understanding of Family Teachings," *National Catholic Reporter*, March 5, 2014, www.ncronline.org.

10. See, for example, Cindy Wooden, "Synod on Family Surveys: German, Swiss Catholics Reject Teachings on Marriage, Sexuality," *National Catholic Reporter*, February 4, 2014, www.ncronline.org.

11. The bishops of England and Wales conducted an assessment both prior to and following the 2014 synod. Catholic Church in England and Wales, "The Call, the Mission, the Journey: A Summary of Responses," September 2015, see www. catholicnews.org/uk.

12. Although the bishops make recourse to their own privately commissioned research reports (and discuss these in closed-conference deliberations), and though some USCCB committees consult sociologists, the U.S. bishops have generally not been overtly welcoming of sociological research and analysis on Catholicism.

13. I want to clarify here that while Catholics' experiences and opinions were solicited—an important innovation—lay Catholics themselves (other than a small number of auditors or experts) did not participate in the Synod deliberations.

14. O'Malley, *What Happened at Vatican II*, 306.

15. Benedict, "Prepolitical Moral Foundations," 265, notes that natural law as an "instrument has unfortunately become dull." The reasons Benedict identifies for its limitations are echoed in the *Summary* (#22).

16. There is greater public support in Western democracies for gender equality than for religious freedom, though both are central tenets of liberal democracy; see Pew, *2015 Global Attitudes Survey*.

17. The "ordained" hierarchical structure is twofold: one, the hierarchy of Church office is based on ordination, in descending order: pope, cardinals, archbishops, bishops, priests, and the nonordained (laity); two, this structure is ordained as being in continuity with apostolic succession: the pope, as bishop of Rome occupies the See of

Peter (and priests are ordained, as discussed in chapter 4, to sacramentally mimic Christ's physical presence). Several public secular sites are also masculinized sites of discourse; see Francesca Polletta and Pang Ching Bobby Chen, "Gender and Public Talk: Accounting for Women's Valuable Participation in the Public Sphere," *Sociological Theory* 31 (2013): 291–317.

18. O'Malley, *What Happened at Vatican II*, 26–27.

19. Gerard O'Connell, "Fourteen Married Couples Among 253 Participants at Synod on the Family," *America*, September 9, 2014, www.americamagazine.org; Joshua McElwee, "Vatican Releases Synod List," *National Catholic Reporter*, September 15, 2015, www.ncronline.org.

20. Specifically, women accounted for 10 percent of all participants at the 2014 Synod and 11 percent at the 2015 Synod.

21. It was established in September 2014, a few weeks before the 2014 Synod opened. See Joshua McElwee, "Pope Creates Vatican Commission to Study Marriage Process," *National Catholic Reporter*, September 20, 2014, www.ncronline.org.

22. See Joshua McElwee, "Francis Institutes Commission to Study Female Deacons, Appointing Gender-Balanced Membership," *National Catholic Reporter*, August 2, 2016, www.ncronline.org.

23. Joe Humphreys, "McAleese: Asking Bishops' Advice on Family Life 'Bonkers,'" *Irish Times*, June 16, 2014, www.irishtimes.com. McAleese served as an adviser to the Irish bishops during the deliberations of the New Ireland Forum in 1984 for North–South cooperation. For additional criticisms of women's exclusion, see Ellen Euclide, "Feminist Catholics Respond to Synod," Call to Action, October 23, 2014; see http://cta-usa.org/feminist-catholics-respond-synod.

24. On the narrowness of lay representation, see also Thomas Reese, "The Makeup of the Synod of Bishops on the Family is Disappointing," *National Catholic Reporter*, September 10, 2014, www.ncronline.org.

25. See the "Midterm Report on the Extraordinary Synod of Bishops on the Family," *Origins* 44, no. 21 (October 23, 2014); and "Final Report of the Extraordinary Synod of Bishops on the Family," *Origins* 44, no. 24 (November 13, 2014), www.originsonline.com. These reports inform my analysis in this section.

26. Catholic News Service, "Margin Notes," *Origins* 44, no. 21 (October 23, 2014), www.originsonline.com; and "Margin Notes," *Origins* 44, no. 24 (November 13, 2014), www.originsonline.com.

27. The 2014 final report has 62 paragraphs. *Origins* 44, no. 24 (November 13, 2014) (www.originsonline.com) reports that all of them received a simple majority, but three— #55 (on homosexuality), and two regarding communion for divorced and remarried Catholics—fell short of the two-thirds approval required for a Synod consensus.

28. Synod of Bishops, "*Lineamenta* for the 2015 Synod on the Family," *Origins* 44, no. 30 (December 25, 2014), www.originsonline.com.

29. Ibid., 19.

30. Ibid., 25, 16.
31. "The Vocation and Mission of the Family in the Church and the Contemporary World," *Instrumentum laboris*, June 2015, #132. http://www.vatican.va/roman_curia/synod/documents/rc_synod_doc_20150623_instrumentum-xiv-assembly_en.html.
32. "The Final Report of the Synod of Bishops to the Holy Father, Pope Francis," Vatican City, October 24, 2015, #76. http://www.vatican.va/roman_curia/synod/documents/rc_synod_doc_20151026_relazione-finale-xiv-assemblea_en.html.

    The Vatican English translation does not use the phrase "homosexual tendency." But the accounts based on the initial Italian summary report document—provided by Gerard O'Connell, "The Synod Approves Final Document, Leaves the Door Open For the Pope to Move Forward on Key Issues," *America,* October 24, 2015, www.americamagazine.org, and Joshua McElwee, "Synod Offers Striking Softening to Remarried Proposing Discernment," *National Catholic Reporter*, October 24, 2015, www.ncronline.org—use "homosexual tendencies" language. Upon further probing, I found that the Italian, French, and Spanish translations use "tendencies" and the German uses "orientation."
33. O'Connell, "Synod Approves Final Document" and McElwee, "Synod Offers Striking Softening," provide the Synod's vote counts. Across the final 2015 report, the number of votes varied by paragraph owing to abstentions among the 270 eligible voters; 258 voted on #76.
34. Bendixen and Amandi International, *Global Survey,* 28, 14, 9.
35. The three relevant paragraphs are #84, 85, and 86. Twenty-eight percent voted against #84, 31 percent against #85, and 25 percent against #86; O'Connell, "Synod Approves Final Document."
36. Cardinal Pell, quoted in Laurie Goodstein and Elisabetta Povoledo, "No Consensus at Vatican as Synod Ends," *New York Times*, October 19, 2014, A14.
37. See Emile Durkheim, *The Division of Labour in Society* (New York: Free Press, 1893/1984).
38. John Paul's *FC* #84 was first invoked in the Synod 2014 final report.
39. The *Catechism* points out that all the "other sacraments are bound up with the Eucharist and are oriented towards it . . . the sum and summary of our faith" (#1324, 1327).
40. These include Cardinal Burke, an American outspoken critic of Francis, and Cardinal Pell, who is Cardinal emeritus of Melbourne and Sydney, and appointed by Francis as Prefect of the newly formed Secretariat of the Economy.
41. Gerhard Muller, "Testimony to the Power of Grace: On the Indissolubility of Marriage and the Debate Concerning the Civilly Remarried and the Sacraments," in Robert Dodaro, ed., *Remaining in the Truth of Christ* (San Francisco: Ignatius Press, 2014), 148–165.

42. Juan Jose Perez-Soba and Stephan Kampowski, *The Gospel of the Family: Going Beyond Cardinal Kasper's Proposal in the Debate on Marriage, Civil Re-marriage, and Communion in the Church* (San Francisco: Ignatius Press, 2014), 23, 38–39.

43. Catholic News Service, "Margin Notes," *Origins*, October 23, 2014, www.origin-sonline.com.

44. Vincent Twomey, "Synod Feeds Secular Agenda Hostile to Traditional Family," *Irish Times*, October 18, 2014, www.irishtimes.com.

45. Catholic News Service, "Margin Notes," *Origins,* November 13, 2014, www.origin-sonline.com.

46. The full letter is published by Sandro Magister on his online blog, "Thirteen Cardinals Have Written to the Pope," October 12, 2015 (English translation by Matthew Sherry, Ballwin, MO), http://chiesa.espresso.repubblica.it/articolo/1351154bdc4.html?eng=y.

47. For a detailed account of the controversy over the letter, see Magister, "Thirteen Cardinals." See also Joshua McElwee, "Cardinals Reportedly Criticize Synod in Letter to Francis, But Signatories Disassociate," *National Catholic Reporter*, October 12, 2015, www.ncronline.org.

48. See, for example, O'Malley, *What Happened*; and Wilde, *Vatican II*.

49. For a critique of the assumptions regarding communicative rationality in public dialogue see, for example, Dillon, "Authority of the Holy"; and Cathleen Kaveny, *Prophecy Without Contempt: Religious Discourse in the Public Square* (Cambridge, MA: Harvard University Press, 2016), 46–74.

50. For example, reporting for one of the English-speaking groups in October 2014, Dublin Archbishop Diarmuid Martin noted that his group included five from Africa, seven from Asia, and one each from Oceania, the United States, and Europe; http://en.radiovaticana.va/news/2014/10/17/synod_on_the_family_reports_of_english_language_working_gro/1108779.

51. Berger and Luckmann, *Social Construction*, 41–46, emphasize the relevance of the stock of lived experience or habituated "recipe knowledge" in the negotiation of everyday reality. As noted earlier (chapter 1, n. 14) Habermas's earlier construal of communicative rationality saw tradition (including religious tradition) as an impediment to rational discourse. On the relevance of tradition and group culture in consensus formation, see for example, Nina Eliasoph and Paul Lichterman, "Culture in Interaction," *American Journal of Sociology* 108 (2003): 735–794; and Rich Wood, "Religious Culture and Political Action," *Sociological Theory* 17 (1999): 307–332.

52. Cardinal Marx, quoted in Catholic News Agency, "Read Today's Report from the German Small Group at the Synod," October 14, 2015, www.catholicnewsagency.com.

53. At a press conference discussing the German-language group's report, Cardinal Marx stated: "Every text [released by] the German-speaking group . . . is unanimous, no vote against it"; quoted in Joshua McElwee, "German Synod Group

Outlines Communion Path for Remarried Catholics," *National Catholic Reporter*, October 21, 2015, www.ncronline.org.

54. In line with the Synod's doctrinal politics, Erdo's remarks received a quick rejoinder from Bruno Forte, the special secretary to the Synod secretariat (and whom Erdo had blamed for the welcoming language on homosexuals in the 2014 midterm report). Forte stated "Although it holds true that this synod must not be expected to change doctrine, it must be said very clearly that this synod is not meeting to say nothing. It is not a doctrinal synod, but it is pastoral"; see Sandro Magister, "First Shot on Target Comes from the Conservatives," October 8, 2015, http://chiesa.espresso.repubblica.it/articolo/1351154bdc4.html?eng=y.

55. The quotes I use in this section are from the content in the sequence of summary group reports published online by Gerard O'Connell in his dispatches from the Synod in *America*, October 9, 2015 (report #1), October 14, 2015 (report #2), and October 21, 2015 (report #3), www.americamagazine.org. The four English group reports are each respective group's actual summary, and the non-English group reports are highlights based on O'Connell's summary of the main points contained in these respective original language groups' reports.

56. For example, two of the three English-language groups convened during the second week of the 2014 Synod commented positively on the spirit of "reciprocal listening" and openness to others' insights and experiences; see http://en.radiovaticana.va/news/2014/10/17/synod_on_the_family_reports_of_english_language_working_gro/1108779. Reciprocal listening is also noted in the 2014 Synod's mid-term (#58) and final (#62) reports, and in the December 2014 post-Synod *lineamenta* (#62). See also Dublin Archbishop Diarmuid Martin, quoted in Paddy Agnew, "Diarmuid Martin Warns Against Unrealistic Synod Expectations," *Irish Times*, October 18, 2014, www.irishtimes.com.

57. For example, Twomey, "Synod Feeds Secular Agenda."

58. See the summaries of English B (#2), C (#2), D (#2), Italian B (#2), and French A (#2).

59. Cardinal Napier (from Durban, South Africa); reported in Catholic News Service, "Margin Notes," *Origins*, October 23, 2014, www.originsonline.com.

60. The (2015) Final Report of the Synod of Bishops, October 24, 2015, #69.

CHAPTER 7

1. *Amoris Laetitia* is available at http://w2.vatican.va/content/vatican/en.html.

2. During his visit to Georgia in October 2016, Francis acknowledged the reality of marital breakdown and divorce, and reiterated that the Church's attitude toward those in situations of irreconcilable breakdown must be to "welcome them, accompany them, promote discernment, and integrate them into the community"; see Joshua McElwee, "Francis in Georgia: 'There Is a Global War to Destroy Marriage,'" *National Catholic Reporter*, October 1, 2016, www.ncronline.org.

3. In 2010 and 2011, there were two dismissals each year, there were four in 2012, fourteen in 2013, and eighteen in 2014 (data based on my analysis of publicized case details, collated by my research assistant Kirsten Kemmerer). The San Francisco diocese, long home to a large number of LGBT individuals and a vibrant LGBT community, and headed (since 2012) by doctrinally conservative Archbishop Cordileone (chair of the U.S. bishops' Sub-Committee for the Promotion and Defense of Marriage; see chapter 5), has been a flashpoint for teacher-contract clauses affirming the upholding of Catholic sexual morality. See, for example, Carol Pogash, "Morals Clause in Catholic Schools Roils Bay Area," *New York Times*, February 26, 2015, A12, 15.

4. See Smith, *Conceptual Practices*, 17–21, on the bifurcation of consciousness required by women's simultaneous negotiation of the divergent realities of home/motherhood and the public-occupational sphere.

5. As Berger and Luckmann elaborate in *Social Construction*, reality maintenance requires an ongoing necessary translation between objective and institutional realities and their subjective and intersubjectively shared meanings.

6. Archdiocese of Philadelphia, "Pastoral Guidelines for Implementing *Amoris Laetitia*," July 1, 2016, www.archphila.org.

7. See, for example, Archbishop Chaput's sharply worded address "Sex, Family and the Liberty of the Church," given as the University of Notre Dame's de Tocqueville Lecture on Religious Liberty, September 15, 2016. Among other points, Chaput stated:

> For the nation's leading Catholic university to honor a Catholic public official [Vice President Biden] who supports abortion rights and then goes on to conduct a same-sex civil marriage ceremony just weeks later, is—to put it kindly—a contradiction of Notre Dame's identity. It's a baffling error of judgment. What matters isn't the vice president's personal decency or the university's admirable intentions. The problem, and it's a serious problem, is one of *public witness* and the damage it causes both to the faithful and to the uninformed. (Emphasis in original, www.archphila.org)

8. Archdiocese of Portland, Oregon, "Pastoral Letter on the Reading of *Amoris Laetitia* in Light of Church Teaching," October 7, 2016, www.archdpdx.org.

9. See, for example, Joshua McElwee, "Four Cardinals Openly Challenge Francis over 'Amoris Laetitia,'" *National Catholic Reporter*, November 14, 2016, www.ncronline.org; and the "Filial Correction," signed by several conservative Catholics and submitted to Francis on August 11, 2017; posted at www.correctiofilialis.org

10. This, for example, is the view of Bishop Kevin Farrell, the Irish-born bishop of Dallas (2007–2016) and appointed in October 2016 as Cardinal and head of the Vatican's restructured Dicastery for Laity, Family and Life. See Joshua McElwee, "New Cardinal Farrell: '*Amoris Laetitia* Is the Holy Spirit speaking,'" *National Catholic Reporter*, October 14, 2016, www.ncronline.org. A similar view is emphasized by Cardinal Wuerl, one of Francis's most outspoken defenders in the United States; see Joshua McElwee, "Cardinal Wuerl: *Amoris Laetitia* Is 'Consensus

Document' Rooted in Tradition," *National Catholic Reporter*, October 4, 2016, www.ncronline.org. Farrell, and other American bishops, continue to reiterate this position; see, for example, Joshua McElwee, "Bishops Deliberate Whether One Rule Applies to All Divorced People after 'Amoris Laetitia,'" *National Catholic Reporter*, October 6, 2017, www.ncronline.org.

11. See Cindy Wooden, "Vatican Newspaper: 'Amoris Laetitia' Is Authoritative Church Teaching," *Catholic News Service*, August 23, 2016, www.catholicnews.com. See also the editorial in *National Catholic Reporter*, "Guidelines Point to *Amoris Laetitia*'s Intent," September 17, 2016, www.ncronline.org.

12. Berger and Luckmann, *Social Construction*, 53–54, argue that "All human activity is subject to habitualization . . . [and] the background of [everyday] habitualized activity opens up a foreground for deliberation and innovation."

13. See, for example, Jones et al., *Exodus*; D'Antonio et al., *Catholics in Transition*, 140–150; Pew, *Catholics Divided over Global Warming*; Pew, *Support for Same-Sex Marriage Grows*; Pew, *Survey of LGBT Americans*; and Pew, *U.S. Catholics Open to Non-Traditional Families*.

14. Vatican Radio, "Pope Writes to Young People Ahead of Synod on Vocational Discernment," January 13, 2017, http://en.radiovaticana.va/news/2017/01/13/pope_letter_to_young_people_for_synod_on_vocational_discernm/1285408; and, Holy See Press Office, Presentation of the Preparatory Document of the Synod on "Youth, Faith, and Vocational Discernment," October 13, 2017, http://youth.synod2018.va/content/synod2018/en.html

15. Cardinal Sean O'Malley, head of the Pontifical Commission for the Protection of Minors, established by Francis, stresses that, despite evidence of foot-dragging, the elimination of clergy sex abuse remains a top priority for the Vatican; see Joshua McElwee, "O'Malley Pledges Pope Still Committed to Rooting Out Clergy Sex Abuse," *National Catholic Reporter*, March 23, 2017, www.ncronline.org.

16. See, for example, Ross Douthat, "The Pope and the Precipice," *New York Times*, October 25, 2014, www.nytimes.com; and Ross Douthat, "The Plot to Change Catholicism," *New York Times*, October 18, 2015, www.nytimes.com.

Index